Good Pastors, Bad Pastors

Good Pastors, Bad Pastors

Pentecostal Ministerial Ethics in Ghana

DELA QUAMPAH

WIPF & STOCK · Eugene, Oregon

GOOD PASTORS, BAD PASTORS
Pentecostal Ministerial Ethics in Ghana

Copyright © 2014 Dela Quampah. All rights reserved. Except for brief quotations in critical publications or reviews, no part of this book may be reproduced in any manner without prior written permission from the publisher. Write: Permissions, Wipf and Stock Publishers, 199 W. 8th Ave., Suite 3, Eugene, OR 97401.

Wipf & Stock
An Imprint of Wipf and Stock Publishers
199 W. 8th Ave., Suite 3
Eugene, OR 97401

www.wipfandstock.com

ISBN 13: 978-1-62564-051-2

Manufactured in the U.S.A.   08/12/2014

Scriptures taken from the Holy Bible, New International Version®, NIV®. Copyright © 1973, 1978, 1984, 2011 by Biblica, Inc.™ Used by permission of Zondervan. All rights reserved worldwide, www.zondervan.com. The "NIV" and "New International Version" are trademarks registered in the United States Patent and Trademark Office by Biblica, Inc.™

To the memory of my parents,
Jane Yawa and Harry Othniel Quampah.

Contents

List of Tables   *viii*

Foreword by J. Kwabena Asamoah-Gyadu   *ix*

Acknowledgments   *xiii*

Introduction   *xv*

Abbreviations   *xviii*

1. Background and Context   1
2. Ghanaian Traditional Leadership Milieu and the Contextualization of Christianity   32
3. Selected Ethical Theories and Systems   49
4. Christian Ethics   65
5. Leadership Structure in Select Ghanaian Pentecostal Churches   89
6. Issues in Pentecostal Ministerial Ethics in Ghana   127
7. Analysis of Information on Pentecostal Ministers   169
8. Summary, Conclusions, and Recommendations   195

Appendices

    Apostolic Church Ghana End-of-Year Performance Review Form   199

    Church of Pentecost Ministers Appraisal Form   203

    Model Ministerial Code of Ethics of Grace Community Churches by Dela Quampah   208

    Questionnaire on the Ethical Dimension of Pentecostal/ Charismatic Church Leadership in Ghana   211

Bibliography   217

Tables

1   Christian Denominational Demography   29

2   Assessment of Moral Standards of Specific Pentecostal Ministers   172

3   General Information on Moral Standards among Pentecostal Ministers   173

4   Ministers' Responses to Some Ministerial and Ethical Issues   187

Foreword

GIVEN THE ENORMITY OF its influence in the world today, Dela Quampah's book, which examines the interface between Pentecostal spirituality and Christian ethics, serves as an important addition to the growing literature on Pentecostal and charismatic Christianity in sub-Saharan Africa. This published doctoral thesis is the first such work devoted entirely to Pentecostal ethics carried out within the Ghanaian context. Pentecostalism has blossomed into a worldwide movement with incredible success in Africa. There are two reasons for this development. First, it has seemed good to God to choose those from the underside of history—the weak and foolish of this world—in order to revive Christian mission by shaming the wise. Pentecostalism is doing well not just in Africa, but also in developed countries—former heartlands of the Christian faith—where Christianity has gone into recession. For even in those contexts in which churches and cathedrals have now metamorphosed into restaurants, non-Christian temples, mosques, ashrams, or recreation centers, many Pentecostal churches and movements are reclaiming such facilities for ministry. The rise of Pentecostalism has therefore been good for the preservation of the faith in the West and its renewal in the global South. Here in Africa, Pentecostalism's infectious forms of worship and empowering message are felt even within the historic mission church traditions.

The second reason why Pentecostalism is doing well as a global movement is its inherent sense of mission. This is a movement that teaches and inspires insiders to be actively involved in witnessing to the saving grace of Christ and the power of the Holy Spirit to deliver, heal, and help people prosper in both physical and spiritual terms. Many have embraced this faith because of the palpable changes that it brings to lives that were previously going nowhere on account of wild living and destructive social choices. Africans have an additional reason for preferring Pentecostalism over liturgically ordered forms of the faith. As Harvey Cox argues in his book, *Fire from Heaven*, Pentecostal piety resonates with traditional African religiosity's strong sense of the power of the supernatural as real and able to possess, heal, and deliver people from sin and the demonic. This book is important because it challenges readers to consider the fact that the success of Pentecostalism has come with its own challenges. One of them is the need for the leadership to take issues of ethics and morality seriously. In this vein, part of the book's importance lays in how Quampah captures within an academic context a discussion that has dominated public discourse for some time.

The core message of the Pentecostal movement is that the experience of the Spirit is real. There are testimonies of moral transformation and spiritual empowerment, signs and wonders, and credible fulfillments of prophetic declarations that underscore the veracity of Peter's Day of Pentecost message: "Repent and be baptized in the name of Jesus Christ for the remission of sins; and you shall receive the gift of the Holy Spirit. For the promise is to you and to your children, and to all who are afar off, as many as the Lord our God will call" (Luke 1:38–39). Pentecostals frown upon cessation theories that denounce modern charismatic manifestations as untenable, and for Africans in particular, the religion that works is the one that brings results. This push for results is what has sometimes led to the sorts of moral waywardness that Quampah discusses in this volume. It is true that Pentecostalism, in all its various streams and shades, has spoken to the spiritual emptiness of our time. It has offered a form of Christian religion in which encounters with the transforming power of Christ and the dynamic presence of God by his Spirit are experienced as active and normative parts of church life.

Testimonies abound—especially among Pentecostal leaders in Africa—of how such transforming encounters with Christ have led to new lifestyles and brought material prosperity. In some cases, the born-again experience has enabled people to re-channel their material resources into more constructive ventures, leading to evident upward mobility in family circumstance. This message, widely articulated by the leadership in sermons and books, is now shared with expectant followers looking to make something out of their lives within oppressive African social and economic circumstances. This book examines the challenges that have come with the success of Pentecostalism in Africa, including ethical issues. In many cases, power has not been handled properly, and a lack of accountability in the use of spiritual gifts and finances has led to moral failures that must be named and dealt with. To that end, Dela Quampah has served us well with an important study that examines the ethical implications of Pentecostal spirituality, ministry, and decision-making.

Foregrounded in a useful interrogation of the relationship between Western philosophical and African traditional ethics, Quampah challenges Pentecostal churches and their leaders on their own theological principles of sanctification and points out the gaps between profession of faith and lifestyle. Indeed, the biggest challenge of contemporary Pentecostalism in African countries like Ghana today is how to translate spirituality into everyday living. This book shows how a critical public responds to some of the dross that has crept into an otherwise very important stream of Christianity. Almost on a constant basis, exposés decrying the commercialization of Christianity, self-serving prophetic declarations, extravagant leadership lifestyles, and moral failures among Pentecostal leaders appear in the media. The matter is made even more complicated by newer Pentecostals who affirm wealth and material things as indicators of divine prosperity. Thus, the desire for the material and the grandiose is behind the many temptations that have befallen pastors and led to moral laxity within the membership.

That newer Pentecostal churches, like the Lighthouse Chapel International, are instituting codes of conduct for pastors even as leading pastors like Bishop Charles Agyin Asare are writing books on ministerial ethics is an indication of both the extent of the problem and the widespread desire to do something about it. One of the many strengths of this book is that Quampah has gathered empirical evidence from both the classical Pentecostal and newer Pentecostal traditions. His conclusion that the presence of solid administrative structures, with their inbuilt accountability, enables classical Pentecostals to deal with religious deviance in more decisive ways than newer churches that are often managed by individuals unaccountable to anybody, is most revealing. Dela Quampah writes as an insider of Pentecostal Christianity, and this book promises to form the basis of a larger discussion and teaching on church, society, and ethics in contemporary Africa.

J. Kwabena Asamoah-Gyadu, PhD
Baëta-Grau Professor of African Christianity
and Pentecostal Theology
Trinity Theological Seminary, Legon, Ghana

Acknowledgments

I REGISTER MY DEEPEST appreciation to my initial supervisors, Dr. Rebecca Ganusah and Rev. Dr. B. Y. Quarshie who have contributed remarkably to my scholarship. Their commitment to this project was a real source of motivation and encouragement to me, and I am perpetually grateful to them. Professor Chris Thomas, who supervised my corrections, has also left his mark on this thesis. He provided much academic material at his own expense and paid me the highest compliment anyone doing corrections under supervision could receive: "You seem to be enjoying it." Thank you, Professor; working with you was exciting academic adventure.

I am much obliged to Apostle Dr. Opoku Onyinah, Chairman of the Church of Pentecost, whose instrumentality helped me embark on this project. I am also thankful to Rev. Dr. E. Anim, my Dean of Faculty of Theology and Mission at Pentecost University College, for his support and invaluable suggestions and contributions to this thesis. I am much indebted to Mr. Francis Broni and Mr. George Danquah, who offered inestimable assistance in data collection. I am also deeply thankful to Mrs. Trish Waller for proofreading portions of this work for free. Madam Misonu Amu of the University of Ghana's African Studies Department deserves special mention for allowing me to use one of the songs of Dr. Ephraim Amu. I am also grateful to the leadership of the Church of Pentecost and the Apostolic Church Ghana for allowing the publication of their ministers' assessment forms.

The individuals who gave me part of their time and provided me with useful information in interview sessions cannot be taken for granted. Although space limitation prevents the enumeration of their names, I am all the same extremely grateful to all of them. Finally, and most importantly, Connie, my wife, and our two boys, Sammy and John, deserve special acknowledgement and gratitude for what they have sacrificed to make this book a reality.

Introduction

IT IS ONE OF the telling tragedies of human history that the comprehensive study of ethics remains an obscure discipline in the academy, often relegated to a remote corner of the philosophy department. This problem becomes further compounded as discourse in moral philosophy is presented in such complicated language that only the initiated can understand it. A critically reflected position, however, should be convinced that character development and moral issues are at the heart of life and the survival of humanity. Moreover, the overall positive impact of our social and commercial institutions is directly proportional to the uprightness of their moral framework. In addition to the challenge of responding adequately to traditional moral issues such as human sexuality, power, and the proper application of resources, the recent media exposure of unethical practices in financial institutions, the Wikileaks scandals, and the Edward Snowden affair suggest the prioritization of moral debate in contemporary times. Consequently, we can appreciate the pressing need for universally accessible moral education. One of my objectives in writing this book is an attempt to make ethical discourse as comprehensible and easily accessible as possible, notwithstanding my exploration of the highly specialized field of Christian ministerial ethics. I have therefore examined some classical ethical theories, such as Kantian ethics, Jeremy Bentham's Utilitarianism, and Fletcher's Situationism to enhance their universal appeal. The enduring value and timelessness of the principles revealed in some of these theories underscore their continuing relevance to life, even in the information age.

Secondly, a fallacious notion seems to exist among Christian leaders that since the main focus of their vocation is moral uprightness, any systematic and structured attempt to expose Christian leaders to ethics is superfluous. By implication, such leaders assume that because they preach and teach others about good morals, they become, by default, icons who need no further instruction in ethics. Another perspective argues that since Pentecostal leaders are "Holy Spirit-filled," the Spirit provides a more than adequate source of moral instruction that brooks no other human or institutional source of moral teaching. However, the validity of such convictions is disproven by the authoritative works of major and classical Christian ethicists, along with the fact that Christian ethics has survived, over the generations, as a discipline in theological colleges. Furthermore, the endlessly breaking of ministerial scandals among Christian leaders—including Pentecostals—underscores the need for a multidimensional approach to the moral training of all Christian leaders.

Moreover, there appears to be a worrying trend among Pentecostal leaders, by which moral concerns receive less preference than they did with their Holiness movement progenitors. The contemporary Pentecostal emphasis on the success and prosperity motif suggests that, to them, enjoying the temporary benefits of relating to the divine takes precedence over the eternal dividend of moral transformation. Furthermore, it appears that to many of these church leaders, public opinion, social status, and reputation take precedence over character issues and moral decency. No wonder the Pentecostal movement is still struggling to generate a compelling theory in moral philosophy, as most of their moral doctrines only reflect a repackaging of traditional Protestant moral concepts. This is supported by the fact that Joseph Fletcher, in developing his concept of Situationism, challenges the Pentecostal movement to develop an authentic, resilient, and Holy Spirit-inspired ethical system—a challenge that is still awaiting a response. Evidently, the functional impact of ethical principles on the personal choices and institutional practices of Pentecostals calls for a more in-depth and comprehensive intellectual reflection than we have encountered so far.

In Ghana, the Pentecostal churches have emerged as prominent institutions that command a considerable level of social and economic influence, but it appears that their positive impact on the moral fiber of the nation has been much less significant. Today's frequent media reports and pronouncements by opinion leaders on ministerial scandals demand academic attention. One answer to this challenge is a philosophical exploration of the possibility of effectively integrating Ghanaian traditional ethics with Christian morality—for, to some extent, the pull of traditional values on contemporary institutions could help explain the travesty being experienced in the moral standards of Pentecostal leadership in Ghana.

A critical examination of the response of Pentecostal leaders to prevalent ethical problems in Ghanaian society undoubtedly reveals a crying need for more exposure to moral philosophy. Among Pentecostals in Ghana, it appears the issue of women's liberation has received inconsistent, inadequate, and variegated attention. The need for heightened institutional focus on gender issues and women's empowerment can therefore not be overemphasized. Within the context of the specific ethical issues navigated here, traditional ideas seem to exert the greatest influence on the Pentecostal application of power and wealth. The power dimensions appreciated by Pentecostals comprise spiritual, economic, and social influences whose application sometimes appears unconstructive. The non-empirical nature of spiritual experience limits any objective analysis of Christian institutions; as a result, spiritual encounters such as visions, dreams, and prophecies have become a ready tool of control and manipulation. The rapid emergence of deliverance ministries that, in certain instances, promote witch-hunting, indiscriminate demonization, superstitions practices, and their attendant negative social impact, demands a moral framework to guide their operations. Furthermore, narratives on the domestic and social relationships of some Pentecostal leaders have emerged as textbook cases in immoral behavior that demand an adequate ethical response.

These perspectives notwithstanding, suggestions that stigmatize all Pentecostal leaders as a moral liability rather than asset to Ghanaian society definitely constitute a false impression. Some of these negative impressions are attributable to stereotyping, ecclesiastical competition, and a media agenda driven by commercial interests. Investigations have uncovered impressive concern for moral rectitude in Pentecostal institutional provisions, programs, literature, sermons and other public pronouncements by such church leaders. Furthermore, there is copious evidence of exemplary leadership that is driven by moral authority among Ghanaian Pentecostals. And no one can fault Ghanaian Pentecostals on their numerous generous charity projects. No wonder my survey of the ethical impact of these leaders has registered a significant endorsement from congregation members.

Are we receiving conflicting ethical signals from the Pentecostal fold? Probably. In the first place, no human institution can escape the reality of the tension of travesty versus ideal. Secondly, the varied nature of Pentecostal phenomenon defies any objective analysis; and attempts at rigid classification, branding, and stereotyping always end in futility. Professor Chris Thomas's observation to me on the situation is perceptive: "Any movement that originates from God cannot be scientifically classified and analyzed." I therefore invite you to join me to celebrate Pentecostal variety, even in their approaches to morality.

Abbreviations

AG	Assemblies of God Church
AICs	African Independent Churches
APP	Association of Pentecostal Pastors
CAC	Christ Apostolic Church
CAFM	Christian Action Faith Ministry
CoP	Church of Pentecost
GPC	Ghana Pentecostal Council
HGPM	House of God Prophetic Ministry
ICGC	International Central Gospel Church
LCI	Lighthouse Chapel International
NACCC	National Association of Charismatic and Christian Churches
REC	Redeem Evangel Church
WMCI	Word Miracle Church International

1

Background and Context

Introduction

THE EMERGENCE OF PENTECOSTAL churches[1] on the threshold of the twentieth century has marked a turning point in Ghanaian Christian discourse. Pentecostals can be regarded as the category of Christians who emphasize an ethos of sudden conversion, a belief in speaking in tongues as evidence of baptism in the Holy Spirit, and further demonstrations of the gifts of the Holy Spirit such as prophecy and healing. Elom Dovlo identifies the Pentecostal and charismatic churches as revivalist movements "who hold their activities to be under the dynamic guidance of the Holy Spirit and use His gifts and fruits to 'minister' to themselves and the Church."[2] A definition of Pentecostalism that hints at what is believed to be the Wesleyan Methodist holiness roots of the movement is offered by Bassett, who claims, "Pentecostalism emphasizes a postconversion experience of spiritual purification and empowering for Christian witness, entry into which is signaled by utterance in unknown tongues (Glossolalia/Speaking in Tongues)."[3] Bassett's reference to "spiritual purification" is pertinent to this work's topic, for it gestures toward the Wesleyan Holiness teaching on sanctification, a theological category that deals mainly with character transformation.[4]

---

1. Here, "Pentecostal churches" also includes churches referred to in Ghanaian parlance as "charismatic churches."

2. Dovlo, "Comparative Overview," 62.

3. Bassett, "Pentecostalism."

4. Scholars who have attempted to depict the Wesleyan Methodist Holiness movement as the immediate context for modern Pentecostalism include Dayton, *Theological*

The Wesleyan tradition teaches that apart from having our sins pardoned through faith in Christ, our sinful nature can be removed through Christ's atoning work, creating the possibility of living without sinning. In his famous transgenerational sermon on Christian perfection, John Wesley claimed, "It remains, then, that Christians are saved in this world from all sin, from all unrighteousness; that they are now in such a sense perfect, as not to commit sin, and to be freed from all evil thoughts and evil tempers."[5] As a result, sanctification has been understood to be a sudden operation of heart purification that follows regeneration but precedes Spirit baptism. Many Pentecostal groups continue to affirm this viewpoint. For example, it is declared in the Church of God's statement of faith, "We believe . . . in sanctification subsequent to the new birth . . . [and in] the baptism with the Holy Ghost subsequent to a clean heart."[6] The Church of God thus subscribes to the "entire sanctification" doctrine wherein it is believed that one may attain sinless perfection as a precondition to baptism in the Holy Spirit. In such a context, sanctification is regarded as a definite discernible crisis event that should occur after conversion but before baptism in the Holy Spirit.

In his *Theological Roots of Pentecostalism*, Dayton endeavors to establish the Wesleyan Methodist Holiness tradition as the matrix that cradled the Pentecostal movement.[7] Discourses on charismatic Christianity after the New Testament era trace its origins to the Montanist movement that emerged in Phrygia around a.d. 175 and was known as "the New Prophecy."[8] In his *Pentecost outside Pentecostalism*, Omenyo examines the trajectory of charismatic Christianity through the history of the church, from the Montanist era to the Azusa Street Revival.[9] Although many Pentecostals would see their tradition as a novelty that emerged from the Azusa Street Revival, we must acknowledge that the revival was triggered by the prevailing religious climate in the United States.[10] This revival was led by William Seymour,

---

Roots of Pentecostalism; Synan, *Century of the Holy Spirit*; Anderson, *Introduction to Pentecostalism*; Lederle, *Treasures Old and New*.

5. Wesley, *Wesley's Standard Sermons*, 173.

6. Church of God International Offices, "Declaration of Faith."

7. Dayton, *Theological Roots*, 35–54.

8. Walker, *History of the Christian Church*, 69. Montanus, the leader of this movement, claimed inspiration by the Holy Spirit to prophecy. He was joined by two women, Priscilla and Maximilla, who shared his inspiration and attracted a sizable following. The Montanist movement spread rapidly beyond Phrygia but was persecuted by the Roman Catholic Church until it fizzled out by the time of Saint Augustine of Hippo (ibid., 69–70).

9. Omenyo, *Pentecost outside Pentecostalism*, 78–90.

10. Synan argues that the Holiness movement, which emerged around the 1830s, emphasized sanctification as a post-conversion experience. The main area of doctrinal

an African-American minister who in 1906 developed a spirituality that led to the Los Angeles Azusa Street Revival, an event most Pentecostal historians credit as the cradle of Pentecostalism.[11] It is generally accepted that this revival was stimulated by the prevailing religious paradigm in America, to which Pentecostalism added a fresh dynamic. Dayton is convinced that in tracing the roots of Pentecostalism, we must begin with Methodism and "pick up the story in such a way as to demonstrate actual historical links and developments that will climax in Pentecostalism."[12] Walter Hollenweger also argues that Wesley left as his legacy the doctrine of sinless perfection to the first generation American Pentecostals, whose religious context was considerably influenced by Methodism.[13]

It is, however, noteworthy that not all Pentecostal churches subscribe to the doctrine of sinless perfection. The Assemblies of God (AG), which emerged from the Azusa Street Revival (and also happens to have been the first Pentecostal foreign mission in Ghana, having arrived in 1931) views sanctification as both given in salvation and progressive throughout the Christian life.[14] Other churches that uphold this view on sanctification include the Elim Pentecostal Churches and the International Church of the Foursquare Gospel.

In Ghana, the classical Pentecostals have been churches with a history of considerable Western missionary effort in their formation—although some of them, such as Christ Apostolic Church (CAC), began as indigenous initiatives. They include the Assemblies of God, the Apostolic Church Ghana, and the Church of Pentecost (CoP). Their inception was signaled by the arrival of the first Assemblies of God missionaries in Ghana. Over the years, these churches have developed sustainable institutional structures to guide them in selecting and training leaders who, for the purpose of this work, are comprised of ordained clergy.

Closely linked to the classical Pentecostals, but slightly divergent in outlook, is a new strand of Pentecostal churches that Ghanaians refer to

---

emphasis of this movement was a return to holy living, and the movement gained currency in the first national camp meeting held in 1867 in Vineland, New Jersey. According to Synan, "The Vineland meeting was destined to change the face of American religion. Although it called for a return to holy living, the call was couched in Pentecostal terms. Those who came were invited to 'realize together a Pentecostal baptism of the Holy Ghost' and 'to make common supplication for the descent of the Spirit upon ourselves, the church, the nation and the world'" (Synan, *Century of the Holy Spirit*, 26).

11. See Dayton, *Theological Roots of Pentecostalism*; Synan, *Century of the Holy Spirit*; Anderson, *Introduction to Pentecostalism*; Hollenweger, *Pentecostalism*.

12. Dayton, *Theological Roots*, 36.

13. Hollenweger, *Pentecostalism*, 145–52.

14. Pearlman, *Knowing the Doctrines*, 252–53.

as "charismatic" churches. These churches emerged out of the evangelical revival of the late 1960s and 1970s and were founded—and are currently led—by significant charismatic individuals such as Bishop Charles Agyin Asare of Word Miracle Church International (WMCI), Rev. Christopher Titriku's Redeeem Evangel Church (REC), Rev. Dr. Mensah Anamuah Otabil of the International Central Gospel Church (ICGC), Rev. Dr. Dag Heward-Mills of Lighthouse Chapel International (LCI), Archbishop Nicholas Duncan Williams of Christian Action Faith Ministry (CAFM), Rev. Nii Apiakai Tackie-Yarboi of Victory Bible Church International, Rev. Bob Hawkson of Jubilee Christian Centre, Rev. Dr. Robert Ampiah-Kwofie of Global Revival Ministry, among others.[15] A difficulty in classification arises from the fact that these churches do not all belong to the same church association. While the majority subscribe to the National Association of Charismatic and Christian Churches (NACCC), a few, such as the Christian Action Faith Ministry and Word Miracle International, identify with the Ghana Pentecostal Council (GPC).

In addition, there is a category of autonomous Pentecostal ministries that do not associate or identify with either the GPC or the NACCC. A good example is Emmanuel Ofosu-Akuamoah's Redemption Faith Ministry located in the Kwashieman neighborhood of Accra, Ghana. According to Ofosu-Akuamoah, the ministry, which he founded in 2001, had a membership of 150 and was led by four full-time ministers as of January 15, 2008. In an interview, Ofosu-Akuamoah revealed that he had not joined any Pentecostal association because he thought his church was too young.[16] In 2005, Pastor Francis Yeboah founded a similar Pentecostal church in Ghana called Living Praise Sanctuary in Kwashieman, Accra. By July 17, 2008, the Living Praise Sanctuary boasted a total membership of eighty and was led by the founder and three associate pastors. Pastor Yeboah likewise claimed that he was considering the possibility of joining the NACCC.[17]

Out of concern for some of these autonomous Pentecostal churches, which need structural and organizational guidance, Apostle Stephen Waye Onyinah, founder of Christian Church Outreach Mission located at Mallam, a suburb of Accra, has established a group called the Association of Pentecostal Pastors (APP). One of the Association's objectives is "to help

---

15. Some of the available literature on the origins and development of these churches include Omenyo, *Pentecost outside Pentecostalism*; Anim, "Who Wants to Be a Millionaire?"; Dovlo, "The Proliferation"; Asamoah-Gyadu, *African: Charismatics*.

16. Emmanuel Ofosu-Akuamoah, Redemption Faith Ministry, interview by Dela Quampah, Accra, Ghana, January 15, 2008.

17. Francis Yeboah, Living Praise Sanctuary, interview by Dela Quampah, Accra, Ghana, January 15, 2008.

younger Pastors through training,"[18] and it has so far registered thirty ministers from the entire country.

Attempts at classification of Pentecostal churches have to reckon with what, for lack of a better terminology, is often called African Independent Churches (AICs). The period between 1920 and 1930 gave birth to a number of AICs, which are called *sumsum sore, mumu sulemo*, which, in the native Ghanain languages of Twi and Ga, respectively translates to "spiritual churches." The earliest ones emerged from the missionary tours of African indigenous prophets such as Wade Harris, whose converts, John Nackaba and Grace Tani, later formed the Twelve Apostles Church. These AICs were mainly founded by former members of the mainline churches who broke away from their mother churches, although others were introduced to Ghana by Nigerian migrants. In addition to the Twelve Apostles Church, major AICs include the Musama Disco Christo Church, the Savior Church (*Memene da Gyidifo*), the Apostle's Revelation Society (*Apostolowo fe Latin Dedefia Habɔbɔ*), the African Faith Tabernacle, the Eternal Sacred Order of Cherubim and Seraphim Society, and the Church of the Lord (*Aladura*).

One of the early comprehensive scholarly works on this category of churches is C. G. Baëta's *Prophetism in Ghana*. These AICs exhibit revivalist tendencies and emphasize faith healing and other Pentecostal features. Although Asamoah-Gyadu thinks the AICs are, with certain exceptions, orthodox Pentecostals, he also admits that some of their practices are rejected by the major Pentecostal denominations.[19] The *sumsum sore* have come under attack from the new Pentecostal churches on suspicion of syncretism due to their reliance on rituals and objects that appear to be a legacy of African traditional religions.

Another significant development in the Pentecostal domain is the influx of Nigerian missionaries who have established numerous branches of their home churches in the country. Notable among them are Rev. William Folorunso Kumuyi's Deeper Bible Life Ministry; the House of God Prophetic Ministry led by Prophet Rowland Odagwe; Winners' Chapel founded by Bishop David Oyedepo; Kingsway International Christian Centre founded by Pastor Matthew Ashimolowo; and Pastor Chris Oyakhilome's Christ Embassy. Some of these churches have huge satellite equipment to transmit the founders' sermons from their Nigerian bases to Ghanaian branches during church services. They have also established a significant electronic media

---

18. *Constitution of the Association of Pentecostal Pastors*, § 2, cl. ii, accessed at APP headquarters in Accra, Ghana, May 5, 2006.

19. Asamoah-Gyadu, *African Charismatics*, 21.

ministry by broadcasting their sermons on almost all the Ghanaian radio and television channels.

It is important to note that there is little doctrinal difference between the classical Pentecostals and charismatic churches. Some scholars, Emmanuel Anim for instance, think the disparity between these two categories emerges in their emphasis on certain theological concepts.[20] The classical Pentecostals stress the doctrines of sanctification, eternal life, and eternal reward, while charismatic churches tend to emphasize issues of prosperity and the development of human potential for an accomplished life. Nevertheless, we cannot ignore Paul Gifford's insightful observation that these two categories of churches are similar in many dimensions. According to Gifford, the view of Apostle Dr. Micheal Kwabena Ntumy, Chairman of the Church of Pentecost, that prosperity is a direct reward from God for faithful service and generous financial support of the church, seems almost indistinguishable from the convictions of charismatic church leaders.[21] The affinity between these two Pentecostal streams is further enhanced by the use of the term "Neo-Pentecostals" in reference to charismatics by scholars such as Cephas Narh Omenyo and Emmanuel Kingsley Larbi. And sometimes there is no attempt to differentiate between the two, as Larbi seems to suggest: "the evangelical/charismatic renewal in the 1960s and 1970s saw the development of new independent *Pentecostal churches*, some becoming huge churches in less than a decade from their emergence."[22] I will refer to both categories as Pentecostals and their practices as Pentecostalism, although they may be differentiated by terms such as classical Pentecostals or charismatic churches where necessary.

The success of the charismatic churches has come partly through the reaction of some of the youth to the rigid ethical practices of the classical Pentecostals. The strict rules concerning dress code, the use of cosmetics, seating arrangements, dancing formation, and general social conduct have caused many young classical Pentecostals to opt for the less legalistic and relaxed atmosphere prevalent in charismatic churches. In some classical Pentecostal churches, such as the Church of Pentecost and the Apostolic Church Ghana, women are compelled to wear headgear to church. However, since some educated ladies prefer to sport stylish hairdos, many such ladies tend to opt for charismatic churches that impose no such restrictions. On certain occasions, the exuberant self-expression of young people singing

---

20. Anim, "Who Wants to Be a Millionaire?" 53–54.

21. Gifford, *Ghana's New Christianity*, 40. Ntumy's opinion on prosperity is expressed in his book, *Financial Breakthrough*.

22. Larbi, *Pentecostalism*, 295, emphasis mine.

and dancing can become an issue in the classical Pentecostal churches, unlike in charismatic ministries in which no such regulations exist. Gerrie ter Haar has rightly observed that charismatic churches are thus in rivalry with the existing Pentecostal churches, which are often seen by the new ones as too legalistic and formal.[23]

Although some charismatic church leaders developed their Christian foundation in classical Pentecostal churches,[24] American preachers such as Oral Roberts, Morris Cerullo, Kenneth Hagin, and T. L. Osborne have appreciably influenced their style of ministry. While a significant number of Ghanaian Neo-Pentecostal leaders embarked on ministry without any level of theological training, a handful of them—including Nicholas Duncan Williams, Nii Apiakai Tackie-Yarboi, and Charles Agyin Asare—trained at Benson Idhahosa's Bible School in Benin City, Nigeria. Many of those who were trained this way found that they did not fit into existing church structures, which led them to found their own denominations.

The validity and appeal of the ministry of charismatic pastors seems to lie in the level of charisma and visionary leadership they can offer. Their captivating influence seems to depend on their giftedness and capacity for effective communication, which attracts followers to endorse their leadership. In such a context, it cannot be denied that the moral vision of the individual leader largely shapes the standards of right and wrong within the church. Marleen de Witte expresses the challenge posed by this approach to ministry, explaining, "in Ghanaian charismatic Christianity, too, there is a constant tension between free spontaneous spiritual expressions and the disciplinary institutionalized 'format' that molds people into 'good Christians.'"[25]

Apart from the personal moral vision of the leader, many churches also have documents that spell out high ethical standards for their ministers. For instance, the largest overseeing body of charismatic churches in Ghana, the NACCC, had registered a total number of 119 member churches by May 5, 2006. Prominent in their prerequisites for membership is this query: "Would you be faithful to ministry by upholding the highest standards of ministerial ethics, moral and financial rectitude, self-sacrifice, living a godly life and cherishing the call of God on your life?"[26]

23. Ter Haar, "Standing up for Jesus," 227.

24. Mensah Otabil was an Assemblies of God congregation member, and Charles Agyin-Asare, founder of the Word Miracle Church, as well as Nicholas Duncan Williams emerged from a CoP background.

25. De Wille, "Altar Media's 'Living Word,'" 174.

26. See the National Association of Charismatic and Christian Churches membership registry and membership application form for churches and ministries, accessed at NACCC headquarters in Accra, Ghana, May 5, 2006.

Similarly, the GPC, which boasted 195 members in 2006, is an umbrella body for many of the classical Pentecostals as well as some charismatic churches that focuses on promoting high moral standards in ministry. The GPC's code of ethics condemns behaviors such as drug abuse, currency trafficking, polygamy, alcoholism, and other kinds of immorality among its ministers.[27] Furthermore, the ministerial moral codes of many denominations likewise demand exemplary conduct of their ministers. For instance, the disciplinary code of the Church of Pentecost stipulates outright dismissal for certain infractions:

> "The Chairman and an Area Head or the Executive Council may summarily dismiss a Minister who commits any of the following offences:
>
> a. Theft
> b. Fraud
> c. Dishonesty
> d. Immorality."[28]

Christine Leonard aptly observes that the Church is especially strict in dealing with matters of marital infidelity—even more so when it occurs among church elders or pastors.[29] Likewise, the constitution of Assemblies of God Ghana details several other offenses that merit disciplinary action:

> a. Any moral or ethical failure, including sexual misconduct;
> b. A failure to represent our Pentecostal testimony correctly;
> c. A contentious or non-co-operative spirit;
> d. A declared open change in doctrinal views.[30]

Nevertheless, these churches still grapple with ethical issues relating to their institutional policies on social responsibility, the position of women, abuse of authority, power struggles, and other forms of misconduct of some functionaries.[31]

---

27. "Ghana Pentecostal Council Code of Ethics," 1–2, unpublished document dated October 1986, accessed at Ghana Pentecostal and Charismatic Council headquarters in Accra, Ghana, May 5, 2006.

28. *Constitution of the Church of Pentecost*, 42, accessed at CoP headquarters in Accra, Ghana, May 5, 2006.

29. Leonard, *Giant in Ghana*, 110.

30. *Constitution of Assemblies of God Ghana*, 40, http://www.agghana.org/hq/gh/index.php/calendar/const.

31. An example is captured in Ebenezer Ato Sam, "Revolt at CAC: Chairman Thrown Out," *New Punch*, March 30–April 12, 2008, 1, 8.

Evidently, what *is* does not often correspond to what *ought* to be in human institutions, and Ghanaian Pentecostal churches are no exception. Although Christians have high moral expectations for their leaders, these leaders' ability to measure up has always been a cause for concern in both the church and in wider society. This observation is underscored by the Ghanaian media's numerous reports of unethical conduct by some Pentecostal ministers. In research reported in *The Daily Dispatch*, the Centre for Media Analysis surveyed fifteen Ghanaian newspapers from July to September 2005 and discovered that 49 percent of the 1,748 news items on charismatic/Pentecostal churches were negative, while 29 percent were neutral, and 22 percent were positive.[32] Items on topics such as evangelism, social responsibility, the development of educational infrastructure, and pastoral roles fell into positive and neutral categories, while negative items covered issues such as promiscuity, fraud, and divorce.

Statement of the Problem

The ethical dimension of church leadership, which is referred to as ministerial ethics, explores the factors that influence a minister's personal conduct at home and in public. This study therefore focuses on the clergy or ordained men and women who officially represent their denominational interests. Ministerial ethical issues will be considered from two perspectives, the first being moral stipulations and how they are implemented within churches' administrative structures. The second perspective will examine the challenges individual ministers experience in ethical decision-making in relation to available institutional support.

Pentecostal church leaders in Ghana have suffered numerous ethical problems, and public opinion often censures them for the ostentatious lifestyles that many suspect may mirror commercialized ministries. For example, in the assessment of George Kinsley Acquah, Chief Justice of Ghana, Pentecostal churches "are profit-making ventures, feeding on the ignorance and plight of the population."[33] Sometimes such ministers are also accused of self-aggrandizement for appending so many titles to their names. In certain instances, Pentecostal ministers have also been criticized for promoting superstition, for they tend to demonize people, events, and objects

---

32. Ben Ephson, "Research Reveals Negative Media on Charismatic Churches," *Daily Dispatch*, October 25, 2005, 8.

33. George Kinsley Acquah, quoted in Edmund Kofi Yeboah, "Churches Feeding on People's Ignorance," *Daily Graphic*, July 29, 2004.

indiscriminately. Promiscuous behavior is yet another often-reported trend in such ministers' immoral conduct.

These negative reports notwithstanding, it would be remiss of any objective observer of the church scene to overlook the significant and valuable contributions of many of these ministers to the progress of Ghanaian society, both morally and socio-economically. The philosophy of ministry, the innovative programs, and the sermons of many of the Pentecostal ministers are having an overall positive impact on society. For instance, Dovlo has aptly observed that the teaching ministry of Rev. Dr. Mensah Otabil provides "spiritual and moral commentary and guidance for public life."[34]

Reflecting upon this quandary of strengths and weaknesses in Ghanaian Pentecostalism, the main focus of this research is to discover how far Christian moral principles manifest in the institutional practices of Ghanaian Pentecostal churches, as well as in the personal choices of individual ministers. This investigation is further supported by the following subsidiary questions:

a. Should ethical standards among Pentecostal leaders in Ghana be considered as ultimately more positive than negative?

b. What moral principles emerge from Ghanaian traditional institutions that could influence church leadership—constructively or otherwise—in contemporary times?

c. What level of awareness do Pentecostal leaders demonstrate in their understanding of moral philosophy?

d. What ethical concepts do their ministerial ethical codes reflect, and how effective are these standards in regulating conduct in ministry?

e. How trustworthy are media reports and public opinion on Pentecostal ministerial ethics, and how have church leaders responded to these moral concerns among their fold?

f. How can society contribute to approximating high standards in Pentecostal ministerial ethics?

---

34. Dovlo, "Proliferation of Churches," 65.

Research Objectives

The objectives of this study are to:
a. Analyze some ethical theories and systems in order to understand their functional role in the practical moral choices Ghanaian Pentecostal Church leaders make;
b. Examine the ministerial codes of ethics of some Ghanaian Pentecostal churches in order to assess their impact on the moral standards of their ministers;
c. Explore the institutional structures of some Ghanaian Pentecostal churches to discover how they promote appreciable standards in ministerial ethics;
d. Interrogate public opinion and media reports on the conduct of Pentecostal ministers to establish their veracity and identify the moral lessons that emerge from such narratives;
e. Design a model ministerial ethical code of conduct that could serve as a reference point for the churches under discussion.

Scope of This Study

Considering the sheer size and wide variety of the Pentecostal community in Ghana, any attempt to exhaustively examine every facet of its ministerial ethics would prove a daunting task. Consequently, I have explored the background and historical development of select Pentecostal churches to identify the principles, significant functionaries, factors, and events that shape their ministerial ethics. The first of these representative institutions is the Church of Pentecost (of the classical tradition), the largest of the Pentecostal churches in terms of membership selected for its unique leadership structure, which blends the hierarchical with the representative (as in Presbyterian polity). The Assemblies of God Church, being the oldest of the classical tradition, was chosen for its size and influence as well as its peculiar semi-autonomous congregational leadership.

The two churches identified for detailed study in the charismatic category are Word Miracle Church International (WMCI) and Redeem Evangel Church (REC). Bishop Agyin Asare's WMCI, headquartered in Accra, has been chosen for this study because it appears to be one of the fastest-growing and influential churches among Ghana's charismatic groups. Rev. Christopher Titriku's REC, headquartered in Ho, Ghana, is one of the few charismatic churches whose headquarters is located in a provincial town rather than a metropolis.

In this study, I have consciously avoided a comprehensive examination of historical trends in the churches and have instead elected to study events and personalities that could possibly influence ministerial ethics. My sociological perspectives on the churches do not necessarily engage with a general classification and evaluation of their social impact. Rather, attempts at categorization take these churches' responses to concepts in Christian moral philosophy and their effects on the moral fiber of Ghanaian society into account.

It is necessary to state that the issues discussed are not restricted to these select churches. To a certain extent, this work engages with a broader context by evaluating reports from other Pentecostal churches that are of national significance, such as those released by Christian Action Faith Ministries International, Lighthouse Chapel International, and Christ Apostolic Church, among others.

The inevitable limitation imposed on this research is due to the very nature of ethics and its practical application. Generally in Africa, issues of morality are so sensitive that one must observe considerable decorum when investigating people's behavior and attitudes, especially those of influential figures such as pastors. Access to such information is limited, and some of those who offer information on other people's conduct are unwilling to have their identity known. These challenges notwithstanding, this research endeavors with all circumspection to uncover critical issues related to Pentecostal ministerial morality while consciously avoiding any temptation towards mudslinging.

Literature Review

Some Ethical Concepts

Undoubtedly, the prevalent ethical ideas in the socio-cultural context within which religious institutions operate have some bearing on the moral standards they maintain. It is therefore necessary, in examining the ministerial ethics of Ghanaian Pentecostals, to engage with moral concepts in the social milieu to identify areas of agreement and conflict with other value systems. One author who has systematically explored Christian ethics from an African perspective is Samuel Waje Kunhiyop, an ordained minister of the Evangelical Church of West Africa who has served as head of South African Theological Seminary's Postgraduate School. Kunhiyop, in appreciating the roots of African ethics, admits that the lack of written records is problematic, but claims this difficulty is overcome by reliance on "customs and the rich African oral tradition."[35] He convincingly ascribes African moral values to a religious source rather than a humanistic one, insisting that to Africans, ethical values and religious beliefs are intimately related. Kunhiyop also engages with the perennial ethical debate on holding personal interests and communal considerations in equilibrium, concluding that in traditional Africa, the communal good holds sway over individual benefit.

Demonstrating an awareness of the influence of external value systems on African traditional values, Kunhiyop examines the impact of Western moral philosophy on African ethics. The slight problem with this approach is that it fails to recognize the common ground between the two value systems; instead, Kunhiyop sounds apologetic in preferring African religious ethics to the secular Western approach. As a result, Kunhiyop is unable to appreciate the legacy of Western secular moral philosophy, whose theories elucidate the concepts of utility, deontology, and virtue, which can provide a useful reference point in examining religious ethics.

In developing a system of morality that is biblically grounded, theologically sound, and relevant to the African context, Kunhiyop's *African Christian Ethics* identifies and incorporates those features of African ethics that he considers biblical into his African Christian moral system. Kunhiyop elaborately examines the crucial role of the community in the Christian redemption narrative and compellingly demonstrates its resonance with the African approach to religion and ethics. Nevertheless, although he applies a comparative approach to Western ethics and finds it deficient in many cases, Kunhiyop seems to be sympathetic with the African system to the extent that he disregards value judgment on certain unsavory practices, as the following passage reveals: "Similarly [to the practice of euthanasia], in some [African] societies, tradition has also laid down that twins are to be murdered because they bring bad luck, and babies with Down's syndrome or deformities are to be killed immediately after birth."[36]

Another book that is relevant to this thesis is *Christian Social Ethics* by Joshua N. Kudadjie and Robert Kwasi Aboagye-Mensah. The co-authors offer one of the most useful approaches in understanding ethics by defining it as "a style of living which reflects the attitudes and values of that individual or of an identifiable group to which he belongs."[37] Kudadjie and Aboagye-Mensah avoid the simplistic approach that views the ethical enterprise

---

35. Kunhiyop, *African Christian Ethics*, 8.
36. Ibid., 9.
37. Kudadjie and Aboagye-Mensah, *Christian Social Ethics*, 1.

as a set of rules to be obeyed. Their method focuses instead on reflection and the personal responsibility of deliberation to ascertain and improve those abstract qualities of self-expression that shape the value systems of an individual or a group of people. Kudadjie and Aboagye-Mensah further emphasize the three cardinal concerns of any worthwhile ethical endeavor, which are decision, action and evaluation, arguing that the ethical agent "must take decisions and act, and be able to evaluate his actions and those of others."[38] They also raise one of the most pertinent question in ethics: "What standards must be used?"[39]

In their attempt to answer this rather knotty question, Kudadjie and Aboagye-Mensah explore some of the factors that influence our ethical standards and value systems, such as the laws of nature, custom and tradition, societal norms, and social pressures.[40] The issue of societal norms is prominent in African traditional ethics due to the strong sense of social bonding. According to these co-authors, these norms "may not always be morally justifiable when carefully considered, but they are generally accepted and enforced."[41] Kudadjie and Aboagye-Mensah reveal certain implications of this communal ethic: "For instance, it is commonly assumed (though erroneously) that people who belong to certain professions, such as lawyers and doctors, are rich; so it is expected that they should live in big and luxurious houses and give big donations at weddings, funerals, and in Church."[42] Consequently, the level of influence such Ghanaian social norms and attitudes have exerted on Pentecostal ministerial ethics is of great interest.

Kudadjie and Aboagye-Mensah give a Christian grounding to their findings by underscoring the separateness of Christians as a faith community that looks to the Scriptures for its ethical standards. Kudadjie and Aboagye-Mensah's assertion is that "the norms and standards of the 'heavenly country' to which Christians ultimately belong are found in the Bible."[43] They lament the immoral practices that bedevil Ghanaian society, observing, "it is a fairly common practice among businessmen to give bribes in order to procure contracts or scarce goods. Those who are determined to remain honest find it almost impossible to cope, since their businesses will collapse."[44] It is within such a context that the Christian leader has been

38. Ibid.
39. Ibid.
40. Ibid., 2–3.
41. Ibid., 1.
42. Ibid., 3.
43. Ibid.
44. Ibid.

called to exemplify and project biblical ethical standards and serve as a check on immoral behavior.

Some Theological and Sociological Perspectives

Two significant works on Ghanaian Pentecostalism that offer a degree of reflection on the ethical aspects of the movement are Kwabena Asamoah-Gyadu's *African Charismatics: Current Developments within Independent Indigenous Pentecostalism in Ghana* and Paul Gifford's *Ghana's New Christianity: Pentecostalism in a Globalizing African Economy*. Asamoah-Gyadu employs a historico-theological method to evaluate current trends in Pentecostal groups in Ghana.[45] He emphasizes the influence of social context on religious movements in insisting that the local versions of Pentecostal expression can be understood only within the context of traditional Ghanaian culture and the religious environment in which they exist. Asamoah-Gyadu corroborates Larbi's attribution of the progress of Pentecostalism in Ghana to a receptive culture.[46] In Asamoah-Gyadu's view, African Pentecostal theology extends beyond the Bible to engage cultural metaphors, for "Although Pentecostal themselves unapologetically appeal to the Bible for explanations of their experience, in the African context there is a significant measure of credibility in the perceived resonance between Pentecostal and African traditional/primal religiosity."[47]

Asamoah-Gyadu demonstrates that the primal African worldview comprises a belief in the reality of both benevolent and malevolent spiritual forces that arbitrarily influence human life. It is Pentecostal theology's capacity to engage with and offer "convincing" responses to these perceptions that accounts for the success of the movement in Ghana. Kwame Bediako, an eminent Ghanaian theologian, also identifies this dynamic as a prerequisite for any impactful soteriological engagement within the African context.[48] Asamoah-Gyadu consequently argues that Pentecostals have creatively responded to the traditional worldview with scriptural validation in the form of the exorcism narratives by Jesus and Paul (Matt 17:14–20; Mark 7:25–30; Luke 9:38–43; Acts 16:16–18).

---

45. Asamoa-Gyadu, *African Charismatics*, 16. This approach traces the trajectory of the movement by examining the socio-cultural, religious, and historical factors that shape Pentecostal theology and identity in Ghanaian Christian discourse.

46. See Larbi, *Pentecostalism*, 31.

47. Asamoah-Gyadu, *African Charismatics*, 17.

48. Bediako, *Jesus in Africa*, 22.

Furthermore, Asamoah-Gyadu explores recurrent themes in charismatic soteriology from theological, ethical, and sociological perspectives in chapters such as "Salvation as Transformation and Empowerment," "Salvation as Healing and Deliverance," and "Salvation as Prosperity."[49] Asamoah-Gyadu's work offers a useful discussion of the benefits and the pitfalls inherent in the application of these theological categories. He is on target with his observation that the concept of salvation as transformation and empowerment is applied holistically in Pentecostal hermeneutics. To the charismatics, salvation does not only secure spiritual benefits, it is also supposed to empower Christians to pursue progress in terms of good health, success, and prosperity.

Asamoah-Gyadu rightly identifies the ethical implication of salvation as liberation from sin, making it relevant to the African context by associating it with freedom from the oppression of evil spirits. In discussing the concept of empowerment, Asamoah-Gyadu further introduces the Pentecostal motif of anointing, which endows ministers with the power to facilitate healing and other miracles to bless people. He raises the perennially debatable issue of the relationship between morality and performance by suggesting that the impact of a minster's anointing is directly proportional to his or her moral standard, saying, "the effectiveness of a person's anointing depends on moral uprightness and enhanced spirituality achieved through fasting, Bible study and prayer."[50] However, this assertion demands further interrogation to determine whether the blessings ordained for God's people necessarily depend on the character of the functionary. Asamoah-Gyadu gives credit to charismatic ministries for pursuing rigorous ethics based on their concept of renewal by the Holy Spirit, who enables the believer to bear the fruit of the Spirit (Gal 5:22–23). This, according to the author, provides a secure anchor against "the moral relativism and permissiveness of modern society."[51]

Although Asamoah-Gyadu seems to suggest that the charismatic practice of ascribing moral failure to demonic activity has some biblical basis (Eph 2:1–2),[52] he also points out that excessive emphasis on the demonic can create a sense of pervasive fear and spiritual insecurity among Christians.[53] The theme of salvation as healing and deliverance, according to Asamoah-Gyadu, is popular among Ghanaian charismatics because

---

49. Asamoah-Gyadu, *African Charismatics*, 132–63, 164–200, 201–32.
50. Ibid., 155.
51. Ibid., 138.
52. Ibid., 136.
53. Ibid., 183.

it responds to the indigenous worldview, which upholds the warding off of evil spirits as a target of religious rituals.[54] He identifies the underlying principle of the deliverance ministry as the firm belief in a "causal relationship between sin, the work of demons and sickness."[55] Therefore the moral benefit of deliverance is appreciated as freedom from "'bondage' to sin and Satan."[56] Nevertheless, in evaluating Pentecostal demonology, which ascribes almost all human problems to the activity of Satan and his agents, the author perceptively posits that the hermeneutics on which such teachings are sometimes based are either arbitrary or forced.[57] Asamoah-Gyadu logically concludes that deliverance ministers' inability to develop an adequate pastoral response to the problem of theodicy underlies this tendency toward excessive demonic ascription.

In reflecting on the concept of salvation as prosperity, Asamoah-Gyadu discerns a direct relationship between this theological category and salvation as healing and deliverance. He claims charismatics believe that, if devoid of sin and demonic activity, there is no reason why the Christian should not live a fruitful life in terms of health and economic success. In examining the biblical and ethical ramifications of the prosperity gospel, Asamoah-Gyadu initially affirms the scriptural basis for a Christian soteriology that promotes the overall wellbeing of humanity. Nevertheless, he identifies the selective hermeneutical method of prooftexting the prosperity message as problematic. This approach, according to Asamoah-Gyadu, produces "truncated, if not erroneous, views on theological issues."[58] The author argues that in modeling the prosperity message, charismatic leaders seem to trade the Christian virtues of humility and service for fame and popularity: "The standard and model of leadership is not that of the humble Christ, identified with the poor and marginalized, but that of the powerful in modern society."[59]

Gifford, a keen observer of the African Pentecostal scene, has undertaken a comprehensive consideration of the institutional structures and major themes of charismatic and Neo-Pentecostal ministries from historical and sociological perspectives. In *Ghana's New Christianity*, Gifford reviews the prevailing socio-political conditions since Ghana's 1957 independence that have made up the matrix of Ghanaian Pentecostalism. This study

54. Ibid., 166.
55. Ibid., 167.
56. Ibid.
57. Ibid., 183.
58. Ibid., 215.
59. Ibid., 229.

informs Gifford's conviction that Pentecostal theological discourse that engages with socio-economic deprivation is responsible for Pentecostalism's mass appeal. Focusing on the problem of governance, Gifford identifies neo-patrimonialism as one of the major factors shaping political culture in Ghana.[60] He points to political leaders' attitudes toward wealth as an indicator of the larger societal attitude to possessions, saying, "Yet the wealth is flaunted; indeed, if the money went into savings or investment, the point would be lost. Wealth and status go together; the former is the sign of the latter. Appearances matter—and appearances, titles and the symbols of office often matter far more than doing a job well or delivering results."[61] This observation's resonance with other critics' views of Pentecostal leadership in Ghana is significant, for it begs the question of whether there is cross-fertilization of attitudes between the political and ecclesiastical establishments in Ghana.

Gifford regards the emergence of Neo-Pentecostalism in Ghana as a paradigm shift in the church scene, justifying this observation by noting the declining influence of the historic Western mission-oriented churches. The main features of the Neo-Pentecostal phenomenon examined by Gifford include its theology, liturgy, and social impact, which diffuse through its remarkable media patronage. He also records his interaction with a segment of Ghanaian society that is not well disposed to the emergence of these churches. Gifford notes the opinion of K. Gyasi, a columnist who identifies one of three societal problems as the proliferation of churches "full (of women), loud, and in competition 'for the limited and not so limited wealth of very often their gullible congregations.'"[62]

Gifford also notes the fluidity of the Pentecostal phenomenon, which transcends church boundaries to impact other Christian persuasions. Referring to this as the "charismatisation" of other churches, Gifford claims that it is expected to stem the exodus of members flocking to join Pentecostal churches.[63]

Gifford attempts a comprehensive examination of what he calls the "recurring emphases" of the charismatic ministries.[64] His approach is backed by an impressive accumulation of primary data in the form of sermons, prayers, testimonies, lyrics, slogans, documents, and interviews that largely

---

60. Gifford, *Ghana's New Christianity*, 7.

61. Ibid., 13.

62. K. Gyasi in *Spectator*, January 20, 2000, 3, quoted in Gifford, *Ghana's New Christianity*, 41.

63. Ibid., 38–39.

64. Ibid., 44–71.

authenticate the author's views on the subject. Most often he deliberately refuses to theorize his opinions and instead presents copious evidence to reveal a particular trend of thought or practice among the church groups studied.

Gifford identifies the recurring emphases of the charismatics as success, wealth, and status. He argues that the new Ghanaian Christianity differs considerably from the Western missionary denominations that charismatic leaders blame for not teaching divine principles of prosperity. Gifford supports his identification of American prosperity preachers as the main influence on Ghanaian charismatic leaders using testimonies from the Ghanaian leaders themselves. Although he acknowledges that the traditional African religious orientation is conducive to the prosperity message's success, he insists that the way it is expressed, even in Ghana, reflects developments in the United States. Gifford identifies examples such as Russell Conwell's sermon on "Acres of Diamonds" and Norman Vincent Peale's *The Power of Positive Thinking* as the main sources of this theological construct.[65] The author likewise analyzes the theme of success in the context of Bishop David Oyedepo's Winners' Chapel branch in Accra. Gifford reveals that the leadership is extremely inclined towards the material success of congregation members, as church pronouncements like "Success is our birthright," and "If you won't succeed, go to another church" seem to suggest.[66]

Furthermore, Gifford discerns a link between traditional religious ideas and the practice of deliverance in Ghanaian Pentecostalism. He perceives the basic idea of deliverance as a situation where a "Christian's progress and advance can be blocked by demons who maintain some power over him, despite his having come to Christ."[67] Gifford further ascribes the proliferation of prayer camps to Ghanaians' desire to break loose of such demonic chains so they can accomplish their dreams. In evaluating the role of prophetic churches as agents of moral transformation, Gifford observes that due to their preoccupation with spiritual phenomena, these churches seem to show a lack of interest in moral or ethical issues. And since spiritual forces are blamed for all misfortunes, people's moral failures are also often attributed to demonic activity, thus considerably diminishing people's sense of responsibility. As Gifford explains, "In Ghana it is not uncommon for those accused of crimes before the courts to attribute their deeds to evil spirits."[68]

---

65. Ibid., 47.
66. David Oyedepo, quoted in Gifford, *Ghana's New Christianity*, 57.
67. Ibid., 86.
68. Ibid., 110.

Gifford's objectivity emerges as he examines the approach Rev. Mensah Otabil, founder of the ICGC takes to ministry. According to Gifford, this approach is devoid of the extreme faith motif and spiritualization that is prominent in many constituencies of the charismatic fraternity, for Otabil avoids the anointing oil practice, demonization, preoccupation with witchcraft, and the excessive stress on the prophetic and miraculous.[69]

Hollenweger, a doyen of Pentecostal studies, has written considerably about the roots and development of Pentecostalism around the globe. In his book, *The Pentecostals*, Hollenweger goes beyond mere description of Pentecostal spirituality's manifestation to examine some of the doctrines and practices that characterize the movement. Of direct relevance to this study is Hollenweger's analysis of Pentecostal ethics. Considering that *The Pentecostals* dates from 1972, a few of Hollenweger's perspectives on ethical issues have become dated, such as: "But Pentecostals consider that fashionable clothes are not for Christians, women's hair should not be waved; powder and make-up should be left to the world."[70] This observation seems dated in light of the current taste among Pentecostal church members and leaders for trendy fashion and elaborate hairstyles, which have become so conspicuous as to attract criticism from the media.[71] Nevertheless, many of the ethical concepts identified in the book are still applicable to Pentecostal churches today. Hollenweger's discussion of Pentecostal attitudes towards issues such as tithing, the observance of Sunday as a day of rest, military service, taboos on pleasure, food, sex, marriage, and women in ministry reveals ethical principles that remain relevant and sometimes controversial in contemporary Pentecostal communities.

Hollenweger suggests that the two main factors that shape Pentecostal morality are ethical prescription and cultural nuances.[72] He contends, "if we look for the origins of Pentecostal ethics, we find on the one hand a constant basic pattern of ethical prescriptions, and on the other hand powerful influences from the national background of each particular group."[73] Hollenweger captures a subtle hermeneutical error in some practices of Pentecostal ethics when he observes, "But the belief is always held that these

---

69. Ibid., 119.

70. Hollenweger, *Pentecostals*, 403.

71. One reporter's complaint about Pentecostal leaders is "Under the guise of serving the Living God, they sport well-sewn three-piece suits [coats] and fix a clerical on their necks" (Ebenezer Ato Sam, "Why Apostle Nimo was Rejected," *New Punch*, July 1, 2007).

72. Hollenweger, *Pentecostals*, 407.

73. Ibid.

distinctive national features have been derived from the Bible."[74] For instance, in Ghana, some of the classical Pentecostal churches such as the Church of Pentecost, and the Apostolic Church Ghana, strictly enforce head coverings for women in church, which they defend with scriptural passages such as 1 Cor 11:1–16. This scriptural provision notwithstanding, we cannot rule out the influence of traditional Ghanaian dress code on this particular practice.

Obviously, Hollenweger, Gifford, and Asamoah-Gyadu offer perceptive theological reflections on Pentecostal doctrines and practices and engage with important moral issues such as the source of ethical concepts, demonization, the judicious application of economic resources, and dress codes, among others. However, guided by their methodology, these authors do not undertake a systematic examination of ministerial ethics among the groups they have studied, which is the task of this research.

Ministerial Ethics

Ministerial ethics is a universal discipline with general concepts that submit to specific applications in diverse church and social contexts. Therefore, although Trull and Carter's book, *Ministerial Ethics: Being a Good Minister in a Not-so-Good World*, is set in the United States, it reveals principles that are universally applicable and resonate appreciably with the Ghanaian situation. Trull and Carter claim the core issue in ministerial ethics is that "the moral ideal for the minister is integrity, a life of ethical wholeness, and moral maturity."[75] To help approximate this standard, Trull and Carter identify one major cause of ministerial moral malaise as the assumption that morality comes instinctively to those who preach the gospel, for "ministerial ethics is neither simple nor automatic."[76] The co-authors reinforce this position by observing that "minsters can only develop moral sensitivity through education and experience."[77]

Trull and Carter argue that a fundamental requirement for ethical ministry is a clear understanding of the minister's calling. To elucidate this point, they explore the concept of vocation in Christian ministry by describing the minister as a person who is set apart and commissioned by God to accomplish a divine mission. Pondering some ideas expressed by Bayles[78] in his *Professional Ethics*, Trull and Carter suggest that the concept of pro-

74. Ibid.
75. Trull and Carter, *Ministerial Ethics*, 19.
76. Ibid., 20.
77. Ibid., 43.
78. Bayles, *Professional Ethics*, 30.

fessionalism derives from the Christian doctrines of vocation and covenant, which create a community in which believers serve the purposes of God by serving others. However, Trull and Carter lament the secularization of these concepts into career and contract in the modern world, a development that they claim poses a threat to the full reclamation of the traditional virtues of professionalism. In isolating these virtues, they highlight Edmund Pellegrino's concern that "the central idea of a profession, altruistic service and effacement of personal reward, are today downgraded."[79]

Trull and Carter focus on the dynamic relationship between devotion to God and the call to serve humanity by asserting that the minster's devotion to God cannot obliterate the obligation of pastoral duties. In their view, "Ministry involves both privilege and responsibility. The minister's calling always must be fleshed out in some kind of community, usually a local congregation."[80] Trull and Carter rightly conclude, "one cannot serve Christ without serving people, for to serve people is to serve Christ (Matt 25:31–46)."[81]

The co-authors make the revealing and relevant observation that because evangelicals depend on the Bible for moral authority, there is a need to recognize that the Bible contains diverse approaches to moral reasoning. In Trull and Carter's opinion, biblical ethics are not limited to a single category; rather biblical ethics variously espouse the concepts of virtue, principle, and consequence to diverse degrees. The co-authors emphasize the role of character or virtue in moral education by advocating, "Character is basic to all ethical decisions. Who you are determines what you do."[82] Trull and Carter refer to William Willimon's definition of character, arguing that the "basic moral orientation that gives unity, definition, and direction to our lives by forming our habits and intentions into meaningful predictable patterns that have been determined by our dominant convictions."[83] Reflecting on this definition, the co-authors suggest that the Christian minister needs to internalize both the obligations and boundaries of the vocation in order to reflexively behave ethically most of the time.

The prominent role of character in moral formation notwithstanding, Trull and Carter agree with the standard observation in moral philosophy that virtue alone is inadequate in achieving ethical maturity. They therefore proceed to examine the ethics of conduct, arguing:

79. Edmund Pellegrino, quoted in Trull and Carter, 30.
80. Trull and Carter, *Ministerial Ethics*, 22.
81. Ibid., 22.
82. Ibid., 46.
83. Willimon, *The Service of God*, 47.

Acting ethically always involves more than just having a sterling moral character. That is certainly basic, but the moral life is more than simply being a good person. Along with a healthy, wholeness of *being*, must be added conduct and its values—the perspectives, obligations, and aspirations that guide the Christian minister in making right choices.[84]

Trull and Carter seem to endorse the universal notion that misconduct in the clergy centers on sex, money, and power.[85] To develop an adequate moral response to these three cardinal areas of ministerial temptation, the co-authors suggest a consistent approach to the cultivation of moral values. First, they claim that the Bible revels "the theological perspectives that ground us, the obligations that bind us, the norms that guide us and the goals that motivate."[86] This opinion lays a foundation for their discussion of the concepts of obligation and consequence in ethics. Kant's categorical imperative provides the framework for Trull and Carter's examination of obligation in ministry. Trull and Carter convincingly argue that the Bible is fraught with obligations and principles; hence they stress the need for the minister to engage with biblical norms, church codes, and governmental edicts. Nevertheless, in taking a comprehensive view of the ethics of duty, the co-authors caution against its potential for extreme legalism.

Secondly, Trull and Carter reveal that biblical ethics have a dimension of teleology, or the ethics of aspiration. They link this idea to John Stuart Mill's idea of Utilitarianism, which aims to bring the greatest good to the greatest number of people. Serving as a bulwark against legalism, teleological ethics are evident in both the Old and New Testaments, as, for example, in the story of the Hebrew midwives and Pharaoh (Exod 1:15–20) and Jesus' Sabbath controversy with the religious leaders (Mark 2:23–27). However, the co-authors do not mention the dangerous slippery slope of relativity that could emerge from teleological ethics.

Third, Trull and Carter suggest that another extremely important aspect of any worthwhile endeavor in ministerial ethics is the ethics of integrity, or what they call "moral vision," describing it as "a Mount Everest on which every minister hopes to stand."[87] They summarize the three critical concepts in moral formation thus: "Our contention is that the morally

---

84. Trull and Carter, *Ministerial Ethics*, 51.

85. Admittedly, these areas of moral susceptibility are universal rather than peculiar to Christian ministers; however they are the most frequently reported issues relevant to ministerial scandals.

86. Trull and Carter, *Ministerial Ethics*, 53.

87. Ibid., 59.

mature minister experiences concomitant growth in three vital areas: character, conduct and moral vision . . . these three elements interface to produce a morally complete person. Each is necessary, and none is complete without the other two."[88]

Based upon these moral precepts, Trull and Carter offer practical counsel on the minister's personal and family life, relationship with congregation, interactions with colleagues, and engagement with wider society—advice that is biblically grounded, ethically sound, and realistic. Yet because Trull and Carter write from an American background, they cannot engage with the particular moral issues that are endemic to the African context, such as witch hunting and demonization, the impact of the prosperity gospel in a third world economy, and the ethical implications of the specific administrative challenges that confront Pentecostal ministers in Ghana. In view of this limitation, this research is an attempt to respond to some of these issues.

Few books on ministerial ethics by Ghanaian Pentecostal leaders exist, and even the handful available are written more from practical ministry and motivational perspectives than from an academic standpoint. That notwithstanding, I have selected Bishop Charles Agyin-Asare's *Pastoral Protocol: A Guide to Ministerial Ethics* for this review because it is highly relevant to the Ghanaian context. Agyin-Asare insists that the minister's relations with family, church, finances, denomination, community, the opposite sex, and colleagues are all guided by well-laid down standards, which suggests a principled-based approach to ministerial ethics. However, the author does not engage with the concern of the authority and sources for these standards. Furthermore, Agyin-Asare does not respond to factors such as motive, aspiration, and external influence, which to a large extent determine the moral choices ministers make.

Agyin-Asare begins his book on an apologetic note by attempting to defend the ministry against some of the unreasonable demands society makes of the functionaries. He captures some of these demands under the heading of the "Pastor's Dilemma," explaining:

> If he [the pastor] drives an old car, he shames his congregation; if he buys a new one, he is setting his affection on earthly things. If he [the pastor] preaches all the time, the congregation gets tired of hearing just one man; if he invites guest ministers, he is shirking his responsibility.[89]

---

88. Ibid.

89. Agyin-Asare, *Celebrating the Pilgrimage*, 26.

The rest of the book covers a variety of issues ranging from the personal manners of the minister to his relationship with his vocational establishment.

Agyin-Asare brings attention to the tension between the personal standards of conduct for pastors and the pressure of society to conform to certain expectations. The present work explores this concern further to reveal how the desires of such ministers and the demands of society could be held in creative tension for effective ministry. In addition, relevant issues such as the principles and sources that inform Christian ethics and ministerial ethics (which Agyin-Asare's book seems to overlook) are examined in this thesis. Other relevant works will be reviewed as we proceed through later chapters.

Methodology

Multi-Disciplinary Approach

Apart from their spiritual focus, religious movements entail socio-cultural, economic, political, and philosophical ramifications. Hence, any meaningful study of ethical issues in Pentecostal church leadership in Ghana demands a multi-disciplinary approach to reach comprehensive and informed conclusions. Philosophy and morality have a symbiotic relationship, with the former providing the tools and methods necessary for any worthwhile ethical endeavor. Geisler and Feinberg are convinced that the most famous area of philosophy is the study of ethics,[90] which is not only concerned with right action, but also focuses on the principles that justify a particular course of action, contending that such principles should "be universally, or at least generally, applicable in similar situations."[91] It is therefore necessary to undertake a logical reflection on the institutional structures of Pentecostal ministries as well as the conduct of some individual ministers in order to identify trends that promote constructive ministerial ethics.

Nevertheless, the parameters of logic are sometimes inadequate to examining the mystery of religion. As Thomas O'Meara observes, "*kingdom*, *Spirit*, or *grace* are words denoting a special divine presence (beyond the universe studied by physics and biology)."[92] Consequently, the existentialist approach to truth-discovery has also provided an essential missing link in this endeavor. Existentialism is a reaction to rationalism, which, while

---

90. Geisler and Feinberg, *Introduction to Philosophy*, 24.
91. Ibid.
92. O'Meara, *Theology of Ministry*, 35, emphasis O'Meara's.

accepting objective scientific fact, holds subjective truth to be important in ontology (matters related to being or existence).[93] Reflecting on Kierkegaard's concept of existentialism, Wyatt suggests that the individual means everything to the existentialist, for the person is revealed as a series of possibilities, and every decision made redefines that individual. Jean-Paul Sartre further developed this idea in terms of "I" defining the "self," whereby each human being creates a "self" who is "independent from all other knowledge and 'truths' defined by other individuals."[94] Wyatt sums up Kierkegaard's view of religion as something illogical, claiming, "paradox was at the center of his faith."[95] By implication, the fact that some of the decisions and actions of Ghanaian Pentecostal church leaders may fail the test of logic and empirical analysis may not necessarily devalue their validity. However, we must be cautious in avoiding the temptation to use the existentialist approach as a camouflage for accepting every erratic decision or act as "genuine" subjective religious experience. The overall positive or negative impact of such decisions must help to determine their value to society. As Jesus put it, "By their fruit you will recognize them" (Matt 7:16).

The historical approach, which focuses on trends in the development of Pentecostalism as both a universal and Ghanaian phenomenon, would go beyond the mere identification of significant events and personalities to uncover some of the historical factors and concepts that fashioned the value system(s) of the movement.

According to Howard Washington Odum and Katherine C. Jocher, social survey offers an objective, "qualitative approach to the study of social processes,"[96] which affords an invaluable method for evaluating the impact of Pentecostal church leadership on individual lives, families, institutions, and communities. I have therefore sampled the views of selected segments of Ghanaian society to help explain their perceptions of Pentecostal ministers through questionnaires, participant observation, and interviews.

I employed a qualitative approach because scholars are increasingly appreciating the important role of the human element as a determining factor in epistemology. In Esogwa Osuala's estimation, "Qualitative research places stress on the validity of multiple meaning, structures, and holistic analysis."[97] By implication, the human interpretation of truth and understanding of facts is recognized as subjective, and these perspectives are

---

93. Osuala, *Research Methodology*, 46.
94. Jean-Paul Satre, quoted in Wyatt, "Soren Kierkegaard," 14.
95. Ibid., 14.
96. Odum and Jocher, *Introduction to Social Research*, 250.
97. Osuala, *Research Methodology*, 170.

largely determined by people's experiential encounter of the world. The task I have undertaken as a qualitative methodologist has been to record what people say and do in relation to my subject matter and interpret the data as logically and objectively as possible.

The Interview

The interview method, which is described as the most important, most effective, and most widely used means of data collection on social phenomenon,[98] is indispensable in navigating the ethical philosophy and conduct of Pentecostal church leaders. I have personally interviewed thirty-seven church leaders, including top hierarchy such as chairmen, presidents, founders, and general overseers or general secretaries of the selected denomination. These leaders were of particular interest due to their level of influence and their supervisory roles on denominational ministerial conduct. A second category of Pentecostal ministers was selected on the basis of their involvement in the specific ethical issues I seek to examine. The third set of interviews, conducted with ministers who were chosen from the rank and file of their denominations and selected at random, were not highly structured, providing the advantage of spontaneity in answers. Other interviewees included academics whose fields of study touch on the issues explored, as well as some journalists who had investigated Pentecostal ministerial ethics. I have also indiscriminately selected some lay leaders and congregation members who have been influenced or affected by the ministries of Pentecostal leaders to discover the impressions they carry of such leaders.

The Participant Observer

In addition to the interviews, I also gathered primary information through participant observation in Pentecostal churches. In Tom Kumekpor's view, the participant observer is "socially, personally and spatially integrated into the group."[99] Consequently, I undertook participant observation by sitting through Pentecostal church services and taking sermon notes, as well as listening to their testimonies, prayers, and songs. I went further to study their administrative structures and investigate how some of their ministerial ethical codes are applied. This direct interaction approach has equipped me to draw conclusions derived from experience, affording some advantages

98. Kumekpor, *Research Methods*, 119.
99. Ibid., 74.

over the external observer's a priori stance. This method has enabled me to watch and note events from within the context in which they occur and it has accorded me access to details that might, as Kumekpor put it, "elude a casual observer."[100]

It is also necessary at this point to mention that my twelve years of experience as a minister of the Church of Pentecost, coupled with four years' work as a lecturer in Christian Ethics at Pentecost University College, have afforded me insights that may not be available to one observing Pentecostal phenomenon as an outsider. However, these perspectives face the criticism of subjectivity, for it can be extremely difficult to extricate one's personal sentiments and denominational sympathies from one's work. As Kumekpor observes, "the probability of bias, improper comprehension of a situation and implicit moral judgment may be high, especially where the study touches matters or issues on which the observer has strong feelings or to which he may be implicitly hostile."[101] I found Kumekpor's insights useful, for they increased my awareness of the potential pitfalls of participant observation. They have helped me considerably as I consciously endeavored to balance objectivity with a healthy quantum of the subjective.

The Questionnaire

Although my methodology was mainly qualitative, it became necessary to collect some quantitative measures to sample congregation members' views on the ministers under discussion in order to determine the popularity or otherwise of certain notions held by the public about such leaders. Accordingly, I gave out two hundred copies of the questionnaire (see Appendix 4) and received 177 back. The distribution of respondents was an indiscriminate selection of 108 members from the chosen churches: the Church of Pentecost, Assemblies of God, and Redeem Evangel. In addition, I surveyed a random selection of fifty-seven people from other Pentecostal churches and eleven from the Historic Western Mission churches who had encountered Pentecostal ministers. The questionnaire consisted of both closed and open-ended questions carefully phrased to elicit the appropriate responses. I used the simple majority approach to analyze the data and identify trends of both the impressions and factual information respondents offered on the conduct of the Pentecostal ministers they had encountered.

---

100. Ibid., 75.
101. Ibid., 79.

Significance of the Study

The progress and expansion of Pentecostalism has made a remarkable impact on Christianity, and the already-high global membership statistics keep rising. David Barrett and Todd Johnson assert that Pentecostals have become a worldwide movement, with an estimated 450 million members across the world.[102] The impact of Pentecostalism on Ghanaian Christianity and other facets of national life has been overwhelming. According to the Ghana Statistical Service's *2000 Population and Housing Census*, Christians comprise 68 percent of the total population, and their denominational distribution is expressed in the table below:

Table 1: Christian Denominational Demography

Persuasion	Percentage
Catholic	15.1%
Protestant (Mainline)	18.6%
Pentecostal	24.1%
Other Christian	11%
TOTAL	68.8%

In a total population of 18,912,079 people, the census found that 13,914,779 identified as Christians, out of which the Pentecostal movement forms a bulk of 24.1 percent.[103]

The membership registers of the GPC recorded 195 different churches in January of 2006.[104] The second group, the NACCC, which consists mainly of Neo-Pentecostal churches, had 119 member churches in May of 2006.[105] These impressive statistics indicate that the Pentecostal strand of the Christian faith is prominent in Ghanaian society. Consequently, the ethical example of Pentecostal leaders can be posited as a significant contributory factor in determining moral standards in society.

Furthermore, the influence of the Pentecostal ethos has traversed the borders of the movement to impact the practices of other Christian traditions. The adoption of full-blown Pentecostalism in some sections of the Catholic and mainline Protestant churches is a widespread phenomenon

---

102. Barrett and Johnson, "Annual Statistical," 24.

103. Ghana Statistical Service, *2000 Population and Housing Census*, 27.

104. See Ghana Pentecostal Council, "Member Churches of GPCC," http://gpcc-ghana.org/list%20of%20members.html.

105. See the National Association of Charismatic and Christian Churches membership registry, accessed at NACCC headquarters in Accra, Ghana, May 5, 2006.

that Omenyo effectively explores in his *Pentecost outside Pentecostalism: A Study of the Development of Charismatic Renewal in the Mainline Churches in Ghana*. Many conservative mainline churches now encourage previously forbidden Pentecostal practices such as drumming and dancing to the tune of Ghanaian choruses, organizing revival meetings, and tithing. According to Asamoah-Gyadu,

> Pentecostalism at the moment represents the most cogent, powerful and visible evidence of religious renewal and influence in Ghana. I would argue that even the new lease on life being experienced by some of the older churches in Ghana is explicable in terms of their, albeit recent, tolerant and open attitude towards Pentecostal phenomena and renewal movements in their midst.[106]

Another scholar who holds a similar opinion is Dovlo, who avers that the influence of Pentecostalism on the mainline churches has far-reaching implications for religion, liturgy, social norms, and the economy as a whole.[107]

Pentecostal churches have also established a formidable presence in Ghana's electronic media, where their sermons frequently feature on almost all the radio and television channels in the country.[108] According to Asamoah-Gyadu, the Pentecostal movement has become highly visible in terms of the number of followers and high-profile leadership. He therefore acknowledges that if a stream of Christianity becomes so popular, there is no way it would escape the attention of scholars.[109]

Evidently, it is not Pentecostal songs and dance forms alone that seep into other Christian traditions and the wider society—their doctrines and

---

106. Asamoah-Gyadu, *African Charismatics*, 14.

107. Dovlo, "Proliferation of Churches."

108. For example, at the time of writing, Mensah Otabil's "Living Word" aired on TV3 at 6:00 pm Sundays, while Agyin Asare's "Miracle Encounter" was also featured on Saturdays at 5:30 pm on TV3, and Matthew Ashimolowo's "Winning Ways" was telecast by Ghana Television at 8:00 am on Saturdays. The Church of Pentecost sponsored "Pentecost Hour," featuring key leaders on Ghana Television at 5:30 am on Thursdays and on TV3 at 5:30 pm on Wednesdays. David Oyedepo of Winners' Chapel appeared regularly on Metro TV at 11:30 am on Sundays, and Stephen Amoaning, Chairman of Christ Apostolic Church, was featured regularly on "The Apostolic Voice" on Ghana Television on Sundays at 8:00 am, while Duncan Williams's "Voice of Inspiration" aired on Ghana Television on Sundays at 7:30 am. Although schedules have since changed, the Pentecostal presence these examples demonstrate is still felt strongly across multiple media platforms in Ghana.

109. J. Kwabena Asamoah-Gyadu, Trinity Theological College, interview by Dela Quampah, Accra, Ghana, June 2, 2009.

ethical principles invariably filter through as well. Nevertheless, there seems to be little evidence of any significant academic investigation into Pentecostal ministerial ethics in Ghana. Most of the available literature on Ghanaian Pentecostalism is confined to the historical, theological or social dimensions of the movement.

Although a handful of authors such as Paul Gifford,[110] Asamoah-Gyadu,[111] and Emmanuel Anim[112] offer critiques of the ethical implications of deliverance and the prosperity gospel, hardly does any of them directly engage with general standards in ministerial ethics in the Ghanaian Pentecostal movement. The low level of research on the ethical aspect of Pentecostalism is not limited to the Ghanaian context. It has also been observed even on the international front that Pentecostal theology has yet to produce an appreciably compelling or clearly articulated moral theory.[113] Currently, only two notable books have been published by Pentecostal ministers in Ghana on ministerial ethics: Charles Agyin-Asare's *Pastoral Protocol: A Guide to Ministerial Ethics* and Dag Heward-Mills' *Ministerial Ethics: Practical Wisdom for Christian Ministers*. Only a few of the numerous Pentecostal churches have produced comprehensive ethical codes for their ministers, although they do hold the ministers accountable for unethical behavior.

Obviously, the Pentecostal churches have become a force to reckon with in the religious, social, economic, and even the political discourses of Ghana. This brings into focus the need to explore the moral theories revealed in the institutional stipulations of such ministries and the conduct of their individual ministers.

---

110. See Gifford, *Ghana's New Christianity*, 140–60.
111. Asamoah-Gyadu, *African Charismatics*, 222–32.
112. Anim, "Who Wants to Be a Millionaire?"
113. Palmer, "Social Ethics," 605.

2

Ghanaian Traditional Leadership Milieu and the Contextualization of Christianity

Introduction

ALTHOUGH THE CENTRAL FACTOR of religious experience is intangible, mysterious, and sometimes unexplainable, its concomitant revelation or message is always communicated through the observable material cultural context within which the encounter occurs. Contextualization, from the Christian perspective, is regarded as the various processes by which a local church assimilates the universal gospel message with its local culture.[1] In this regard, David Bosch[2] claims the indigenization model is effective in translating the gospel message into the idioms and metaphors of the host community. Pentecostals seem to be successful in Africa because they have responded creatively to the socio-cultural and religious heritage of the communities. The scriptural relevance of this kind of engagement is supported by Bediako, who suggests that understanding Christian soteriology through the African worldview is as biblical and convincing as any other theological perspective.[3]

It can therefore be postulated that traditional Ghanaian institutions and the values they promote still have a significant influence on contemporary Ghanaian institutions, including Pentecostal churches. This informs Kwame Gyekye's assertion that "most of the traditional ideas and values have, generally speaking, not relaxed their grip on modern African life and

---

1. Luzbetak, *Church and Cultures*, 69.
2. Bosch, *Transforming Mission*, 421.
3. Bediako, *Jesus in Africa*, 22.

thought."[4] These values and forms of thought are considered in the enculturation process as convenient vehicles for the communication and depositing of truth.[5]

This chapter therefore explores some of the traditional institutions and leadership structures that constitute the social matrix of the twentieth century Pentecostal revival in Ghana. The family, as the basic unit of society, is analyzed to isolate ethical principles that guide individuals in their communal interaction. Traditional political and religious leadership trends are also examined to better discover how their value systems relate to contemporary Pentecostal leadership.

Traditional Ghanaian Family

The role of the family in value formation and ethical education in any society is paramount. Since the family provides the initial grid through which a person views the world, experiences and values imbibed within that context have an enduring and defining impact on the individual's life and personality. Social anthropologists often emphasize the impartation of moral values to a child, and in many cultures a large proportion of this responsibility falls on the family.[6]

Students of the Ghanaian family structure readily distinguish between the nuclear and extended family systems. The extended family includes parents, siblings, uncles, aunts, cousins, and grandparents. The nuclear family, however, is comprised only of a father, mother, and a child or children. Max Assimeng offers a functional definition of the nuclear family as "a group of sexually interacting adults and their children who occupy statuses, perform roles and are responsible for the economic, social and emotional welfare of one another, especially the children."[7] This functional definition provides an adequate framework for an analysis of the basic ethical principles that manifest in the family structure. The specific issues that arise in the context of traditional family values include status, responsibility, and the use of titles. Since the extended family is more heavily emphasized in Africa than the nuclear family,[8] I find it worthwhile to examine these ethical ideas in relation to the extended family structure.

4. Gyekye, *Unexamined Life*, 69.

5. Bevans, *Models of Contextual Theology*, 37.

6. Grunlan and Mayers, *Cultural Anthropology*, 145; Nukunya, *Tradition and Change*, 51.

7. Assimeng, *Understanding Society*, 31.

8. This has been demonstrated in Ganusah, "Community Versus Individual Rights," 1–21.

The Extended Family Structure

In Ghana, marriage is considered as a contract among four clans rather than between just two individuals, as the extended family embraces grandparents, uncles and aunts, cousins, nephews and nieces, and so on. In Rebecca Ganusah's view, "The two [prospective couple] are being married not just onto [sic] themselves as a couple, but into four families of the man's father and mother, as well as those of the woman's father and mother."[9] This extended family system has its own leadership structure, which defines the rights, duties, and responsibilities of the individual to the lineage. The Akans refer to the lineage, or extended family, as *abusua*, the Eves call it *fome*, and the Gas designate it as *weku*. The central figure in *abusua* among the Akans is *Abusua Panyin*, or the head of the lineage, who is normally a man, even in a matrilineal context.[10]

The lineage's leadership structure ensures the mutual support and cooperation of its members. It also regulates behavior by insisting on conformity to social norms, with its inherent ability to punish and reward accordingly. Members depend on the lineage for their identity (normally revealed in their surnames), appreciation, and moral support in the normal pursuits in life—be it in developing a career, arranging a marriage, in childbirth and training, or in travelling abroad. In tragic times such as bereavement, protracted illness, or accidents and loss of property, the whole lineage rallies around the individual to offer help in the recovery and restoration process.

Nevertheless, this positive practice of socialization in the lineage can generate tensions that cause adverse social reverberations. Peter Sarpong, for instance, has observed that "the African family may have wonderful values, but the same African family may have counter-values that are causing problems in Africa—ethnocentrism, tribalism, excessive particularism."[11] Financial obligations to the extended family, such as caring for underprivileged relatives, sometimes make unrealistic demands on the individual. Furthermore, almost the whole lineage is expected to attend social functions such as weddings and funerals, making the cost of a reception a drain on the host's resources. In addition, lineage affiliation can lead to nepotism, for a person of influence is expected to please his or her kith and kin by favoring them with appointments and contracts, even over more qualified applicants.

---

9. Ibid., 3.
10. Nkansah-Kyeremateng, *Akan Heritage*, 67.
11. Sarpong, *Peoples Differ*, 80.

The Status and Role of Women in Traditional Ghanaian Society

Traditionally, the position of married women within the various Ghanaian ethnic groups is not an enviable one. The very structure of traditional marriage subordinates the status of women to that of men. A study of family values demands the identification of the two family systems of marriage, namely the monogamous and polygamous. While many Ghanaian cultures are tolerant of polygyny (wherein a man marries more than one wife), polyandry (wherein a woman takes more than one husband) is unheard of among any Ghanaian ethnic group. One Christian feminist ethicist's account of Kenyan Parliamentarians' strenuous objections to a bill aimed at proscribing polygamy poignantly reflects the position of African women, even in the twenty-first century. Prominent among these male politicians' reasons for rejecting the bill was their strong conviction that the man is supreme in African marriage since he is the one who swears to take the wife. A first wife therefore has no right to object when her husband decides to take another wife.[12]

This male-dominant factor and the attendant abuse of women in the African family unit are not limited to polygamous marriage. The cultural practice of taking a bride-price[13] from suitors seems to reduce women to chattel and exposes them to every kind of imaginable domestic maltreatment. K. Nkansah-Kyeremateng, a social commentator on Akan culture, is convinced that by paying the bride-price, a woman effectually becomes part of her husband's estate.[14]

Traditional philosophy, as expressed in this Akan maxim, further highlights the low status of women in African society: ɔbaa tɔ etuo a etwere ɔbarima ɔdan mu. This translates, "If a woman acquires a gun, she keeps it in a man's room." This maxim, despite its origins in a matrilineal society, does not only project the idea that a woman's achievement is transferred to her husband (or sometimes to her male relative), it also betrays the fact that

---

12. Njoroge, *Kiama Kia Ngo*, 81.

13. According to Nukunya, the bride-price among the Eʋes, for instance, comprises of twelve bottles of assorted drinks, cash, kente cloth, and wax printed cloth (Nukunya, *Tradition and Change*, 43).

14. Nkansah-Kyeremateng, *Akan Heritage*, 118. Sarpong, however, argues that the bride-price is not equivalent to the commercial value of the woman, but it is rather a symbolic "gift" of appreciation and compensation for the loss of a female helping hand in the family (Sarpong, *Ghana in Retrospect*, 83). However, since there is no documentation on the whole practice, we can fairly conclude that the practice is subject to various interpretations and each view could be equally valid.

women could not own property in the traditional setting.[15] This patriarchy is by no means peculiar to the Akans, for even among the Eve's who inherit paternally, a woman has virtually no property rights.

It is noteworthy that some modern institutions such as industry, politics, and academia have provided the necessary leverage for Ghanaian women to attain national and international fame. It was the industrial sector that projected the late Dr. Esther Nkulenu Ocloo to international recognition when she co-won (with General Olusegun Obasanjo, President of Nigeria) the Africa Prize for Leadership for Sustainable End of Hunger award in 1990. Another remarkable example of a Ghanaian woman whose achievements were empowered by education is Professor Florence Abena Dolphyne, who rose to the high office of Pro-Vice Chancellor of the University of Ghana from 1996 to 1998 and also served as President of the West African Linguistic Society. The gender neutrality of the academy has been further enhanced by the appointment of the first female Ghanaian Vice Chancellor of the University of Cape Coast, Professor Jane Naana Opoku-Agyemang, in 2008. Yet the church in Ghana, with the exception of a few denominations that ordain women, has still not produced a female church leader of national or international acclaim.

The Status and Role of Children in Traditional Ghanaian Society

Most sociologists agree that Africans place much value on childbearing, and barrenness or sterility can be a cause for either divorce or polygyny. A large family size is popular in Africa to enhance personal reputation and a desire to be remembered after death. In addition, children become an important factor in determining one's economic progress, for they provide the labor needed in traditional agriculture. Ultimately, children also serve as social security in old age. The ethical question that is generated by these attitudes to childbearing is whether one should consider the offspring as a means to an end or we should value them as ends in themselves?

From a constructive perspective, child training in the traditional Ghanaian context inculcates in them respect for elders. Children are encouraged to obey their parents and to respect their elders in order to enjoy their favor and appreciation. Nevertheless, it could be taken to the extreme in certain cases, where respect is often demanded rather than earned.

---

15. It is noteworthy that Kwame Gyekye ignores the issue of women's rights in his much-acclaimed book, *African Cultural Values*, while G. K. Nukunya seems to support the status quo in his *Tradition and Change*.

Although respect between adults and children is supposed to be reciprocal, most often, children are compelled to be obedient and dutiful, no matter how they are treated.

These underlying traditional principles to child upbringing are, to some extent, responsible for institutional neglect and sometimes gross abuse of children, even in contemporary Ghanaian society. Although Ghana prides itself on being the first nation to ratify the United Nations Convention on the Rights of the Child and the Children's Act 560, the protection of the rights of children in the country is lamentable, even in official circles. In 2007, the year marking the fiftieth anniversary of Ghana's independence, the Executive Director of Children's Rights International, Ghana, a non-governmental agency working in the interest of children, wrote a rather scathing news commentary against the partial attitude of the judiciary to child abuse cases. Here is an excerpt:

> The child who seeks justice is also perceived as truant in the context of tradition. About 90 percent of children in Ghana never get the opportunity to be heard in the traditional justice administration . . . The reality is that children whose cases are in court do not receive due attention and prompt judgment. In Ghana, 80 percent of cases involving children are withdrawn and settled under the traditional justice system. Twenty percent take between one and three years before justice is delivered.[16]

The Status and Role of Men in Traditional Ghanaian Society

Traditional Ghanaian society is largely patriarchal, with men dominating the social institutions and regulating almost every facet of family and communal life. This situation is in place for two reasons, namely the military factor and the strenuous demands of manual work. The military factor became relevant as ancient Ghanaian communities were exposed to frequent attacks from other tribes. The need to mobilize members of the community to ward off such provocations became paramount, and because in many cultures women are insulated from military service, traditional communities in Africa hardly ever allowed women to become combatants.[17] As a

---

16. Children's Rights International Executive Director, "Ghana and the Dawn of 50."

17. An exception to this norm occurred among the Asante when Yaa Asantewa, the Queen Mother of Ejisu, led men to battle against the British in 1900.

result, those men who defended the communities became opinion leaders and regulators of political, economic, and social life.

Secondly, traditional modes of economic sustenance were supported by vocations that were physically taxing, such as the manual cultivation of land to raise crops, fishing, hunting, and trading with far-off communities without the convenience of modern means of transport. Obviously, many of these economic ventures were too physically demanding and hazardous for females to undertake. Because men dominated major economic activities in this traditional setting, economic empowerment extended their influence and diminished women's with financial deprivation. Consequently, almost all leadership positions in traditional institutions became a kind of male preserve among many ethnic groups in Ghana. The chieftaincy, for instance, is controlled by men from generation to generation, making them the communal potentate.

Titles and Status in Traditional Family

The functional role of personal titles is an integral part of family, and for that matter, community life in Ghana, where people are more readily identified by their titles than their names. These titles help to identify social position and define relationships between people to facilitate their social intercourse. For example, among the Eʋes, the title *enyrui* not only depicts a man as an uncle, but specifically points to a maternal uncle. Similarly, *nɔdɛ* not only identifies a maternal aunt, but reveals that this aunt is one's mother's younger sister, while *nɔgã* or *nanagã* suggests she is senior to one's mother. *Tɔdɛ* denotes a paternal uncle younger than one's father, while *tɔgã* stands for a paternal uncle older than one's father. The use of *efo* suggests the one being addressed is a senior brother, while *daa/davi* refers to a sister or any woman who is senior in age. Hence, titles are crucial in the family, communal, and institutional lives of traditional Africans, and they remain relevant today, even in the church.

Relevance of a Traditional Sense of Community to the Church

Kinship ties in Africa produce communal bonding, and this sense of belonging is such a prominent feature in African communities that every social institution has to reckon with it. Theologians such as Philomena Mwaura see a biblical reflection in this sense of community and suggest that it not only approximates the tribal ties of the Old Testament, but also reflects the concept of *koinonia*, or community, which characterized the early Church.[18] This sense of community resonates well with Pentecostalism, which Jackie David Johns claims transforms the affections of the individual, making them relational in character: "Thus the model of godly affections is community, the *koinonia* of the saints, and orthopraxy is always shared orthorpraxy."[19] Asamoah-Gyadu, in exploring the success story of the Church of Pentecost, observes that communal bonds and the "welfare system of support for members is key to their ability to attract and hold members."[20] Similarly, Ganusah examines the rights of the individual in the African communal setting and suggests that charismatic churches' response to traditional communal life reflects a paradox of rejection of traditional bonds and the re-creation of a new community. As she explains:

> So that the Christian faith, in a seemingly paradoxical way, is contributing to the decline in the traditional communal spirit of partaking in every communal practice, while at the same time it is helping to enhance some communal expectations in the society like rejoicing with those who rejoice and mourning with those who mourn.[21]

Dr. John Kpikpi, a New Frontiers minister and former lecturer at the University of Ghana, has developed an approach to contextualization that relates the concept of tribal affiliation to Christianity by regarding the Christian community as a kind of tribe. In his book, *God's New Tribe*, Kpikpi suggests that in Ghana, "the effects of tribal identities can be seen in the very structure of marriage and family life, business, politics, national life and religion."[22] Nevertheless, he insists that if taken to the extreme, tribalism could be destructive; hence he promotes the concept of God's "new tribe," a community that upholds biblical values that do not particularize tribal identity. Agyeman-Nkansah takes a similar view in suggesting that since traditional life is communal and the church is also a community, the

---

18. Mwaura, "New Religious Movementss," 10. It is noteworthy that the initial attempts in the Book of Acts to establish an authentic Christian community revealed imperfections that led to the death of Ananias and Sapphira (Acts 5:1–11) and discrimination against the widows from the Jewish Diaspora in the distribution of material support (Acts 1:1–6).

19. Johns, "Yielding to the Spirit," 77.

20. Asamoah-Gyadu, "Pentecostalism and the Missiological Significance," 44.

21. Ganusah, "Community Versus Individual Rights," 16.

22. Kpikpi, *God's New Tribe*, 11.

church in Africa can emphasize this commonality to enhance its indigenous identity.²³

In such a context, the implications of communal affinity for moral value formation become obvious, as the interest and values of society are projected above those of the individual. In support of this position, Gyekye argues that social life, as a robust feature of the African communitarian society, mandates a morality that emphasizes duty to others and to the community.²⁴ However, Gyekye comprehensively examines the concept of personhood in another article in which he takes issue with any ethical system that diminishes the moral autonomy of the individual by subjecting them to "the activities, values, projects, practices and ends of the community."²⁵

The challenge, in such a context, is to discover how the rights of the individual are recognized in personal value formation and held in equilibrium with communal interest. Consequently, the Ghanaian Christian leader is challenged to respect social norms without trampling the rights and interests of the individual.

Ghanaian Traditional Political Leadership

Attempts to contextualize the Christian gospel by applying traditional Ghanaian political leadership imagery and nuances have yielded some stimulating results. For instance, Ghanaians' familiarity with their royal establishments has produced imagery and accolades that are readily transferable to Christ to better project his royal status, as revealed in a praise song by Afua Kuma, a Ghanaian Pentecostal:

> [Christ] Chief of young women:
>
> They have strung a necklace of gold nuggets and beads, and
> hung it around your neck.
> So we go before you,
> Shouting our praises, "*Ose, Ose!*"
> Chief of young men:
> They are covered with precious beads
> And gold pendants worn by princes
> They follow you, playing musical instruments.²⁶

---

23. Agyeman-Nkansah, "Deeping the Roots of Christianity," 32–42.
24. Gyekye, "African Ethics."
25. Ibid., "Person and Community," 102.
26. Kuma, *Jesus of the Deep Forest*, 23.

In many African communities, the position of a traditional ruler is believed to be invested with a sacred power that makes the chief a representative of the deities and ancestors of the community. According to Douglas Waruta, "in African society, leadership was never purely political or mere civil authority. It always carried with it a religious aspect in which the leaders of the people exerted ritual and religious authority as well."[27] Hence, it is easy for the Ghanaian to accord human leaders supernatural attributes, for they have long been regarded as the physical representatives of benevolent supernatural forces that provide for and preserve the community.

The origin of the institution of chieftaincy in many Ghanaian communities is rather hazy; however, in certain cases it is ascribed to the founding fathers or families (who became the monarchs) of early settlements.[28] Some contemporary scholars who have analyzed Ghanaian chieftaincy seem to have done a certain disservice to the institution by using Western democracy as their yardstick. Researchers such as Oseadeeyo Addo Dankwa III[29] and Alexander Frempong[30] argue that the selection and administrative structure of the chieftaincy institution, for example that of the Akans, is comparable to democratic establishments anywhere. This insight is revealed in Frempong's suggestion that "the absence of the ballot box in African villages did not necessarily imply that Africans were ignorant of democracy."[31] To better appreciate the institution of chieftaincy, I think it would be preferable to consider it on its own merit, rather than pitting it against modern Western democracy. The rationale is that the Ghanaian context and experiences that gave shape to the institution are uniquely different from the Greek setting that molded Athenian democracy. The strength of the Ghanaian system lies in the fact that, unlike other contexts wherein succession devolves to the leader's firstborn, the Ghanaian establishment normally draws potential candidates from a number of clans, out of which the kingmakers select the most resourceful person.[32]

The Ghanaian chieftaincy provided the essential unifying pivot for vulnerable and scattered settlements before the colonial European scramble and partitioning of Africa. The chiefs became a source of identity and ethnic pride, for they afforded protection from external aggression and provided internal stability while serving as custodians of the values and principles

27. Waruta, "Jesus Christ for Africans Today?" 60.
28. Dankwa, *Institution of Chieftaincy in Ghana*, 11.
29. Ibid., 16.
30. Frempong, "Chieftaincy, Democracy and Human Rights," 380.
31. Ibid.
32. Ibid., 383.

that sustained vital social institutions. The chieftaincy also preserved the intellectual property, aesthetic values, and the creative accomplishments of the community. More importantly, the chief was expected to serve as the moral icon of the community, exemplifying and safeguarding their value system. In his article on religion and traditional leadership, Abraham Akrong explains that the numerous taboos attached to chieftaincy worked to set the high ethical standard the chief is expected to observe as a moral model for the community.[33]

Because titles are crucial to social interaction in Africa, they become even more important in the socio-political establishment. The meaning of chieftaincy titles among the Akans becomes clear through an examination of the specific roles and functions of the title holders: The *Omanhin* is the supreme leader of the community; the *Adontenhin* is the next in line; the *Gyasihin* is the person in charge of the domestic arrangements of the *Omanhin*, the *Ankobeahin* is leader of the *Omanhin*'s personal body guards. Besides these functional titles, Ghanaian chiefs are sometimes designated by attributes such as *Oseadeayɔ* (the one who keeps his word), *Otumfuɔ* (the mighty one), *Osabarima* (the mighty warrior), *Odenehu* (the independent one), *Osagyefo* (the deliverer), *Okasapraku* (once he makes a declaration, his word goes unchallenged). Such attributes convey the traditional philosophy of leadership, which expect chiefs to embody these attributes in order to exemplify the "spirit" of the community.

The significance of the iconic role of the traditional ruler in exhibiting the moral values of society has attracted some academic attention. G. K. Nukunya emphasizes the chief's moral duty to maintain law and order in society, insisting that he symbolizes the moral and ritual purity of his people. Nukunya further argues that this responsibility of moral and spiritual leadership places serious taboos on the chief to enable him maintain his ritual purity.[34] Akrong is also convinced that the chief, as a *de jure* ancestor, is bound to demonstrate the moral qualities of the ancestors and emerge as the moral paragon of the community. Akrong further identifies the function of taboos as the regulatory factor on the social and moral life of the chief, which empowers him to "articulate the values and ideals of the society."[35]

Thus, in both the traditional setting and some contemporary institutions, the challenge of moral excellence is regarded as a benchmark for those in leadership. However the ability of the occupants of the throne to live up to these moral standards has often been called into question. Some of

---

33. Akrong, "Religion and Traditional Leadership," 200.
34. Nukunya, *Tradition and Change*, 70.
35. Akrong, "Religion and Traditional Leadership," 200.

the concerns raised over the less attractive aspects of traditional leadership include the institutionalization of polygamy, the autocratic use of power, human rights abuses, misapplication of communal resources, and chieftaincy disputes.[36]

Traditional Religious Leadership

Harold Turner conceives of religion as something "existing in the interplay between revelation of the transcendent and the response of the human, both set always, of course, in a particular milieu."[37] This concept identifies the three crucial factors of deity, individual, and community, whose interplay generates and sustains any significant religious narrative. Turner's opinion is instructive in studying religious functionaries and their social impact within the traditional African setting as "a particular milieu." The African worldview, which is keenly aware of the constant dynamic interaction between the spiritual and physical realms, makes traditional religion pervasive, influencing almost all aspects of personal and communal life.

Emanuel Bolaji Idowu regards African traditional religion as one of reciprocal relationships by which humankind relies on the deity for the fulfillment of personal and basic needs that are both material and spiritual.[38] This practicality and pervasiveness of religion in Africa is further enhanced by the idea of mystical causality, or the belief that occurrences in the physical realm are predetermined and influenced by supernatural forces—either benevolent ones, such as deities and ancestral spirits, or malevolent ones, such as witches. This widespread religious inclination makes priests and other sacerdotal functionaries indispensable in the traditional setting, for they play intermediary roles between deities and communities.[39] In the traditional Ghanaian setting, priests and priestesses, diviners, mediums, medicine men, magicians, and herbalists comprise the set of religious functionaries whose roles often overlap and do not respond readily to Christian categories. However, for the purposes of the present work, I would like to give attention to the office of priests and priestesses, whose functions, in certain dimensions, seem to be reflected in aspects of Pentecostal ministry.

Mbiti, in examining the traditional priesthood, appreciates these functionaries as embodying what is the best in the religion, for they become

36. Some of these criticisms are captured in Perbi, "Servitude and Chieftaincy in Ghana," 353–78; Hagan, "Epilogue," 663–73.
37. Turner, "Way Forward in the Religious Study," 13.
38. Idowu, *African Traditional Religion*, 190.
39. Mbiti, *African Religions and Philosophy*, 162–84.

living symbols of the presence of God as well as the spiritual beliefs and moral values of the people.[40] Mbiti further suggests that as the repository of the religious heritage of their communities, they are "wise, intelligent and talented people, often with outstanding abilities and personalities."[41] This suggests that traditional religious leaders are charismatic and resourceful individuals who protect and project the religious ideas and practices of their communities—qualifications which are not alien to Christian leadership.

The Calling and Training of Priests

K. A. Busia delineates the calling of traditional priests in his seminal work on Asante society, in which he explains that the Asante candidates for priesthood are chosen directly by the spirit of the *bosom*, or deity, through special revelation.[42] John David Kwamena Ekem, who has extensively explored the status and roles of the ɔkɔmfo (plural: akɔmfo), the traditional priest, to identify parallels in Christian nomenclature, also argues that the call to the priesthood is the prerogative of the deity.[43] Principal among the criteria for a genuine call to the priesthood is possession by the spirit of a particular *bosom*. But this has to be attested by more experienced *akɔmfo*.[44] Thereafter, the candidate is sent to a shrine for training. The training period varies from about six months to four years[45] and can be rigorously exacting, sometimes demanding extreme self-discipline in dietary and sexual matters. According to Opoku Onyinah, the training process is quite elaborate, instructing candidates in "the laws, taboos, dances, songs and idiosyncrasies of the gods, as well as general priestly duties."[46] The moral dimension of this training is further enhanced by the instructions trainees receive when they graduate, which include such injunctions as "not to kill, not to steal, not to deceive, not to be proud, to obey parents and elders, to be discreet and not to quarrel even when provoked."[47]

---

40. Mbiti, *Introduction to African Religion*, 153.
41. Ibid.
42. Busia, "Ashanti," 193–94.
43. Ekem, *Priesthood in Context*, 48.
44. Ibid.
45. Ibid., 49.
46. Onyinah, "Akan Witchcraft," 56–57.
47. Mbiti, *African Religions and Philosophy*, 171.

Functions and Roles of the Priest

The interpretation of scholars such as Green, who suggests that Africans may not necessarily engage in religious activities unless calamities cause them to seek explanations from their spiritual and moral framework,[48] seems to limit the social impact of traditional religion and its functionaries. To reiterate, religion permeates every facet of African life, and shrines are regularly consulted for protection and prosperity not only in the hereafter, but more importantly, in the present age. According to Gyekye, "emphasis on the pursuit and attainment of human well-being is unrelenting. Indeed, religion is considered essentially as a means of attaining the needs, interests and happiness of human beings in this life."[49] This issue is discussed later in connection with the prosperity gospel. Africa's pervasive religious attitude underscores the indispensability of shrines and their functionaries in observing ceremonies, rituals, and rites of passage of traditional communities.

Beyond the performance of rituals on behalf of the community, groups, and individuals, traditional priests play an important intermediary role between the deities and their devotees. The priests plead with the gods on behalf of petitioners, and in turn reveal to them the divine will, especially in terms of pacification requirements, which the acolytes help worshippers to carry out after the prescribed objects have been provided. Onyinah describes the process of consultation, explaining that the spirit of the deity of a particular *bosom* is invited to possess the ɔkɔmfo. The ɔkɔmfo receives esoteric messages from the *bosom*, which are then deciphered by an interpreter to the clients.[50] The content of these messages, according to Onyinah, include "the type of treatment of a disease, or causes of mishaps, such as barrenness, an accident, a sudden death or origin of conflicts in marriage."[51] Another important function of the priest is that of prophecy, for the priest is expected to predict the future and speak the will of his or her deity under divine inspiration.

Normally, a high standard of ethical behavior is expected of priests because of the prominent role they play in society. Such behavior may include self-discipline in sexual expression as well as the observance of other personal and social taboos.

---

48. Green, "Religion and Morality," 6.
49. Gyekye, *African Cultural Values*, 14. In addition, see Larbi, *Pentecostalism*, 50.
50. Onyinah, "Akan Witchcraft," 56–57.
51. Ibid.

Moral Influence of Religious Functionaries

Linking traditional African morality to religion has generated a polarized debate among scholars. Mbiti,[52] Ganusah,[53] and Akoto[54] argue for a religious basis for traditional morality, while Gyekye[55] and Wiredu,[56] for instance, insist on a non-religious traditional value system. Considering the pervasiveness of religious ideas and the rejection of the dichotomy between the sacred and the secular in the traditional African context, this researcher supports a religious foundation for traditional African ethics, and consequently locates religious functionaries at the center of morality for the community.

The traditional religious establishment often provides the context for rewards and sanctions in response to moral choices in the community. Chris Abotchie undertakes an elaborate exploration of the various mechanisms for social control among the southern Eʋes by isolating the relevant factors of lineage identity, rites of passage, traditional leadership, and what he calls the "magico-religious mechanism."[57] Abotchie's magico-religious category emphasizes that the Eʋes hold criminal acts as offensive to the gods, who consequently engage supernatural forces to regulate human behavior in the community.[58] Abotchie postulates that the Eʋes consider sickness and tragic occurrences as aberrations attributable to spiritual forces. Their occurrence, therefore, calls for causal identification, which requires that priests and diviners consult the deities, pronounce the cause, and prescribe the appropriate remedy.[59] Some of the popular causes are the breaking of a taboo, for which the diviner may recommend animal sacrifice to appease the aggrieved spiritual forces. Other magical methods of enforcing moral behavior, in Abotchie's view, include *nukaka*, or oracle consultation, *akadodo*, trial by ordeal, and *ame dede trɔ me*, or hexing.[60]

The subject of witchcraft features prominently in any discussion of traditional African religions. The reality or otherwise of the phenomenon is, however, beyond the scope of this study. Generally, witches are branded

---

52. Mbiti, *Introduction to African Religion*, 174–79.
53. Ganusah, "Impact of Religion on Morality," 69–82.
54. Akoto, "Religion, Morality," 83–99.
55. Gyekye, *African Cultural Value*, 56–57.
56. Wiredu, "Moral Foundations," 193–206.
57. Abotchie, *Social Control*, 4.
58. Ibid.
59. Ibid., 63.
60. Ibid.

as evil people, especially old ladies, who use psychic powers to harm others or destroy their possessions. It is extremely difficult, if not impossible, to prove that someone has dabbled in witchcraft. Nevertheless, witchcraft accusations are frequent features of traditional religion; some priests and shrines even specialize in witchcraft detection and subsequent exorcism. The person identified by a priest or diviner as the witch responsible for someone else's calamity is exposed to all kinds of humiliating treatment and is sometimes ostracized from the community or even surreptitiously killed. The emergence of this trend in contemporary society and the response of Pentecostal leaders to the phenomenon are discussed further in chapter 6.

Considering the function of religious leaders in determining the moral gauge of society, we might expect them to exemplify the morality they mediate. Acolytes in training observe certain moral prohibitions and taboos that they are often expected to uphold even after graduation. The emphatic moral slant of the Christian gospel, with its subsequent demand that practitioners serve as moral icons, seems to run parallel to these qualifications for traditional religious leaders. Hence, the public outcry against unethical conduct among Pentecostal ministers appears to be an extension of traditional attitudes towards religious leaders.

Inherent Challenges in Traditional Leadership

The positive influence of traditional political and religious leadership notwithstanding, concerns about how the veneration of such leaders could result in the abuse of followers and mismanagement of resources are widespread. Such abuses could likewise characterize contemporary Christian leadership, as Waruta succinctly explains:

> Some priests and bishops have definitely exploited this African cultural heritage of reverence to their spiritual leaders for their own personal glory and enrichment. Even in political circles, leaders tend toward personality cult[s,] which they know will easily develop in the context of the African cultural respect for their leaders. This tendency may explain why in the African church and state, people in authority do not easily relinquish power. Authority in Africa is held as a sacred rather than as a public trust . . . Taken by fallen human beings, the African reverence for authority can become a source of great abuses and sufferings.[61]

61.

Conclusion

The Christian gospel's contextualization is emerging as a fresh dynamic among Pentecostal churches, especially in Africa, where significant strides are being made in the indigenization of doctrine, ritual, and ecclesiastical structure. In some instances, traditional ideas seem to resonate well with Christian concepts and practices that reflect an African sense of community, a sharp awareness of spiritual reality, and submission to leadership. The examination of Ghanaian traditional institutions, namely family, chieftaincy, and religion has revealed ethical issues such as women's and children's rights, the balance between communal and personal interests, and the responsible application of political and religious authority. Obviously, these concerns still manifest in contemporary institutions, not least of all in Pentecostal churches.

3

Selected Ethical Theories and Systems

Introduction

THE STRUCTURE OF SOCIETY compels Christian ethics to interact with other ethical systems such that no comprehensive discussion of the former is complete without an appreciable reference to the latter.[1] Consequently, this chapter focuses on general ethical theories and systems to identify parallel principles and explore the dynamics of Christian ethics' interrelationship to secular moral philosophy. This study closely examines select relevant ethical theories to help discern their possible manifestation in Ghanaian Pentecostal ministerial ethics. In addition, the formulation of traditional Ghanaian ethical philosophy is also explored in order to detect its influence on the moral standards of Ghanaian Pentecostal leaders.

Various definitions for ethics have been offered. Depending on the orientation of the ethicist, understandings of ethics may either emphasize principle over consequence or vice versa. From another perspective, some ethicists promote the interests of society over those of the individual, while others do the opposite. For instance, John and Paul Feinberg define ethics as "the branch of philosophy that reflects on such issues as the source of moral norms and how to justify one's rules for governing action in moral

---

1. Since Christians do not live in isolation of people of other faiths and ideologies, the cross-fertilization of moral concepts between them becomes inevitable. This interaction could be beneficial or detrimental, contingent to the Christian community's response. A constructive comparative approach could identify parallels on the one hand, and areas of conflict on the other hand, thereby facilitating the necessary reflection that would resource the Christian to appreciate his or her ethical convictions from a better informed position.

matters."[2] The use of "norms" and "rules" in this short definition implies an approach to ethics that is more inclined towards duty and principle than consequence.[3] Let us also consider Wiredu's definition, which explains ethics as "simply the observance of rules for the harmonious adjustment of the interests of the individual to those of others in society."[4] This definition from an African, apart from its inclination towards obligation, also seems to subject the interests of the individual to those of society. Applied to ministerial ethics, the pertinent issues include whether ministers' conduct should be principle-based or consequence-driven, and whether ministers should be guided by conscience to define their own moral standards or they ought to conform instead to society's expectations. This investigation defines ethics as a discipline that focuses on the rectitude of human behavior by examining the motives, principles, and consequences of a particular act or general conduct. I have attempted to use an inclusive definition that recognizes the place of rules as well as outcomes in the ethical debate, without necessarily projecting the interests of society over those of the individual, or vice versa. I seek to maintain this sense of balance in exploring Ghanaian Pentecostal ministerial ethics.

Deontological Theories

Deontological (from the Greek *deon*, or "duty," and *logos*, for "word") ethical theories are defined by the principles of duty and obligation; such ethical systems do not necessarily consider the outcome or result of a particular choice in establishing ethical norms. They are usually based on principles and laws that regulate human interaction with nature and the dynamics of human relationships that constitute the structure of society. By observing nature and the structure of society, deontological ethicists identify certain unconditional norms that are deemed crucial for the stability and survival of humanity. Many Christian ethicists have a bias towards this deontological approach in practicing ethics, insisting that Scripture is full of divine commandments that we are obliged to obey without due consideration of the consequences. The main examples of Christian ethical systems in this category include Karl Barth's ethical absolutism, which holds up biblical ethics as inviolable.[5] The secular deontological approach is referred to as

---

2. Feinberg and Feinberg, *Ethics for a Brave New World*, 18.
3. Ibid.
4. Wiredu, "Moral Foundations," 191.
5. Barth, *Church Dogmatics VI*, 793.

ethical rationalism, which happens to be an ethical system based on human reason. The most prominent proponent of this system is Immanuel Kant, whose theory is examined in the next section.

Trull and Carter, in applying the ethics of obligation to Christian ministry, seem to suggest that the observance of rules—be they scriptural commandments, ecclesiastical codes, or governmental edicts—cannot be ignored by the Christian leader.[6] It is therefore significant that the oldest book on ministerial ethics, *The Rule of Saint Benedict*, is replete with moral obligations, such as Saint Benedict's first step in humility: "The first step of humility is unhesitating obedience, which comes naturally to those who cherish Christ above all."[7]

Kantianism

Kant's Moral Theology

Immanuel Kant (1724–1804) has developed an argument for the existence of God that is predicated on morality by insisting that reason can neither prove nor disprove the existence of God.[8] In Marie Zermatt Scutt's view, the traditional interpretation of Kant's moral theology is the establishment of "the truth of the existence of God based on distinctively moral considerations."[9] According to Kant, "Even the Holy One of the gospel must first be compared with our ideal of moral perfection before he is recognized as such."[10] Scutt's interpretation of Kant's moral theology reveals that pure reason serves as an authority that legislates moral law as the absolute principle binding all rational beings in the natural world. Furthermore, the object of the moral law is identified as the highest good, which is impossible in the natural world. Therefore, the possibility of the highest good can only be realized with the purposive unity between nature and morality, which presupposes God as the moral author of nature.[11] Michael Austin is also convinced that Kant has indirectly contributed to the "Divine Command theory" by claiming that morality requires faith in a God who can help humans meet the demands of morality.[12] Although Montague Brown endorses

6. Charlesworth, *Philosophy and Religion*, 100.
7. Benedict, *Rule of Saint Benedict*, 29.
8. Charlesworth, *Philosophy and Religion*, 100.
9. Scutt, "Kant's Moral Theology," 611.
10. Kant, *Ethical Philosophy*, 21.
11. Scutt, "Kant's Moral Theology," 619.
12. Austin, "Divine Command Theory".

Kant's perception of God "as a principle of unity of all things," he rejects Kant's idea that we must necessarily acknowledge God in order to acquire a moral sense, which is an insightful limitation to Kant's moral theology.[13] Nevertheless, by emphasizing morality as contingent upon the acknowledgement of God, Kant reinforces a position that demands a higher moral standard of people in religious vocations.

The Goodwill

Kant's approach to duty-based ethics has much in common with the Christian ethical concept of Divine Command theory, which is popular with the Pentecostal Holiness movement (their tradition and ideas are discussed in the next chapter). The key principles of Kant's ethical system that resonate with this book are the ideas of "good will," "human dignity," and "the categorical imperative," or the realization of an absolute moral law.[14] Kant based his moral philosophy on the concept of good will, which according to him is the only quality that has intrinsic value. This approximates what the Christian would refer to as good character. Kant argues that only one thing can be called good without any qualification, and that is good will, for as he explains,

> There is no possibility of thinking of anything at all in the world, or even out of it, which can be regarded as good without qualification, except a *good will*. Intelligence, wit, judgment, and whatever talents of the mind one might want to name are doubtless in many respects good and desirable, as are such qualities of temperament as courage, resolution, perseverance. But they can also become extremely bad and harmful if the will, which is to make use of these gifts of nature and which in its special constitution is called character, is not good.[15]

Tom Bailey has observed that all the virtues identified by Kant in this quotation could become evil unless they are applied in a context of good will; consequently, good will is the only virtue which is good irrespective of other conditions and which also, conterminously, provides the context for the goodness of every other virtue.[16] Evidently, the idea of possessing and maintaining one's moral rectitude provides the only premise under which

---

13. Brown, *Restoration of Reason*, 157.
14. Kant, *Ethical Philosophy*.
15. Kant, *Ethical Philosophy*, 7.
16. Bailey, "Analysing the Good Will," 18(4) 2010, (635–662), 638

anything else is worth having or pursuing.[17] This has called into question the value of qualities such as courage, which, when applied without good will, could be destructive.[18] Bailey, reflecting on Kant's concept of duty, avers, "to act 'from duty' is to act precisely because the action is morally good, irrespective of whether or not the action also coincides with the satisfaction of inclination."[19] Duty may sometimes oppose inclination, for "The obligations we impose on ourselves override all other calls for action, and frequently run counter to our desires. We nonetheless always have a sufficient motive to act as we ought."[20]

Human Dignity

Kant's second maxim, which is extremely relevant to contemporary times and especially useful in dealing with minority groups and the underprivileged in society, is his concept of human dignity. The Kantian formula for human dignity instructs us to "Act in such a way that you always treat humanity, whether in your own person or in the person of any other, never simply as a means, but always at the same time as an end."[21] Kant is convinced that only rational agents or persons can be ends in themselves, for they alone can have an unconditioned and absolute value. He insists that it would be morally wrong to sacrifice human beings with absolute value as a means of realizing an end whose value is only relative. Reflecting on this concept, Hill contends that no human being thinks his or her self-worth depends entirely on class, popularity, or utility to society; rather everyone is convinced that he or she has worth simply as a human being.[22] Kant further insists, "Every man has a rightful claim of respect from his fellow men, and he is also bound to show respect to every other man in return. Humanity itself is a dignity, for man can be used by no one (neither by others nor even by himself) merely as a means, but must always be used at the same time as an end."[23]

17. Johnson, "Kant's Moral Philosophy," 5–6.
18. Wood, *Kant's Ethical Thought*, 22.
19. Bailey, "Analysing the Good Will," 640.
20. Schneewind, "Autonomy, Obligation and Virtue," 309.
21. Kant, *Moral Law*, 33.
22. Hill Jr., in Hinman, *Ethics*, 191.
23. Kant, *Ethical Philosophy*, 127. The practice of using people as a human shield in a conflict situation to protect others who are "more important" provides an example of using human beings as a means to an end. In addition, certain institutions sacrifice the interests and rights of individuals, as when personal resources of employees are

The Categorical Imperative

Kant's categorical imperative considers duty to be an unconditional factor in moral action. It is what a person identifies as the reasonable moral duty in any particular situation, one that could be recognized by all rational beings and applied to similar situations universally. As Kant declares, "Act according to that maxim which can at the same time make itself a universal law."[24] He argues that if we cannot extend a moral duty into a universal rule, then we should never act upon it. In J. B. Schneewind's opinion, what stands out in Kant's moral vision is that to the autonomous adult who has the free will to choose, it becomes obvious that there are some actions that we are simply obligated to carry out.[25] Thus, the idea of moral obligation stems from unconditional necessity based on the very structure of society and the demands of human interaction, which needs no external factors for validation.

Relevance for Ministerial Ethics

To reiterate, the moral theology of Kant, which insists that the existence of God is contingent on morality, acknowledges ethical principles as a dominant component of the Christian faith. This position all but equates Christianity with morality. In addition, Kant's idea of the good will as the unconditionally good context that lends value to other virtues resonates with Paul's hymn on love in 1 Corinthians 13, wherein the exercise of charismatic gifts without love is regarded as vain and valueless. Obviously, Kant's moral philosophy ascribes intrinsic value to moral obligations, and this runs parallel to the Christian approach of classifying moral injunctions in Scripture as doctrine. Popkin and Stroll have rightly observed that Kant's concept of morality is not simply a matter of inclination, desire, or preference, but is instead objective.[26] It cannot be denied that Christian moral philosophy is enriched by some of these Kantian concepts. Moreover, they can also be extended to ministerial ethics to help practitioners appreciate the value of ecclesiastical moral codes as objective principles that define and sustain institutional structures.

---

used to further institutional interests without the individuals' consent. Practices such as widowhood rites and witchcraft accusations that dehumanize the victims, also use human beings as a means to an end.

24. Kant, *Ethical Philosophy*, 42.
25. Schneewind, "Autonomy, Obligation, and Virtue . . ." 320.
26. Popkin and Stroll, *Philosophy*, 48.

Selected Ethical Theories and Systems

Nevertheless, the Kantian position does not adequately respond to conflicting values, or cases in which it becomes necessary to break one moral law in order to uphold the other. Furthermore, limiting Christianity to an ethical code is too asphyxiating for the dynamic influence and empowering capacity of the Holy Spirit. O'Meara, for instance, objects to any position that regards Christ merely as an ethical teacher. To him, locating "Jesus within the kingdom of God need not reduce Jesus to an ethical teacher; for he presents himself not only as the incarnation of the presence of God but as the sender of God's Spirit now and in the future."[27] Beyond moral obligations, Christianity responds to moral failure with forgiveness, which is coupled with empowerment to help believers meet the ethical demands of the faith. O'Meara perceptively captures the liberty, wide expanse, and variety of Christian spirituality by explaining, "God was experienced in a vastness, freedom, and goodness flowing through a world of diversity, movement, and order, while Christ appeared in a more human way, filled with a personal love, redemptive and empowering."[28] In this regard, Kant's view of moral objectivity may appear somewhat restrictive;[29] a moderate view of moral objectivism would insist that moral rules are supposed to be interpreted and that strong absolute claims are not always applicable in real life and ministry situations. This observation creates room for the teleological theories that receive attention in the next section.

Teleological Theories

Teleological (from the Greek *telos*, or "end," and *logos*, "word") ethical theories use the value of the end result of an action to determine the rule or obligation that regulates that action. Teleological ethics "derives duty or moral obligation from what is good or desirable as an end to be achieved."[30] According to the teleological viewpoint, it is the outcome of an action that determines its moral rectitude; therefore, no action is by its very nature right or wrong. Trull and Carter argue that this kind of "consequentialism is present in the Bible, and it has the value of compelling the moral actor

27. O'Meara, *Theology of Ministry*, 36.
28. Ibid., 30–31.
29. One wonders whether Kant's idea of "a rational being" can embrace all human beings, and whether all "rational" beings can possibly approximate the one objective standard of morality, given different conditions. In this regard, Fletcher's counsel to avoid absolute claims such as "always," "never," "perfect" etc, may provide the moderating factor.
30. "*Encyclopædia Britannica Online*, s. v. "teleological ethics," http://www.britannica.com/EBchecked/topic/585940/teleological-ethics.

to consider every factor, especially the end result, before implementing a decision."[31] The most prominent example of secular teleological theories is Jeremy Bentham and John Stuart Mill's Utilitarianism, which is discussed in the next section.

Utilitarianism

Bentham: The Greater Pleasure Principle

I have selected the works of two prominent Utilitarian philosophers, Jeremy Bentham (1748-1832) and John Stuart Mill (1806-1873) for discussion. The Utilitarians argue from the premise that human life is governed by two sovereign masters, namely pain and pleasure.[32] The principle acclaimed by utility is, according to Bentham, the one "which approves or disapproves of every action whatsoever, according to the tendency which it appears to have to augment or diminish the happiness of the party whose interest is in question."[33] Bentham did not only use pain and pleasure to explain the motivation for human action; to him they also provide the very basis for defining what is good and moral. As he attempts to demonstrate in his book, *An Introduction to the Principles of Morals and Legislation*, this pleasure and pain dichotomy provides the basic framework for social, legal, and moral transformation of society. Paul Weirich appreciates the Utilitarian position as one that attempts to maximize utility, for as he explains, "every reason for an act is a reason to prefer it to alternative acts and so a reason to increase its utility relative to the utilities of alternative acts."[34]

In order to calculate the quantum of pleasure that justifies the morality of an act, Bentham developed a pleasure calculus, albeit a nebulous one.[35] Bentham and Mill were concerned with legal and social reform, and this interest has sustained the relevance of their concepts even in contemporary times. Julia Driver suggests that for Bentham, what constitutes a bad law is its lack of utility and its tendency to "lead to unhappiness and misery without any compensating happiness. If a law or an action doesn't *do* any good, then it *isn't* any good."[36]

---

31. Trull and Carter, *Ministerial Ethics*, 57.
32. Bentham, *An Introduction to the Principles*, 11.
33. Ibid., 12.
34. Weirich, "Utility Maximization Generalized," 283–84.
35. Bentham, *An Introduction to the Principles*, 38–39.
36. Driver, "History of Utilitarianism," 6, emphasis Driver's.

The intense focus of Bentham's Utilitarianism on pleasure and enjoyment seems to promote a tendency toward hedonism, which has drawn much criticism. Critics target Utilitarianism because it seems to divorce morality from divine revelation and from natural law. Utilitarianism has been regarded as "pigs' philosophy" for its emphasis on sensual pleasure.[37]

Mill: The Greater Happiness Principle

John Stuart Mill developed Utilitarian philosophy further by responding to some of the criticism leveled against Bentham. Mill preferred to define utility in terms of happiness rather than pleasure, where the greatest happiness principle "holds that actions are right in proportion as they tend to promote happiness; wrong as they tend to produce the reverse of happiness."[38] Mill departs from Bentham's hedonism by grading pleasures in terms of quality, and by preferring intellectual pleasures to mere sensual or emotional ones, arguing that Utilitarians "have placed the superiority of mental over bodily pleasure."[39] Walter Sinnot-Armstrong explains that Mill "distinguished higher and lower qualities of pleasure according to the preferences of people who have experienced both kinds."[40]

The Utilitarian position is, however, not one of lawlessness. Mill acknowledges that since we cannot always accurately calculate the result of our actions, rules and norms are necessary to guide behavior. Utilitarians acknowledge the role of moral principles and beliefs, but argue that such principles are not universal or absolute because there are exceptions to the rule. Any of these rules can be broken to serve the principle of utility, especially to satisfy the purpose of the greater good.

Relevance for Ministerial Ethics

Utilitarianism has gained much currency in the West, emerging as a basic philosophy that guides legislation on many ethical issues.[41] Even in Christian moral philosophy, we cannot rule out considerations of consequences in ethical decision-making. This implies that Christian ethics is dynamic, and any attempts made to limit it to one theory—normally principle-based—can

---

37. Hinman, *Ethics*, 137.
38. Mill, *Utilitarianism*, 18.
39. Ibid., 18.
40. Sinnot-Armstrong, "Consequentialism," 5.
41. See Rae, *Moral Choices*, 92.

be frustrating. O'Meara thinks Jesus challenged absolute religious claims, for the Savior "broke through sacral caste to welcome all as he questioned religious rules as divinely guaranteed absolutes and flared up in anger more at religious hypocrisy than at ethical sin."[42] Trull and Carter have also identified some instances of Utilitarianism in biblical ethics:

> Wisdom literature seldom takes the imperative form, but usually gives practical advice about how to achieve the good life (Prov 9:10). Hebrew midwives who "feared God" made their decision to deceive Pharaoh on the basis of the consequence: to save the male babies, God apparently approved of their decision (Exod 1:15–20) . . . In the Sermon on the Mount, Christ stressed motives, noting that good deeds may be corrupted by wrong reasons. The Apostle Paul often evaluated consequences before making a final decision.[43]

Utilitarian considerations becomes relevant to ministerial ethics when, for example, deciding how much of the truth a minister should disclose concerning confessions that could lead to breakdowns in family relationships. In a hypothetical case of consequential morality, Graham Greene presents us with a priest who committed fornication and fathered a daughter. During the period of persecution of Roman Catholic clergy in Mexico, which serves as the setting for his philosophical novel *The Power and the Glory*, the daughter's identification of the priest as her father saved his life—he was spared because it was assumed that Roman Catholic priests did not have children.[44] From a Utilitarian perspective, the priest's promiscuity may appear justifiable because it saved his life.

However, Utilitarianism is an ethical system that focuses mostly on results and may not offer any objective standards for moral assessment. Moreover, the value of the so-called good consequence is relative; from various perspectives this outcome could be judged as good or as evil.

Virtue/Character Ethics

So far the ethical systems we have discussed have focused on the evaluation of either the method of the moral act or its end results, overlooking the moral agent—that is, the human initiator of the act. However the state of mind and condition of the moral agent in any decision-making process

---

42. O'Meara, *Theology of Ministry*, 39.
43. Trull and Carter, *Ministerial Ethics*, 57.
44. Greene, *The Power and the Glory*, 73.

cannot be ignored. This concept, which is much appreciated in Christian ethics, is referred to as character development or sanctification.

The Character Factor

Virtue theorists think morality exceeds merely doing one's duty to involve the whole character and disposition of the moral agent. Central to this position is determining the uprightness of behavior by evaluating the agent rather than the act performed—thus, a person's character becomes the key issue in virtue ethics. In his evaluation of ethical theories, Scott Rae has identified the main differences between virtue ethics and act-oriented ethics. He observes that while act-oriented ethics emphasize doing, virtue-oriented ethics stress being. Secondly, act-oriented ethics focuses on following rules or probing results, as opposed to virtue ethics, which points to people who have consistently demonstrated outstanding moral character for emulation. Rae further observes that virtue theorists place emphasis on a person's motives rather than sharing act-oriented theorists' focus on the act itself.[45]

To appreciate the full impact of character ethics, the first step is to develop a concept of the ideal person as the standard that fulfills the purpose of existence. This is what Plato refers to as determining "how life may be passed by each one of us to the greatest advantage,"[46] both for the benefit of the individual and society. In Aristotle's view, only when a person performs the essential purpose for which he or she was created can that person lead an ideal life.[47] Second, the character theorist has to develop a list of virtues necessary for people to realizing their proper purpose, which the ancient Greeks identified as courage, humility, loyalty, respect, and justice, among others. Third, this theory has to show how these virtues can be developed, whether by divine grace, training, discipline, emulation, education, or a combination of all of the above. For instance, in Aristotle's view, virtues are developed through emulation by following the examples of people who have distinguished themselves as paragons of virtue.

Relevance for Ministerial Ethics

To reiterate, Christian ethics is multifaceted, and so far we have identified its dimensions of deontology, utility, as well as character considerations. Virtue

---

45. Rae, *Moral Choices*, 92.
46. Plato, *Republic*, 26.
47. Aristotle, *Nichomachean Ethics*, 13.

ethics resonate with Christian morality, for both systems focus on internal factors such as the intentions, mindsets, emotions, attitudes, and motivations that culminate in action or inaction, as the case may be. In addition, the virtue theory provides inspiration for character development by holding up moral exemplars whose biographies have become models for society. Some contemporary examples are Mahatma Gandhi's nonviolent resistance leadership and Mother Teresa's selfless service to the poor, destitute, and terminally ill in Calcutta, India. Nelson Mandela's courage in standing for the truth and his magnanimity towards those who oppressed blacks during South African apartheid regime provides another worthy example. The laudable lifestyles of such people become a resource-base of information for both theoretical and practical moral education.

Consequently, character considerations comprise the criteria of society in validating the life and ministry of Christian leaders. Indeed, Christian leaders, even more than other professionals, are expected to emerge as moral exemplars. The approach of imitating the virtues of the heroes of the faith is emphasized in the Bible: "Therefore I [Paul] urge you to imitate me" (1 Cor 4:16); "We do not want you to become lazy, but to imitate those who through faith and patience inherit the promise" (Heb 6:12). It is generally assumed that character is central to clergy role,[48] a viewpoint that is supported by many ethicists. According to Nolan Harmon, "The Christian minister must be something before he can do anything . . . His work depends on his character."[49] In Darrell Reeck's view, character concerns enable leaders to show calmness in making the right choices and boldness in resisting wrongdoing.[50]

Ghanaian Traditional Ethics

As stated in chapter 2, Ghanaian traditional ideas still have a strong hold on contemporary institutions, including Pentecostal churches. It is therefore important, in examining their ministerial ethics, to appreciate the interaction of tradition moral philosophy with Pentecostal ethics. Studies in African traditional ethics, however, face the challenge of lack of documentation and the absence of significant moral theorists.[51] To overcome the challenge

48. Harmon, *Ministerial Ethics*, 34.
49. Harmon, *Ministerial Ethics*, 34.
50. Reeck, *Ethics for the Christian Profession*, 47.
51. In an interview with Rev Professor Joshua N. Kudadjie, a Ghanaian ethicist in Accra on 11th June 2007, he ascribed this situation to the fact that African traditional ethics is a young discipline in the academy.

of sparse documentation, contemporary scholars have scanned folklore for proverbs, witty sayings and axioms, songs, and cultural artifacts to help discover traditional ethical concepts.[52]

Concepts and Nomenclature

A perennial intellectual debate is underway over the classification of major ethical concepts in Africa, and for that matter, Ghana. Various scholars, depending on their orientation, argue that traditional African ethics is either deontological, teleological, or virtue-based. Pieter Coetzee's conviction that African moral philosophy is perspective-driven, resulting in pluralistic and heterogeneous ethical contours, therefore becomes relevant.[53] Kudadjie, for instance, thinks both teleological and deontological elements manifest in African traditional ethics.[54] Scholars such as Akoto[55] and Wiredu[56] insist that traditional African ethics is teleological. Akoto claims, "Actions are judged right or wrong depending on how positively or negatively they affect a person's relationship to the Supreme Being, lesser gods and members of the society both living and dead."[57] In Wiredu's view, both religion and ethics have a utilitarian purpose in the Akan context. He claims a separation of moral values from religion is useful, for nothing is intrinsically good unless it promotes human interest.[58]

Among those who argue for a deontological basis for African ethics are Danquah, Mbiti, and Idowu. Danquah's understanding of deontology in Akan moral philosophy reflects something of the strict principle-based ethics of Kant. According to Danquah, Akan ethics expresses,

---

52. Some of the contemporary philosophers who employ this methodology include, C. A. Ackah, Akan Ethics. Accra: Ghana Universities Press, 1988; Kwasi Wiredu, "Moral Foundations of an African Culture" Eds. Kwasi Wiredu and Kwame Gyekye, Person and Community: Ghanaian Philosophical Studies, I. Cultural Heritage and Contemporary Change Series II. Africa Vol. 1. Washington DC: The Council for Research in Values and Philosophy, 1992; N. K. Dzobo, "Values in a Changing Society Man, Ancestors and God." Eds. Kwasi Wiredu and Kwame Gyekye Person and Community: Ghanaian Philosophical Studies, I. Cultural Heritage and Contemporary Change Series II. Africa Vol. 1. Washington DC: The Council for Research in Values and Philosophy, 1992.
53. Coetzee, "Morality in African Thought," 273.
54. Interview by Dela Quampah in Accra, 11th June 2007.
55. Akoto, "Religion, Morality," 90.
56. Wiredu, "Moral Foundations," 194.
57. Akoto, "Religion, Morality," 90.
58. Wiredu, "Moral Foundations," 194.

> The justice and necessity which will make a universal appeal, at least to all lovers of good who, without knowing or asking the reason why, feel that goodness in itself is preferable to wickedness, even if the way of the wicked looks like leading a pleasurable hedonistic existence, an existence which, however felicitous, is empty of true contentment or genuine and abiding satisfaction.[59]

Danquah thus reveals a duty-based approach that insists on the intrinsic value of morality rather than wagering on the consequences of individual moral acts. He is convinced that pursuing justice for justice's sake, irrespective of the outcome, is preferable to compromising moral principles in order to enjoy the fleeting pleasures of life. Similarly, Mbiti's perspective runs parallel to the divine command approach: "It is believed in many African societies that their morals were given to them by God from the beginning. This provides an unchallenged authority for the morals."[60]

A third school of thought is represented by Kunhiyop, who avers that African traditional ethics reflects the virtue approach.[61] This position is supported by Gyekye, who agrees that "good character is the essence of the African moral system, the lynchpin of the moral wheel. The justification for a character-based ethics is not far to seek."[62]

Communal and Individualistic Ethics

The strong kinship ties that characterize traditional African communities lend support to a preference for communal over individualistic ethics. Coetzee defines the social structure of African ethics as a system under which "an individual's choice of way of life is a choice constrained by the community's pursuit of shared ends."[63] In examining the moral foundation of Akan society, Wiredu suggests communal morality demands that the individual conform to the harmony required by society, even when it calls for the "abridgement of one's own interests."[64] Furthermore, Wiredu sees Akan society as "a type in which the greatest value is attached to communal

---

59. Danquah, *The Akan Doctrine of God*, 92.
60. Mbiti, *Introduction to African Religion*, 174.
61. Kunhiyop, *African Christian Ethics*, 41–42.
62. Gyekye, "African Ethics," 6.
63. Coetzee, "Morality in African Thought," 275.
64. Wiredu, "Moral Foundations," 287.

belonging."65 Gyekye is also convinced that the sole criterion of goodness in Akan moral philosophy is the welfare or wellbeing of the community.66 This excessive focus on communal ethics is, however, sometimes censured for obliterating individuals' moral sense by treating his or her personal values as the mass-product of a social ethical system.

Religious Source of Traditional Ethics

In direct contrast to the non-religious approach to traditional African ethics stand those who contend that since religion pervades every facet of traditional society, the moral foundation of African ethics cannot be ascribed to any source apart from religion. J. Omosade Awolalu and P. Adelumo Dopamu reject the notion of regarding morality as a human invention, arguing that conscience is a witness to God's law, which gives humanity the capacity to discern God's commandments.67 Opoku also argues for a religious foundation for traditional African morality:

> Generally, morality originates from religious considerations, and so pervasive is religion in African culture that the two cannot be separated from each other. Thus, we find that what constitutes the moral code of any particular African society—the laws, taboos, customs and set forms of behaviour—all derive their compelling power from religion. Thus morality flows out of religion.68

We cannot deny the availability of evidence that Ghanaian traditional ethics derives from religion. This position is supported by empirical evidence on the underpinnings of the African sense of justice and the principles that guide social relationships. Aside from the fact that religious consciousness permeates every facet of traditional life, African ideas of morality reflect a deep religious consideration. For instance, an Eʋe person who has been wronged and does not desire to litigate will simply submit his or her cause to God by saying *EdrSla li*, an idiom that is difficult to translate because it is both a statement and an invocation, but literally means, the "One who will judge my cause abides." Idiomatically, these words imply that the aggrieved party is invoking divine justice to rule upon the case.

---

65. Ibid., 291.
66. Gyekye, *An Essay on African Philosophical*, 132.
67. Awolalu and Dopamu, *West African Traditional Religion*, 212.
68. Awolalu and Dopamu, *West African Traditional Religion*, 212.

Conclusion

We have examined some pertinent ethical theories and systems because we know Christian value systems do not exist in isolation of the value systems of receptor communities. The significance of principles and utility in the development and application of ethical systems have also been evaluated in the Western secular and traditional African contexts to discern their relevance for Pentecostal ministerial ethics. We have discovered that although Kantian ethics could provide a rational and objective grounding for ministerial ethics, it can also result in a legalism that is not realistic to life and ministry. The Utilitarian system, which could provide a balance to this ethical rigidity, is also susceptible to an extreme relativity that provides no standards for moral assessment. The virtue approach cannot stand alone either without appealing to act-oriented systems for validation. Furthermore, we have assessed the available evidence on the sources of traditional Ghanaian ethics and concluded that evidence for a religious source is overwhelming. The next chapter explores some of the Christian ethical philosophies that are supposed to define moral standards for Christians in general, and Pentecostal ministers in particular.

4

Christian Ethics

Introduction

THE JUDEO-CHRISTIAN RELIGION IS a highly ethical one that teaches us that our commitment to God should reflect our obedience to God and behavior towards our neighbors. From the creation story through the historical narratives, wisdom literature, and prophetic pronouncements of the Old Testament, the themes of holiness, righteousness, sanctity of life, fairness, justice, self-control, and compassion for the vulnerable and faithfulness, among others, are prominently projected. Israel's response to these ethical stipulations defined the quality of the Israelites' relationship with Yahweh and with one another within the covenant community. The New Testament, in recounting the life and ministry of Jesus and the apostles, upholds these same moral concerns by emphasizing motives and personal responsibility as well as the empowering activity of the Holy Spirit in moral transformation. Needless to say, this extensive heritage of biblical morality provides the primary source of information and motivation for those engaged in Christian leadership, especially for ordained ministers. Consequently, this chapter examines the wider contours of biblical values and approaches to moral formation expounded in the Bible. That notwithstanding, since Christian ethics blends moral philosophy with theology, selected ethical theories developed within a Christian framework are also explored for their relevance to clergy conduct.

Biblical Basis of Morality

The issue of moral responsibility is prominent in the creation narrative in Genesis where, due to mankind's disobedience, humanity's relationship with God and with one another became distorted. Adam shifted blame to Eve and ultimately to God as the cause of his moral failure, while Eve also blamed the serpent for causing her disobedience (Gen 3:1–19). Laird Harris, reflecting on this passage in his commentary on Leviticus, observes, "To err is human; to deny responsibility is as old our first parents."[1] Humanity's moral degeneration reached a climax in the fratricide of Cain, who killed his brother Abel. When Cain was plotting the murder, God warned him, saying, "If you do right, will you not be accepted? But if you do not do right, sin is crouching at your door; it desires to have you, but you must master it" (Gen 4:7). This reveals that even before the law of God was directly given to Israel at Sinai (Exodus 20), humankind was aware of sinful acts such as murder. Indeed, Gordon Wenham asserts that compressed into this Cain and Abel narrative is a "whole theology whose principles inform much of the criminal and cultic law of Israel."[2]

God's progressive revelation was taken a step further when he entered into covenant with Israel through the mediation of Moses. This covenant, which was ratified at Sinai with the delivery of the Ten Commandments, is universally acclaimed as a most remarkable ethical code. This set of laws forbids disrespect to parents, murder, adultery, theft, falsehood and covetousness, among other transgressions (Exod 20:1–17). Hans Küng suggests that God's covenant relationship and the revelation of the Decalogue provide the theological motivation for ethical behavior inspired by gratitude, love, the prospect of long life, and the gift of liberty.[3] Durham also appreciates the import of the Ten Commandments as a set of principles regulating the individual's relationship with Yahweh and with mankind, as well as outlining what that relationship demands from the community of Israel.[4] Obviously, the first four commandments of the Decalogue deal with humanity's duties toward God, and the remaining six with people's duties toward one another. Gerhard Von Rad appreciates the principles behind the social focus of the second segment of the Decalogue thus: "At the head of this latter section stands the command to honor parents, which is followed by ordinances safeguarding the life, property, and honor of one's neighbor.[5]

Walter Brueggman insightfully suggests that the Torah not only issues instructions on obedience to God, but also offers sacramental and spiritual energy to the community to meet the stringent ethical demands of

1. Harris, "Leviticus," 522.
2. Wenham, *Genesis 1–15*, 107.
3. Küng, "Criterion for Deciding," 122.
4. See John I. Durham in Wenham, *Genesis 1–5*, 284.
5. Von Rad, *Israel's Historical Tradition*, 191.

Yahweh.[6] To Brueggman's mind, "Whereas Torah as command is focused on the ethical dimension of existence, Torah as instruction, guidance, and nurture is preoccupied with the aesthetic and artistic, a realm that comes to be expressed as the mystical and sacramental. That is, Torah is as much concerned with the inscrutable mystery of presence as it is with the non-negotiability of neighbourly obedience."[7] This implies that the cultic establishment constituted a symbolic representation of a transcendental Being that provided the inspiration to meet the demands of the law. Leviticus, to a considerable extent, emerges as the ministerial manual and ethical code for priests in Judaism. Harris, in analyzing the contents of Leviticus, intimates that the book reveals God's laws for the conduct of the people that were to be administered by the priest, not only in sacerdotal matters, but also in civil issues such as incest and adultery.[8] Harris further asserts that Lev 17–26 is referred to as "the holiness code" because it emphasizes God's moral standard for the community.[9]

It is notable that the Bible presents Israel's history from a theological perspective, whose holy and just God constantly required that both King and subject strictly observe the stipulations of the covenant law. Von Rad emphasizes the King's role in upholding the moral heritage of the community in relation to Yahweh: "In what the Old Testament has to say about righteousness, focal points came to be occupied by the king and the monarchy: this again is not surprising, for as head of the people the king was regarded as the guarantor and protector of everything in the land, making for faithfulness in community relationships."[10] When Ahab, king of the Northern Kingdom, took possession of Naboth's vineyard after his wife had conspired and killed Naboth, Elijah, as God's messenger, pronounced this harsh sentence on the King: "I am going to bring disaster on you . . . because you have provoked me to anger and have caused Israel to sin" (1 Kings 21).

Another segment of the Old Testament that records extremely valuable moral teachings is the prophetic books, whose discourses are grounded in the covenant relationship with Yahweh, which demanded obedience to God as well as ethical neighborliness. Furthermore, the prophets were often inspired to pronounce judgment upon Israel for transgressing the covenant laws. The approach of the prophets, according to Séan Freyne, is a "repeated appeal to apodictic laws like those in the Decalogue in order to confront

---

6. Brueggman, *Theology of the Old Testament*, 582, emphasis Brueggman's.
7. Ibid.
8. Harris, "Leviticus," 502.
9. Ibid.
10. Von Rad, *Old Testament Theology*, 191.

Israel with her moral failures."[11] According to Walter Kaiser, "it was the writing of the prophets who gave some of the severest rebukes in Scripture against exploiting the poor."[12] For instance, Amos declares:

> For three sins of Israel, even for four, I will not turn back my wrath. They sell the righteous for silver, and the needy for a pair of sandals. They trample on the head of the poor as upon the dust of the ground and deny justice to the oppressed. Father and son use the same girl and so profane my holy name. (Amos 2:6–7)

In Carl Laney's view, the prophets were ethical reformers, for "The prophets of Israel were greatly concerned with social issues, both moral and religious. In fact, for the prophets' social and moral concerns lay at the heart of religion. Repeatedly, they rebuke idolatry, formalistic worship, failure to support temple worship, oppression of the poor, murder, usury, and dissipation."[13]

Wisdom literature[14] constitutes a special segment of the Hebrew Bible in which, to drive home their moral lessons, the sages of Israel refrain from issuing commands and instead summon us to think and infer.[15] Bruce K. Waltke and David Diewert argue that while wisdom appeals to the mind, it issues more from a loving heart, which is the core of both the individual's physical and "emotional-intellectual-moral activities, than from a cold intellect."[16] Because Wisdom literature hardly invokes Israel's covenant relationship with Yahweh, some critics equate its approach to natural theology. Waltke and Diewert, however, refute this by insisting upon Wisdom literature's distinctive inspiration, by which the sages viewed creation and social order "through the lens of Israel's covenant faith" to deduce timeless moral principles. Responding to W. McKane's claim that wisdom literature was utilitarian and eudemonistic, Wlatke and Diewert insist that the "wisdom literature corpus qualifies eudaemonism in the same way the rest of the Old Testament does (cf. Leviticus 26; Dueteronomy 27–28)."[17] H. Wheeler Robinson defines Israel's wisdom as "the discipline whereby was taught the application of prophetic truth to the individual in the light of experience."[18]

---

11. Freyne, "Bible and Christian Morality," 13.
12. Kaiser, *Toward Old Testament Ethics*, 160.
13. Laney, "Prophets and Social Concern," 109.
14. These comprise of Job, Proverbs, Ecclesiastics, and Song of Songs.
15. Kidner, *Wisdom of Proverbs, Job, and Ecclesiastes*, 11.
16. Wlatke and Diewert, "Wisdom Literature," 300.
17. Ibid., 298.
18. Robinson, *Inspiration and Revelation*, 241.

Henlee H. Barnette expresses a similar opinion by arguing that Wisdom literature has a profound theological basis that is expressed in practical rather than speculative terms.[19] For instance, in Prov 24:30–34, the sage engages the sluggard's field as his laboratory, and upon observation, coins the proverb, "A little sleep . . . and poverty will come on you as a bandit and scarcity like an armed man" (vv. 33–34).[20]

There appears to be a link between Old Testament and New Testament morality, insofar as Jesus' ethical concepts are presented within a framework of Jewish moral heritage. Richard Jones confirms this by arguing that the ethical teaching of Jesus was similar to that of the Jewish tradition.[21] Davies finds the fulfillment of the ethical monotheism of Judaism in Jesus' ministry and teaching, insisting that the ethical aspirations of the Law and prophets are fully accomplished rather than abolished in Jesus' moral discourse.[22] The ethical teaching of Jesus therefore testifies to the inception of the kingdom of God promised in the Old Testament, for Jesus' moral standard and discourse demonstrate an "overwhelming conviction that the kingdom of God was 'at hand.'"[23]

Central to the concept of kingdom ethics is the virtue of grace. This informs Davies' position that "because the rule of God is an expression of grace, the moral demands of Jesus are the counterpart of God's grace."[24] This grace is made manifest not only in healings and exorcisms, but also in forgiveness and the moral transformation of both the believing individual and the faith community. The Beatitudes (Matt 5:1–12) therefore constitute the expression of God's grace that precede the moral requirements of the Sermon on the Mount.[25]

Jesus' Sermon on the Mount (Matthew 5–7), according to Barnette, is "a systematic statement of the main elements of the Christian ethic."[26] The sermon stresses inner attitudes such as humility, compassion, purity of heart, and willingness to sacrifice personal rights or endure suffering in order to identify with Christ as a true disciple. In these teachings of kingdom ethics, a more challenging code of conduct than the external righteousness of the Pharisees and teachers of the Law was established.[27] According to Richard

---

19. Barnette, *Introducing Christian Ethics*, 35.
20. Wlatke and Diewert, "Wisdom Literature," 301.
21. Jones, *Groundwork of Christian Ethics*, 27.
22. Davies, "Ethics in the New Testament," 168.
23. Ibid.
24. Ibid.
25. Ibid.
26. Barnette, *Introducing Christian Ethics*, 50–51.
27. Pierce, *Ministerial Ethics*, 68.

Hays, the Sermon on the Mount reveals the sketch rather than legislation of the character of the Christian community.[28] The motivation for morality for the Christian, unlike the Jew, was the love issuing out of a grateful response to the redeeming love of God: "The Jew aimed to satisfy the *law* of God; and to the demands of law there is always a limit. The Christian aims to show his gratitude for the *love* of God; and to the claims of love there is no limit."[29] Grenz also emphasizes the relational dynamics of Christian ethics over a mere legalistic response to commands: "Jesus knew that inward piety and not outward conformity to the law marks true obedience to God, because God's intent focused on establishing relationships."[30]

However, restricting Jesus' ethical message to the didactic or teaching passages presents a limited view of the extensive scope of his moral concerns. The moral focus of some of the parables presents us with such piercing ethical assessments that no direct teaching could lend more force; an example of this kind is seen in Jesus' concealed attack on racism in the parable of the Good Samaritan (Luke 10:30–37). In Hays' estimation, "stories form our values and moral sensibilities in more indirect and complex ways, teaching us how to see the world, what to fear, and what to hope for; stories offer us nuanced models of behaviour both wise and foolish, courageous and cowardly, faithful and faithless."[31] This position finds support in Amos Wilder's observation that the route to moral judgment is by way of the imagination.[32] Hays takes a comprehensive view of Jesus' ethical heritage by intimating that the total moral significance of his life and ministry should not be gleaned only from his pronouncements and parables, but from the complete Jesus narrative of the incarnation, ministry and selfless service, passion, crucifixion, and resurrection presented by the individual evangelists.[33]

For lack of space, I must limit myself to Paul's books in discussing ethical principles in the Epistles, for he has bequeathed to humanity a wealth of information for ethical reflection, even if it occurs sporadically in response to specific events in individual churches. In pondering Pauline ethics, Grenz suggests that Jesus' teaching provided the source and inspiration for Paul, who contextualized the gospel in the first-century Greco-Roman world.[34]

28. Hays, *Moral Vision*, 96.
29. Barclay, *Gospel of Matthew*, 133, emphasis Barclay's.
30. Grenz, *Moral Quest*, 109.
31. Hays, *Moral Vision*, 73.
32. Wilder, *Early Christian Rhetoric*, 60.
33. Hays, *Moral Vision*, 74.
34. Grenz, *Moral Quest*, 119.

Grenz further intimates that Paul's ethics issues from the soteriological activity of the sovereign God, who acted definitively to rescue humanity from moral failure and sinful depravity. This redemptive purpose is revealed in the incarnation with a singular focus on the crucifixion as the pivotal event that facilitates the present activity of the Holy Spirit in the moral transformation of Christians. In Paul's view, this has an eschatological bearing, for the behavior of believers reveals the new life that God has graciously given them and which will one day be theirs in fullness.[35]

So it is that Paul does not formulate an ethical code, but rather responds as the occasion demands to the pressing pastoral problems that arise in his churches.[36] As a result, scholars such as Martin Dibelius[37] argue that there is little connection between Paul's ethical prescriptions and his theological convictions. Hays, however, refutes such arguments and develops a theological framework for Pauline ethics based on the concept of new creation which generates his eschatological ethics. In stating Paul's position, Hays avers, "the death and resurrection of Jesus was an apocalyptic event that signaled the end of the old age and portended the beginning of the new. Paul's moral vision is intelligible only when his apocalyptic perspective is kept clearly in mind."[38]

This panoramic review of biblical ethics reveals it as a unique category by which God does not only issue a moral code to be obeyed, but also empowers the Christian to meet the demands of divine edicts. This is accomplished through the ministry of the Holy Spirit, for as Rae suggests, the Spirit "provides an internal source that assists in decision making and enables one to mature spiritually."[39] This emphatic and significant ethical focus of the Bible reflects high moral standards that no one in Christian ministry can afford to ignore. Hence, in developing his concepts of character and calling in the ordained ministry, Willimon appeals to Hay's three focal biblical images, "community, cross, and new creation."[40] In the same

35. Ibid.
36. Hays, *Moral Vision*, 17.
37. Dibelius, *Fresh Approach*, 143–44, 217–20. Betz, who also insists that Paul does not provide the Galatians with a specifically Christian ethics, supports this view. Indeed, Betz thinks Paul's ethics is a reflection of the moral precepts of his educated Hellenistic context (Betz, *Galatians*, 292).
38. Hays, *Moral Vision*, 19.
39. Rae, *Moral Choices*, 31.
40. Willimon, *Character and Calling*, 52. Hays applies these biblical concept to ethics by first arguing that the church is a countercultural community, constituting the primary addressee of God's imperatives. Second, Hays regards the cross as the paradigm of faithfulness to believers. Third, Hays views the church as the organism that embodies the power of the resurrection in a not-yet-redeemed world (Hays, *Moral Vision*, 196–200).

vein, Richard Gula's theological foundations of ministerial ethics comprise the biblical concepts of covenant, image of God, and discipleship.[41] Consequently, it appears any clergy whose calling and ministry would remain relevant would have to acquire an appreciable knowledge of biblical ethical concepts and model them as an example to the community of faith.

Select Christian Ethical Theories

Christian ethics appears to be dynamic, defying any attempts to cast it in a rigid mold. To various degrees, Christian moral philosophy shows trends in deontology, teleology, and virtue ethics. This variegated nature of Christian ethics has generated various systems and theories that are relevant to life and ministry. The theory selected for discussion in the deontological category is the Divine Command theory, while the approach chosen under teleology (whose Christian value could be objectionable to some ethicists) is Fletcher's Situationism. The Christian concept of sanctification is also examined as an approach in virtue ethics.

The Divine Command Theory

The Divine Command theory centers on God, insisting that obedience to moral obligation conditions our relationship with God. By implication, since moral laws are grounded in the unchanging character of God, they are always relevant and cannot be broken. This informs Gula's conviction that "God is the ultimate center of value, the fixed point of reference for the morally right and wrong, the source and goal of all moral striving."[42] The ultimate foundation for morality is therefore the revealed will of God, the commands of God as found in Scripture. This approach to Christian moral theory is reminiscent of Kant's categorical imperative, by which the agent is obligated to perform moral acts as duties irrespective of the prevailing conditions. Phillips Edgcumbe Hughes, for instance, thinks Christian ethics is always based on principles, arguing that Christian ethics is "prescriptive, not simply descriptive, its domain is that of duty and obligation, and it seeks to define the distinction between right and wrong, between justice and injustice, and between responsibility and irresponsibility."[43]

---

41. Gula, *Ethics in Pastoral Ministry*, 14–30.
42. Ibid., 9.
43. Hughes, *Christian Ethics*, 11.

This link between theology and ethics demands that we examine the role of religion in society as well as the nature of moral discourse. The pertinent problem, therefore, is how to maintain a balanced relationship between reason and religion in ethics. Reflecting on this question, Lawrence Hinman has identified three positions: supremacy of religion, compatibilist theories, and supremacy of reason. The supremacy of religion position insists that all morality is based on divine commands; compatibilist theories consider reason and religion to be identical; and the supremacy of reason position, arguing from an atheistic or agnostic stance, derives its ethics solely from reason.[44] The main justification for a religious ethics is the metaphysical grounding for justice, by which it is believed that God rewards morally upright people in the afterlife and subjects the morally deficient to eternal punishment. This resonates with Kant's idea of moral theology as discussed in the previous chapter.

The litmus test applied to those who hold divine commands as moral absolutes is a response to the question posed by Plato in *Euthyphro* as to whether things are good because God commands them or whether God commands them because they are good.[45] If we were to argue that things are good because God commands them, then we would have to respond to the critical question: What if God orders something evil, like torture or infanticide? However, if God wills something because it is good, then the standard of goodness is located outside of God.

One school of thought suggests that God ordains Christian moral values because they are good. Rabbinic Judaism and the Roman Catholic tradition hold that God is not free to command anything he so desires, as he is bound by his moral attributes to only order what is good. This implies God will only act in ways consistent with his character. From this perspective, morality is not ultimately grounded in God's commands, but in his character, which expresses itself in his commands.[46] This position insists that the very moral values discernible in the natural order must agree with the commandments of God, for "Not only must his commands be consistent with his character, they must also be consistent with the values he has revealed in general revelation."[47]

The Divine Command theory in ethics has stimulated interesting responses from scholars. J. C. Thomas has extensively examined the moral deterministic position, which does not permit any intellectual reflection

---

44. Hinman, *Ethics*, 83–84.
45. Allen, *Euthyphro*, 29–30.
46. Rae, *Moral Choices*, 32.
47. Ibid.

on "God's goodness," in his article entitled "The Supernautralistic Fallacy Revisited." He convincingly argues against the position that assumes God's goodness and therefore insists that attempts to discuss the uprightness of God's choices are unnecessary. To Thomas' mind, "This amounts to the claim that there are no qualities over and above the will of God to which the word 'good' can be applied. Perhaps the term 'ethics' might be replaced by the term 'theodics'?"[48]

Elizabeth Anscombe also argues that moral terminology such as "should" and "ought" acquired rigid aspects due to Christianity's legalistic approach to ethics and wide influence. In her view, the use of such legalistic expressions seems to reveal a verdict on action, which presupposes the existence of a judge, the divine law-giver. To her mind, since society has given up the existence of God, approaches in moral philosophy that are based on a theistic worldview should be abandoned.[49] The Divine Command theory is further criticized for failing to provide a universal understanding of ethical demands in Scripture. The challenge of deriving moral absolutes from the Bible is emphasized by Josef Fuchs, who argues that identifying specific moral absolutes from Scripture is subject to interpretation: "Thus we are inevitably faced not only with the question as to which moral imperatives are actually to be found in Holy Scripture, but also with the question by which hermeneutic rules they are to be understood and evaluated."[50]

A relatively strong position against the Divine Command theory is that "there is something inadequate about punishment and reward orientation of moral motivation."[51] Morality, it is suggested, has to justify itself without depending on the external factors of reward or punishment, it has to possess its own internal unconditional value, for as Kant argues, it should be an end in itself rather than a means to an end. Austin's presentation reinforces the point: "if the motive for being moral on Divine Command theory is to avoid punishment and perhaps gain eternal bliss, then this is less than ideal as an account of moral motivation, because it smacks of moral immaturity."[52]

In spite of these revealing objections to Divine Command theory, the theory has also been defended for providing an "objective" spiritual foundation for morality. [53] Austin is convinced that any commitment to the value of objective moral truths can only be sustained in a conceptual framework

---

48. Thomas, "Supernatrualistic Fallacy," 21.
49. Anscombe, "Modern Moral Philosophy," 1–19.
50. Fuchs, "Absoluteness of Behavioral Norms," 489.
51. Austin, "Divine Command Theory," 3.
52. Ibid.
53. Ibid.

that believes in the existence of God: "That is, if the origin of the universe is a personal moral being, then the existence of objective moral truths are at home, so to speak, in the universe."[54] It is therefore difficult to oppose Austin's conclusion that rejecting a personal moral mind behind creation can only lead to the conclusion that out of the non-moral, nothing moral can emerge.[55]

In addition, the Divine Command theory seems to provide an adequate reason for human morality. Those who believe in the existence of God work under a moral framework that holds humanity accountable for our actions, rewarding the righteous and punishing the wicked, suggesting that ultimately good will triumph over evil and justice will win out.[56] Austin raises this perceptive argument in pointing out that the motivation to act in ways that oppose one's self-interest finds a "deep significance and merit within a theistic framework."[57] To him, under "Divine Command theory it is therefore rational to sacrifice my own well-being for the well-being of my children, my friends and even complete strangers, because God approves of and even commands such acts of self-sacrifice."[58]

Relevance for Ministerial Ethics

In applying this Divine Command approach to ministerial ethics, Langdon Gilkey has observed that since Scripture comprises the law and gospel, the clergy are expected to become authorities who interpret the divine law and in turn regulate the proper morals of the community.[59] In his view, the Reformed tradition in Calvinist and Methodist churches have emphasized the guiding role of divine law for the community, which compels the clergy to "become moral legislators and executive implementers of the moral rules governing the community."[60] Consequently, the minister is expected to model the divine law: "In a sense, now, the holy abides not only in Word (and sacraments) but also in the holy community and especially in and through the *holy person*."[61]

---

54. Ibid.
55. Ibid.
56. Ibid.
57. Ibid.
58. Ibid.
59. Gilkey, "Forgotten Traditions," 47.
60. Ibid.
61. Ibid., emphasis mine.

Robert Anderson suggests that the vestiges of Methodism manifest in the literal approach Pentecostals take to the interpretation and application of Scripture, which can foster legalism, saying, "This extreme literalism is quite consistent with Pentecostalism's roots in the Holiness and healing movements, where there tended to be the same literalistic, legalistic approach."[62] Gula avers that in life and ministry, we need to respond to God as the ultimate center of value, insisting that God's "way of acting and his words, his deeds, and his command are the moral rule of the Christian life."[63] Although Gula appreciates the contribution of social conventions and professional codes to the concept of ethical responsibility in ministry, speaking from a theological perspective, he insists that it is God alone who regulates morality.[64]

Rebekah Miles has also demonstrated the conviction that rule ethics is prevalent in conservative churches, where strict attention is given to what she calls an "arbitrary assortment of rules."[65] She is open to the thought that rules define clear boundaries about right and wrong, serving as guideposts in moral crises,[66] but nevertheless, Miles underscores the less constructive aspects of rule ethics, such as the tendency to become rigid and legalistic. She further suggests that those unable to observe the rules could become paralyzed with guilt, and the righteous could become arrogant in their judgmental attitude.[67] Trull and Carter express a similar conviction: "legalism almost always hinders moral maturity and stimulates egoistic pride. Ethical bed-babies and the self-righteous are undocumented aliens in God's kingdom."[68] O'Meara's reflection on Jesus' response to the priestly application of absolute religious norms is rather revealing: "Jesus faced opposition from the priests of his people; for Jesus broke through sacral caste to welcome all as he questioned religious rules as divinely guaranteed absolutes and flared up in anger more at religious hypocrisy than at ethical sin."[69]

Trull and Carter, reflecting on Karen Lebacqz's views, acknowledge that a system of strict obligation can manifest in ministry, where it is suggested that clergy should uphold absolutes such as promise-keeping,

---

62. Anderson, *Introduction to Pentecostalism*, 226.
63. Gula, *Ethics in Pastoral Ministry*, 25.
64. Ibid., 9.
65. Miles, *Pastor as Moral Guide*, 23.
66. Ibid., 22.
67. Ibid.
68. Trull and Carter, *Ministerial Ethics*, 56.
69. O'Meara, *Theology of Ministry*, 39.

truth-telling, beneficence, non-maleficence, and justice.[70] They also expand the scope of moral absolutes that can be applied to cover church codes and governmental edicts.[71]

Fletchers' Situationism

Fuchs offers a convincing opinion on the response of some Christians to the rigid normative ethics seen in Divine Command theory:

> No small number of convinced Christians are allergic to "absolute" norms—not, indeed, to the possibility of "right," "objective," and therefore "absolutely" binding judgment in concrete instances, and consequently the possibility of moral imperatives too, but to "universally binding," and in *this* sense, absolute norms of moral action.[72]

This observation seems to provide adequate justification for a Christian ethical system that is flexible enough to respond to the moral complexities of contemporary society. I have decided to make a brief exposition here on Situationism, a theory regarded by its main proponent, Joseph Fletcher (1905–1991), as an aspect of Christian ethics, although some Christians would not recognize it as such.

According to Fletcher, there are three approaches to moral philosophy. The first is legalistic, comprising the methods used by the Jews, Catholics, and Protestants. The Jews, under the post-exilic Maccabeans and Pharisaic leadership, lived by the Law (Torah) and its oral tradition (halakah), which constituted a law code of 613 precepts.[73] Joseph Fletcher contends that Catholics have developed a system of legalistic reason based on nature or natural law. He also accuses Protestants, who claim their ethics to be based on the Bible, of initiating a method of legalistic revelation by developing inflexible moral codes that have culminated in ethical absolutism.[74] Similarly, Fletcher regards Pentecostal morality, with its emphasis on holiness, as another legalistic system of ethics: "The Moral Re-Armament ethic is of the kind one would logically expect to find in the Holiness and Pentecostal movements, and yet, in spite of their self-styled pneumatic character,

---

70. Trull and Carter, *Ministerial Ethics*, 55.
71. Ibid.
72. Fuchs, "Absoluteness of Behavioral Norms," 487.
73. Fletcher, *Situation Ethics*, 18.
74. Ibid., 21.

they are for the most part quite legalistic morally."[75] By implication, we might think that the spiritual-consciousness and experiential emphasis of Pentecostalism would allow for a flexible approach in morality, but Fletcher argues that they also take a stern and unyielding approach to ethics.

Reflecting on these concepts, Thomas aptly observes, "Fletcher regards any set of rules which prescribes what is right and wrong as legalistic ethics."[76] Obviously, in rejecting principle-based ethical systems Fletcher seems to engage in oversimplification and stereotyping, since it is impossible to do ethics without any reference to morally defensible positions.

In direct contrast to the legalists, according to Fletcher, are the antinomians who have no laws. He regards them as living in a condition of moral chaos, with no method of differentiating right from wrong.[77] Antinomian moral decisions are, in Fletcher's view, "random, unpredictable, erratic, quite anomalous."[78] While the legalist enters a moral decision-making process armed with guidelines, the antinomian has "no principles or maxims whatsoever, to say nothing of *rules*."[79]

Fletcher offers Situationism as the third alternative, as the median between legalistic and antinomian ethics. For the Situationist, only the command to love is unconditionally good. As far as moral rules are concerned, they are regarded as helpful, but not unbreakable. In making an ethical decision, the Situationist engages with the ethical principles of his or her community and its heritage, treating them with respect in helping to understand the problem at stake. Nevertheless, the Situationist is allowed in any situation to compromise these ethical principles or set them aside if love is better served by doing so:[80]

> Christian situation ethics has only one norm or principle . . . that is binding and unexceptionable, always good and right regardless of the circumstances. That is "love"—the *agape* of the summary commandment to love God and the neighbor. Everything else without exception, all laws and rules and principles and ideals and norms, are only *contingent*, only valid if they happen to serve love in any situation.[81]

---

75. Ibid., 24.
76. Thomas, "What Is Situation Ethics?" 26.
77. Fletcher, *Situation Ethics*, 27–28.
78. Ibid., 23, emphasis Fletcher's.
79. Ibid., 22.
80. Ibid., 26.
81. Ibid., 30, emphasis Fletcher's.

Fletcher derives his single norm concept of love from Bible passages such as "You have heard that it was said, 'Love your neighbor and hate your enemy.' But I tell you: Love your enemies and pray for those who persecute you" (Matt 5:43–48), "The entire law is summed up in a single commandment: 'Love your neighbor as yourself'" (Gal 5:14), and "'The most important one [commandment],' answered Jesus, 'is this: "Hear O Israel, the Lord our God, the Lord is one. Love the Lord your God with all your heart and with all your soul and with all your mind and with all your strength." The second is this: "Love your neighbor as yourself." There is no commandment greater than these'" (Mark 12: 28–34).

Fletcher's supposedly flawless single norm ethical system, according to Thomas, fails to ascribe intrinsic value to moral acts and principles, for "Any action Fletcher thinks is only right as a means to an end. An action which produces the greatest possible degree of love in a situation is morally right; and an action which fails to produce the greatest degree of love in a situation is morally wrong."[82] Thomas thus discerns a subtle link between Fletcher's position and that of Rule Utilitarianism, which respects traditional moral principles and employs them only when they produce the greatest happiness for the greatest number.[83] It is noteworthy that Fletcher actually admits to his reliance on Utilitarianism for social policy formulation: "As the love ethic searches seriously for a social policy it must form a coalition with Utilitarianism. It takes over from Bentham and Mill the strategic principle of the greatest good of the greatest number."[84]

Thomas perceptively identifies the contrived introduction of Kantian concepts into Fletcher's Utilitarian arguments, which is evident in Fletcher's idea of "Personalism."[85] Fletcher's Personalism, as Thomas has aptly revealed, is a modification of Kant's second maxim, which insists that people should never be treated as a means to an end. According to Thomas,

> This simple theory is complicated, however, because Fletcher introduces elements of Kant's ethical philosophy at several points in his arguments. For Situation Ethics puts people at the center of concern, not things. A person is ultimately valuable and must be treated as an end in himself, and never as a means to an end.[86]

---

82. Thomas, "What Is Situation Ethics?" 28.
83. Ibid., 29.
84. Fletcher, *Situation Ethics*, 95.
85. Ibid., 50.
86. Thomas, "What Is Situation Ethics?" 29.

Fletcher's arguments thus become cloudy as he almost identifies the human personality with agape. Thomas critiques this complication further, writing that Fletcher "provides no arguments to show that either agape or persons are good in themselves under all circumstances. He seems to expect his readers to accept his intuitions about what is ultimately valuable."[87] Reflecting on Situationism, David Cook also observes that the ethical person is right to be suspicious of any moral system built on exceptional life situations.[88]

Grenz seems to demonstrate an appreciative disposition toward Situationism. He apologetically suggests that opponents to Situationism appear to either misunderstand Fletcher or to be overreacting to some of his more radical statements on human sexuality.[89] Jones is also convinced that this lack of understanding is responsible for the branding of Situationism as a permissive system of ethics.[90] According to Jones, "the love which he [Fletcher] advocates is a most demanding requirement, involving immense capacity for self-sacrifice and a very high view of the value of other human beings.[91] Generally, Situationism is acclaimed for its emphasis on love and the value of persons, for as Fletcher reveals:

> Nevertheless, this is what Christian love is. It does not seek the deserving, nor is it judgmental when it makes its decisions—judgmental, that is, about the people it wants to serve. *Agape* goes out to our neighbors not for our own sakes, nor for theirs, really but for God's. We can say quite plainly and colloquially that Christian love is the business of loving the unlovable, i.e., the *unlikeable*.[92]

Fletcher's affirmation of the value of human beings is further enhanced by his idea that it is only when virtues, such as patience are applied to human beings that their tangible value could be best appreciated.

Relevance to Ministerial Ethics

In Miles' opinion, goal ethicists think moral faithfulness comprises the capacity to discover and pursue the highest human goals, as a result, many

---

87. Ibid., 30.
88. Cook, *Moral Maze*, 73.
89. Grenz, *Moral Quest*, 178.
90. Jones, *Groundwork of Christian Ethics*, 148.
91. Ibid.
92. Fletcher, *Situation Ethics*, 105, emphasis Fletcher's.

pastors have lately taken to emphasizing this kind of therapeutic approach to direct people towards individual happiness and self-fulfillment.[93] In words that appear to echo Fletcher's, Miles observes, "Christian goal ethics often insist that the ultimate goal is happiness, this ultimate happiness comes from loving and serving God and others."[94] She appreciates the benefits of such approaches for their dynamic flexibility in allowing Christians to be guided by the Holy Spirit or to respond to the peculiar needs of the situation. Miles is convinced that this approach is useful in pastoral care to help people "relate the immediate moment to their highest goals and ultimate relationship to God."[95]

Similarly, Gula develops a covenant framework for ministerial relationships and insists that all such relationships should be mediated by the love of God.[96] Gula thus supports Fletcher's position by rejecting prescriptive ethics, writing, "But a ministerial relationship is open to services that are not so predictable and so cannot always be spelled out in advance. Ministers need to be flexible. Ministry must allow for spontaneity. When we act according to a covenant, we look beyond the minimum."[97] The application of consequential ethics in ministry comes into focus in such cases as when a pastor faces the dilemma of keeping or disclosing information about an adulterous husband, possibly imperiling the marriage.[98]

Virtue Ethics in the Christian Tradition

Weist and Smith appreciate the essential effect of character as the moral sensor that shapes life into "meaningful and predictable patterns" of behavior that demand that the Christian minister internalizes the moral standards of faith in order to behave ethically.[99] What seems to be the most comprehensive view of Christian ethics is captured by the term "sanctification," which connotes a process of moral transformation that is geared towards ethical maturity. Both the Hebrew term *qodesh* and the Greek equivalent, *hagiasmos*, translated as sanctification, mean separation or setting apart. Sanctification expresses the dynamics of divine-human interaction in terms of character growth and ethical maturity. The divine dimension of Christian

93. Miles, *Pastor as a Moral Guide*, 22.
94. Ibid.
95. Ibid.
96. Gula, *Ethics in Pastoral Ministry*, 15.
97. Ibid.
98. Trull and Carter, *Ministerial Ethics*, 58.
99. Wiest and Smith, *Ethics in Ministry*, 182.

character development introduces mystery into moral philosophy. Since discussions in the study of reality (ontology) do not necessarily exclude the superhuman or supernatural, we can comfortably introduce spirituality into this discourse. Invariably, the tangible evidence of this divine-human association is attested to by the positive moral transformation of the individual concerned.[100]

Sanctification implies a conscious effort to avoid unwholesome and sinful behavior in endeavoring to lead a morally upright life that conforms to the standard of righteousness revealed in Scripture. Holiness is an attribute of God that expresses itself in his purity, transparency, and immaculate nature and is not tainted by any kind of evil. God demands that human beings who want to have a relationship with him should be sanctified—that is, they must be people who are focused on rising to the same standard of holiness: "The Lord said to Moses, 'Speak to the entire assembly of Israel and say to them: Be holy because I, the Lord your God, am holy'" (Lev 19:1–2).

It is important to emphasize the prominent role of the Holy Spirit in sanctification, wherein the Spirit provides instruction and conviction that leads to repentance: "When he [the Holy Spirit] comes, he will convict the world of guilt in regard to sin and righteousness and judgment" (John 16:15). According to Paul, the Holy Spirit ultimately produces in the believer the fruit of the Spirit, for "the fruit of the Spirit is love, joy, peace, patience, kindness, goodness, faithfulness, gentleness and self-control" (Gal 5:22–23). These are character traits of the ethically mature Christian, revealing that it is the Spirit of holiness who generates and sustains moral purity among Christians.

Evidently, in spite of the availability of these divine resources to humankind to help us overcome moral shortfalls, there are wide differences in individual standards of morality, even among pastors. This situation is difficult to explain; however, we can ascribe these differences to the level of sensitivity of the individual in applying these equally distributed and readily available divine resources for character transformation.

Relevance to Ministerial Ethics

Invariably, Christian ethics is biased towards the virtue approach, as revealed in the doctrinal concept of sanctification. Sanctification connotes moral exemplars; that is, the recognition of people who excel in the expression of specific virtues, such as integrity, honesty, courage, fidelity, and a

---

100. A practical example of how moral transformation occurred in a sinner who encountered divinity is captured in Agyin-Asare, *Celebrating the Pilgrimage*, 3–4.

progressive maturity in ethical decision-making. Nevertheless, since sanctification is a process that lasts for a lifetime, it is possible for even a mature Christian and human moral exemplar to fall into error occasionally. Hence the accidental moral failure of some Christian leaders could be explained in the light of this character development process. In other words, such leaders are not plaster saints; they remain people of flesh and blood who keep striving to attain the challenging goal of God's standard of moral perfection.

Gula devotes the third chapter of his book, *Ethics in Pastoral Ministry*, to "The Minister's Character and Virtue" in arguing that the character of the minster speaks louder than his or her sermons. He further argues that Christian ministry is one field of human endeavor where "the medium and the message are so closely tied together" that it is not reasonable for a minister to preach on morality and do something different.[101] Gula proceeds to define character as "the *kind of person* who acts in a certain way,"[102] explaining that character focuses on the inner realities of self, including motives, intentions, and attitudes.[103] Like many others, Gula is convinced that character quality is an extremely important qualification for ministry:

> Clearly, good character is a prerequisite for ministry. Ideally, people who chose to enter the ministry have woven into the fabric of their lives the values and habits that make them caring, generous, and trustworthy people committed to promoting the good of others. The public assumes that ministers have good character. No wonder, then, that when a minister is caught up in self-centeredness, it is taken as such a shocking disappointment.[104]

Gyekye, in challenging theological institutions to raise moral leaders for society, intimates that character quality and the capacity for moral guidance are critical in ministry. He further insists that there is a general presupposition that such leaders model the desired moral values and virtues of the community in order to inspire and direct others to chart the same course.[105] In Gyekye's estimation, the minister's "moral life has become a moral paradigm and a point of reference for others."[106] Willimon likewise locates character ethics in the wider context of the ethical debate by suggesting that it is complementary to act-oriented ethics. He insightfully posits

---

101. Gula, *Ethics in Pastoral Ministry*, 31.
102. Ibid., 33, emphasis Gula's.
103. Ibid.
104. Ibid., 35.
105. Gyekye, "Spiritual and Moral Leadership," 34–40.
106. Ibid., 35.

that it is impossible to divorce the question, "What ought I to do?" from "Who do I hope to be?" [107] Willimon uses this complementary approach of "being" and "doing" to examine the concept of character and calling in the ordained ministry, and I have employed the same model in navigating Ghanaian Pentecostal ministerial ethics.

Pentecostal Ethics

Assimeng insightfully observes that the Pentecostal movement did not expound new truths or new applications, but rather Pentecostals seem to be revivalists who recovered popular religious convictions.[108] If Assimeng is correct, we must test Pentecostal ethics. Typical of the Protestant tradition, Pentecostals claim that their ethics is based on the authority of the Bible. However, the unique distinguishing factor of Pentecostal ethics is an intense awareness of the active role of the Holy Spirit in moral formation. The key moral terminologies in Christian doctrine, such as "sanctification," "righteousness," "purity," and "holiness," are very much applicable in the Pentecostal context, although with extra spiritual emphasis. Pentecostals would ascribe ethical maturity to the dynamic and practical work of the Holy Spirit, who becomes the agent of moral transformation. The Spirit is expected not only to teach, but also to empower both the individual and the community to make the right moral choices. In certain cases of moral failure, such as persistent alcoholism or promiscuity, the problem is ascribed to spiritual causes and the Holy Spirit is often invoked in deliverance sessions to cast out (as is often claimed) the "demon" of alcoholism or dishonesty, as the case may be.[109]

Evidently, the Pentecostal experience is highly subjective, as it tends to place much value on the individual's ability to engage with the Holy Spirit. Moreover, the religion is also easily adaptable in that it develops more out of experience than doctrinal formulation; consequently, it may be difficult to apply neat doctrinal considerations to examine the various kinds of spiritual manifestations of Pentecostal expression. These factors of subjectivism and adaptability could allow certain personal and cultural traces to leak into

---

107. Willimon, *Character and Calling*, 12.

108. Assimeng, *Saints and Social Structures*, 133.

109. This approach of spiritual emphasis in ethical formation has promoted a unique focus on demonization and exorcism popularly referred to among Pentecostals as "deliverance ministry." The spiritual value of this ministry notwithstanding, it has generated some level of abuse of suppliants by some of the deliverance ministers, which is discussed further in chapter 6.

the ethics of Pentecostals/charismatics, with positive or negative implications. Sometimes a Pentecostal interpretation of Scripture may produce a kind of severe and regulated morality. This approach to Christian morality leads congregations like the Deeper Christian Life Church to proscribe self-adornment with jewelry to its members. As stated above, Fletcher takes issue with such an application of rigid moral codes in a religious tradition that is supposed to be more experiential and subjective than doctrinal and sacramental.

Hollenweger argues that Pentecostal ethics reveals a basic pattern of ethical prescriptions as well as demonstrating the significant influence of the cultural background of each particular group.[110] Menzies has also made the revealing observation that Pentecostals often use narrative material from the Bible for their theological foundations without questioning their doctrinal value.[111] According to José Míguez Bonino, the assertion that Pentecostal faith is a Bible-centered one is not self-evident because although their hermeneutic is often literalistic, their focus is basically inspirational, seeking direction to solve mundane problems rather than doctrinal formulation.[112] This fluid approach in Pentecostal hermeneutics seems to inform Steven Land's opinion that the Pentecostal concept of salvation emphasizes "salvation as participation in the divine life more than the removal of guilt," which implies that enjoying the benefits of "sharing in divinity" receives more attention than striving for moral uprightness.[113]

Pentecostal Concepts of Sanctification

Sanctification as an Event

The classical Pentecostals who emerged from the Azusa Street Revival had their roots largely in the Wesleyan Holiness tradition's strong emphasis on sanctification. The Wesleyan tradition teaches that apart from having our sins pardoned through faith in Christ, our sinful natures may be eradicated through Christ's atoning work. Wesleyans believe that this holy work secures an experience of entire sanctification, which is also known as sinless perfection. Thus, sanctification is regarded as an event rather than a process—a sudden act of heart purification that occurs after conversion, but is necessary before Spirit baptism. This historic link between the Holiness

---

110. Hollenweger, *Pentecostals*, 407.
111. Menzies, quoted in Ma, "Biblical Studies in the Pentecostal Tradition," 55.
112. Bonino, "Changing Paradigms," 117–18.
113. Land, *Pentecostal Spirituality*, 23.

movement and Pentecostalism is much attested to by scholars: "Pentecostalism," according to Johns, did not "appear 'suddenly from heaven,' but rather quite naturally from well-documented Wesleyan perfectionist precedent upon which it built."[114] Anderson is also convinced that the nineteenth-century movement that emerged from the teaching of John Wesley provided the immediate background for modern Pentecostalism.[115]

The Wesleyan concept of entire sanctification is still upheld by the Pentecostal Holiness Church and the Church of God in Christ in the United States. It appears that no Pentecostal church in Ghana currently sticks rigidly to this three-stage process of spiritual growth from conversion to sanctification to Spirit baptism. Nevertheless, traces of the Wesleyan Holiness moral codes are still discernible in the strict ethical standards maintained by churches such as the Apostolic Church Ghana and the Church of Pentecost. It is interesting to know that one of Ghana's foremost scholars on Pentecostalism, Professor J. Kwabena Asamoah-Gyadu, a Methodist minister and Dean of Graduate Studies at Trinity Theological Seminary in Legon, Ghana, is convinced that true Wesleyan Methodist holiness is more discernible today in the Church of Pentecost than in the Methodist Church.[116] By implication, the public exposure of sin and strict moral codes upheld by this Pentecostal church is closer to primitive Methodism than many other church traditions.

Sanctification as a Process

Evidence of instability in the Pentecostal concept of sanctification manifested when another tradition emerged within the movement, one which taught that sanctification is a process that one experiences over a life time. The foremost proponent of this position was William H. Durham, who in 1910 challenged the entire Wesleyan sanctification doctrine by arguing that sanctification began at regeneration and continued as a process of growth.[117] According to Land, Durham's rejection of the perfectionist doctrine generated tension between some Pentecostals and the Holiness movement that cradled it.[118] Durham preached what he called the "finished work of Calvary," purporting that believers in Christ are justified and sanctified in

114. Johns, "Yielding to the Spirit," 5.

115. Anderson, *Introduction to Pentecostalism*, 25.

116. J. Kwabena Asamoah-Gyadu, Trinity Theological College, interview by Dela Quampah, Accra, Ghana, June 2, 2009.

117. Land, *Pentecostal Spirituality*, 185.

118. Ibid., 186.

Christ, making the beliefver complete in all that is relevant to salvation.[119] To the "finished work" proponents, sanctification became positional and progressive.[120] Other Pentecostal churches, such as Assemblies of God, the Elim Pentecostal Church, and the International Church of the Foursquare Gospel view sanctification as both given in salvation and progressive throughout the Christian life.

Myer Pearlman insists that sanctification is progressive and not instantaneous:

> Sanctification is absolute and progressive—absolute in the sense that it is a work done once for all (Heb 10:14), progressive in the sense that the Christian must follow after holiness (Heb 12:14) and perfect his consecration by cleansing himself from all defilement (2 Cor 7:1).[121]

This category of Pentecostals, unlike the Wesleyan Holiness group, does not insist on external expressions of moral purity in terms of dress codes or the like. However, this does not imply that they have no concern for moral standards—far from that, they uphold Christian moral principles of sexual propriety, honesty, integrity, decency, and decorum. In Ghana, the Assemblies of God and many charismatic churches such as ICGC, WMCI, and CAFM, among others, identify with this "finished work" category.

This seemingly flexible position of the "Finished Work Pentecostals" has led some scholars to think that they do not take issues related to morality seriously. However, the fact that the Finished Work category does not insist on rigid ethical formulations does not imply they have little concern for ethical issues. Their approach is not a community-regulated ethics; the community's role is to mentor and encourage rather than to impose strict controls and sanctions. Christian moral values are taught in sermons and during Bible study sessions, and the choice and responsibility for moral action is left up to the individual's application. For instance, a manual for Assemblies of God adult Sunday school teachers lists Christian growth as one of its objectives: "to grow mature Christian character, people who believe the Bible and apply its principles for guidance in matters of conduct."[122]

---

119. Horton, "Pentecostal Perspective," 107.
120. Land, *Pentecostal Spirituality*, 186.
121. Pearlman, *Knowing the Doctrines*, 254.
122. Amankwa, *Assemblies of God Sunday School*, 13.

Conclusion

In this chapter, I have attempted a brief overview of biblical approaches to ethics and identified the unique emphases the various segments of the Bible reveal. In addition, I have explored some systems in Christian moral philosophy, namely Divine Command theory, Fletcher's Situationism, and the virtue ethical approach known as sanctification in Christian terminology, and then attempted to establish their general relevance to ministerial conduct. Furthermore, the two Pentecostal concepts of sanctification, namely "entire sanctification" and "finished work," have been examined to understand their influence on communal ethics. The implications of Pentecostal communal morality for ministerial conduct shall be discussed further in the next chapter.

5

Leadership Structure in Select Ghanaian Pentecostal Churches

Introduction

As we have already observed, Christian ethics is communal; therefore, no adequate reflection on ministerial morality can be undertaken without an understanding of church polity or the administrative framework within which ministers operate. According to Gilkey, "Polity connotes the institutional structure of the community: its patterns of authority and responsibility, its governing bodies or persons, their rights and obligations, the institutional roles and functions of its officers, committees, and so on."[1] This assumes the existence of institutional structures that equip, support, and guide ministers, in addition to stipulating disciplinary procedures that hold such leaders morally accountable. The relevance of Gula's opinion to institutional accountability is best expressed in his own words:

> The presence of structures of accountability implies the existence of a distinct professional organization which establishes the qualifications for the admission of new members, the course of their preparation, the standards of competence for licensing, standards for peer review, and the disciplinary procedures and sanctions for controlling deviant behavior.[2]

Consequently, we will examine the three approaches in church governance—congregational, presbyterian, and episcopalian—to help us understand their response to ministerial accountability. It is worth mentioning

1. Gilkey, "Forgotten Traditions," 39.
2. Gula, *Ethics in Pastoral Ministry*, 62.

that factors such as theological and church background of the founder(s), cultural context, and certain defining events in the formative stages of a church considerably influence the polity of the denomination. This chapter therefore examines the historical background that has shaped denominational polity and ministerial ethical standards in the selected churches. Furthermore, Gilkey's model of polity categorization into "the Sacramental Church," "the Church of the Word" and "the Churches of the Spirit" provide us with a useful framework for the discussion of the possible interrelatedness between ministerial morality and ministerial efficacy.[3] Finally we will analyze the administrative structure and ministerial ethical codes of the selected churches for their responsiveness to ministerial ethical problems.

Three Approaches to Church Governance

The congregational system of church government places authority in the hands of the congregation, who, to a large extent, decide what the leadership can do. The appointment of church officials is undertaken by popular vote and the congregation must ratify major decisions before they are implemented. The scope of the pastor's authority varies with the congregation, and the Deacons Board may play a mainly advisory role. In most cases, decisions in the church are subjected to open ballot. The multiple-elder system of church leadership is ruled by a board of deacons who have the authority to hire or fire a pastor. Thus, the pastor's authority is subject to the Deacons Board, although in many cases the pastor is given considerable authority to make certain decisions and implement them with the support of the Deacons Board.

The presbyterian system of church governance is led by representatives chosen by the congregation or by the clergy with the approval of lay members. The selected lay leaders, who may be variously called elders, deacons, and deaconesses, constitute the Session of the local church who work in consultation with one prominent, but equal, elder or pastor. Delegates from the local church are in turn selected to represent the congregation at higher levels, covering a wider geographical area called a Presbytery. Furthermore, members of the various Presbyteries are elected to the General Assembly, which constitutes the national decision-making body of the church.

The episcopalian, or hierarchical,[4] approach to church leadership places the clergy, as distinct from the laity, as the governing council of the

---

3. Gilkey, "Forgotten Traditions," 43–53.

4. The word "hierarchy" means priestly governance, deriving from the Greek *hierus* for "priest" and *arche*, or "rule."

denomination. In such cases, important decisions, appointment to church offices, and discipline of church functionaries becomes the prerogative of this hierarchical body. This system of church government is practiced mainly by the Roman Catholic Church, although it occurs to varying degrees in other churches. Kevin Conner has observed that many "Independent" or "Autonomous churches" practice this kind of government in cases when the founder becomes the monarchical church leader and may not be held accountable to anyone.[5]

It is noteworthy that each system is charged with different levels of moral accountability to congregation members. In the hierarchical system, where authority and appointment to church office is the preserve of the clergy, a considerable level of responsibility resides with the clergy to be self-critical in striving to maintain appreciable standards of ethics in ministry. It also has the advantage of a high level of confidentiality, which protects the privacy of the individual clergy member from excessive public invasion. However, the conspicuous lack of accountability to the laity in the episcopalian style of leadership can be a recipe for abuse and manipulation. The presbyterian system of church government has the advantage of achieving a balance of power between the clergy and laity insofar as lay representatives are selected by the congregation to help pastors exercise authority both locally and over a wider geographical area. The lay members of the Presbytery share responsibility with the clergy, and each category may hold the other accountable for ethical standards in Christian leadership. Furthermore, this system affords the clergy with a degree of confidentiality, for the lay members of the Session bear the responsibility of protecting the privacy of the minister. Of the three options, congregational governance, which gives considerable power to congregation members in appraising ministerial performance and preventing abuse of authority, appears to be the most effective in regulating ministerial conduct. Nevertheless, the minister becomes extremely vulnerable insofar as his or her vision and private affairs are always subjected to public scrutiny. Although the congregational approach has the highest probability of effective regulation of morality in ministry, its potential lack of confidentiality can be rather challenging from the minister's viewpoint.

It is, however, noteworthy that these systems of church governance, which developed initially in the North African and West European contexts, have gone through a process of adaptation in sub-Saharan Africa. Reflecting on the impact of cultures on church forms, O'Meara suggests that the Spirit's dynamic influence should be allowed to birth approaches to church

---

5. See Conner, *Church in the New Testament*.

governance relevant to various cultural contexts, arguing that "the forms of church life exist on that edge where revelation meets civilization. The constellations of culture are the catalysts of ecclesial forms. From history we gain not a unique model of ministry divinely given but an understanding of the adaptability of the church."[6] Unfortunately, the scope of this study does not permit a thorough analysis of the various church governance approaches and how they interact with Ghanaian culture. However, it is noteworthy that, in some cases, the process of adaptation has yielded in its wake a kind of a hybrid of system that employs almost all the three approaches concurrently—a system we can conveniently consider as the dynamic and relevant Ghanaian approach to church governance.[7]

Linking Ministerial Morality to Ministerial Efficacy

The thought of predicating the efficacy of ministerial functions on the personal morality of the functionary has triggered an inconclusive debate in the Christian community since the Donatist controversy of around AD 312.[8] The Donatists held a puritan view of the church, insisting that it should be a totally holy and exclusive community in its physical reality.[9] Consequently, they were convinced that the validity of the sacraments depends on the proper moral standing of the minister, rather than any essential quality imbued by ordination.[10] Scholars who sympathize with Donatism tend to appreciate the Donatists' attempt to establish high ministerial ethical

---

6. O' Meara, *Theology of Ministry*, 80.

7. For instance, in an interview with Rev. Charles Appiah-Boachie, General Secretary of Assemblies of God Ghana, the Reverend indicated that because comprehensive congregationalism was not relevant to Ghanaian culture, they have adapted it by requesting that the local secretary only assess a pastor's performance by responding to a questionnaire (Charles Appiah-Boachie, Assemblies of God Church, interview by Dela Quampah, Accra, Ghana, June 22, 2007). Similarly, both Rev. Dr. E. Anim, Pentecost University College's Dean of Theology, and Apostle Alfred Kodua, General Secretary of the Church of Pentecost, agree that CoP polity demonstrates traits of all the three approaches in church governance (E. Anim, Pentecost University College, interview by Dela Quampah, Accra, Ghana, February 15, 2012; Alfred Kodua, Church of Pentecost interview by Dela Quampah, Accra, Ghana, June 7, 2007).

8. This controversy emerged in North Africa, where Donatus, a churchman, objected to the consecration of Caecillian as Bishop of Carthage by Felix, because the latter apostatized during the Diocletian persecution. To Donatus, failure to remain faithful during persecution invalidated Felix's authority to ordain because he had committed the unpardonable sin (Frend, *Donatist Church*, 12).

9. Chadwick, *Early Church*, 221.

10. Ibid.

standards. James Stitzinger, for instance, suggests that the main issue for the Donatists was the purity of the church and the holiness of its pastors, which were to match biblical standards.[11] The mainstream church, however, rejected the Donatist position when the AD 411 Conference of Carthage, presided over by Count Marcellinus, endorsed the Catholic position that "the Church on earth was a mixed body containing good and evil, and not, as the Donatists claimed, a society of the elect 'without spot or wrinkle.'"[12]

This informed the Roman Catholic Church's position that the validity of a sacrament does not necessarily depend on the character of the one administering the sacrament. Gula locates this doctrinal position in the Roman Catholic Church, which, according to him, has "enshrined one form of the power of official appointment in its sacramental theology of *ex opere operato*,"[13] which is to say that the validity of the sacrament depended more on the ordination rite of the minister than personal worthiness. This position is confirmed by O'Meara's conviction that "the ministry serving the church and the community is sacramental, and there is a sacramentality of ministry."[14] The Roman Catholic Church's catechism declares, "As in the case of Baptism and Confirmation, this share in Christ's office is granted once for all. The sacrament of Holy Orders, like the other two, confers an indelible spiritual character and cannot be repeated or conferred temporarily."[15]

Gilkey's classification of the "Sacramental Church" includes Orthodox, Roman, and High Anglican,[16] for such churches emphasize the sacramental mediatory role of the priesthood over their moral vision. What sustains that role, in Gilkey's opinion, is the apostolic succession, the episcopal lineage that is believed to extend unbroken back to the founding of the church. No sacrament is believed to be valid or even conceivable if it is not sponsored by that line. According to Henry Chadwick, this doctrine is traceable to the Augustinian school, which taught that "in the sacraments . . . the priest's actions belong to God who at the moment of ordination has imprinted upon the priest an indelible mark (*character*); therefore, ordination

11. Stitzinger, "Pastoral Ministry in History," 34.
12. Frend, *Donatist Church*, 287.
13. Gula, *Ethics in Pastoral Ministry*, 70.
14. O'Meara, *Theology of Ministry*, 199.
15. *Catechism of the Catholic Church*, sec. 1582, http://www.vatican.va/archive/ccc_css/archive/catechism/p2s2c3a6.htm#VII.
16. Gilkey, "Forgotten Traditions," 43. It is noteworthy that these categories are not watertight. To varying degrees, almost all church traditions reflect certain aspects of the sacramental, the homiletic, and the pneumatic. Nevertheless, Gilkey's approach is useful in identifying the broad outlines that characterize and help define significant traits in church polity.

is independent of the moral and spiritual condition of the person ordained, and the efficacy of the sacraments does not depend on the devout state of mind of the baptizing or celebrating priest."[17] This doctrine seems to condition the direction of their ministerial ethics, for "the ethics of the clergy is primarily directed at the preservation of this divinely established structure of the church."[18] Therefore the priest, as long as he met the outward demands of obedience and order in his role as mediator, was "free from the burden of total personal sanctification if he was to do his professional task."[19] A remarkable illustration of this extreme sacramental pose is seen in Graham Green's "whiskey priest" in his novel, *The Power and the Glory*. In spite of his loss of faith, the village folk compel the "whiskey priest" to say mass, since all the other priests had either fled or officially apostatized to escape persecution. He complied because of his obligation to office, though to the communicants, the validity of the mass had no link to his questionable faith and morals.[20]

Gilkey's extreme sacramental emphasis notwithstanding, a more comprehensive view of such churches acknowledges the rigorous and ascetic discipline of those monks whose pattern of life has bequeathed to the church a rich and enduring heritage in ministerial self-control. For instance, *The Rule of Saint Benedict*, which is acknowledged as one of the most influential documents on European Christian morality, originated from the monastery tradition. Likewise, the Catholic Church has produced some of the saintliest personalities in church history as well as in modern times, such as Mother Teresa.

The second kind of church polity identified by Gilkey is what he calls "the Church of the Word," a tradition that was rediscovered during the Reformation. In his view, such churches recognize the invisible presence of Christ in proclamation of the Word: "The Holy within the community was no longer the sacramental gift of healing grace; rather it was the preserve of the gospel of justification of the sinner and the promise of reconciliation with God contained therein."[21] The Word captured in Scripture and its proclamation provided the locus for the believer to directly encounter God's indescribable presence.[22]

---

17. Chadwick, *Early Church*, 222, emphasis Chadwick's.
18. Gilkey, "Forgotten Traditions," 43.
19. Ibid.
20. Green, *Power and the Glory*, 67–69.
21. Gilkey, "Forgotten Traditions," 46.
22. Ibid.

In the Reformation-type church context, preaching or proclamation of the Word becomes the focal point of the church and the minister's main task. According to Gilkey, the Reformers did not emphasize the clergy's inner perfection or saintliness; rather they demanded fidelity to the Word, "which requires obedient study of Scripture and commitment to the role of obedient proclamation."[23] MacArthur laments the outcome of this polity in suggesting that it has resulted in doctrinal purity and not moral purity: "We have people with the right theology who are living impure lives."[24] In such a context, Scripture displaces the authority of church tradition; as a result, the clergy reject episcopal instructions when it conflicts with Scripture.[25] The authority of the priests therefore depends on their knowledge of Scripture and their faithfulness to its true meaning. Thomas Oden, for instance, forcefully upholds the authority of Scripture in defining the pastoral ministry:

> Pastoral theology lives out of Scripture. When the pastoral tradition has quoted Scripture, it has viewed it as an authoritative text for shaping both the understanding and its practice of ministry. We do not put Scripture under our examination, according to criteria alien to it, in order to understand ministry. Rather, Scripture examines our prior understandings of ministry. It puts them to test.[26]

In contrast to his limited perspective on sacramental ministerial ethics, Gilkey offers a broader view of the evangelical position by acknowledging that since the Scriptures comprise the law as well as the gospel, the clergy were bound to interpret the divine law and consequently define the proper morals for the community of believers.[27] To Gilkey's mind, Reformed church traditions such as that of Calvinist churches regarded the clergy as "moral legislators and executive implementors of the moral rules governing the community."[28] This implies that in this context, "the holy abides not only in Word (and sacraments) but also in the holy community and especially in and through the person."[29] This provides the historical precursor to the extremely high moral demands Pentecostals make of their clergy.

The third category of churches, according to Gilkey's model, is "the churches of the Spirit," which he intriguingly locates among black

23. Ibid.
24. MacArthur, "The Character of a Pastor," 68.
25. Gilkey, "Forgotten Traditions," 46.
26. Oden, *Pastoral Theology*, 11.
27. Gilkey, "Forgotten Traditions," 47.
28. Ibid.
29. Ibid.

communities.[30] Gilkey describes such congregations as "a new synthesis of spirit-centered churches with a worldly, liberationist task, uniting types now a bit worn out in mainline churches or warped into fundamentalist forms in many evangelical congregations."[31]

The main characteristics of Gilkey's "Spirit churches" are subjectivity, transformation unto perfection, and fellowship. By subjectivity, the author means the evidence of the transforming power of the Holy Spirit in the believer, which is manifest in conversion and in an overriding concern for high moral standards. In Gilkey's estimation, this authentic Christianity is valued more than sacraments, ceremonious robes, creeds, liturgy, bishops, learning doctrines, and cathedrals.[32] By implication, although there may be some observance of sacraments and the use of sacred objects, these are overwhelmed by concerns for the influence of the Holy Spirit in the practical real-life choices of the believer. Gilkey further explains that the Spirit church "is holy simply because it is made up of authentic Christians, real believers and real followers who have the Spirit and know they have it, and who follow its leading."[33] This intimate relationship with the Spirit, as described by Gilkey, defies logical and scientific investigations. However, in their testimonies, such believers lay claim to personal spiritual encounters that impact their life choices significantly. Gilkey, in explaining his idea of moral transformation in the Spirit churches, suggests that there is no higher ethic for the clergy than there is for the laity: "If anything, the community, not the clergy, is set apart. Here in principle the whole congregation equally is called to perfection."[34] The clergy in such churches find themselves in a

---

30. The sense of intrigue relates to the resonance of the polity of these black churches in the United States to their counterparts in Ghana, which constitute the subject of this work.

31. Gilkey, "Forgotten Traditions," 49.

32. Ibid., 50. It is, however, necessary to mention that one of this study's focuses is the variety of expression in the Pentecostal movement, which appears to be a strength revealed in its diversity. Some of these ceremonial expressions listed by Gilkey, which the Holiness movement and the progenitors of Pentecostalism rejected, have resurfaced in the movement. I argue in the next chapter that the pomp and pageantry currently expressed in some Pentecostal churches has drawn criticism from certain segments of society as an injudicious use of resources. This is collaborated by Asamoa-Gyadu's assertion, "In the African context within which I work, renewal movements have been described as movements of reformation in their own right, but they have developed a certain penchant and proclivity for things that reflect glory and power, including seeing material things as reflective of God's favor" (Asamoah-Gyadu, "Way to Pentecost Is Calvary," 69).

33. Gilkey, "Forgotten Traditions," 50.

34. Ibid., 51.

paradoxical role, for the clergy are expected to be more than perfect to make up for the moral lapses of the congregation.[35]

This issue of relating clergy morality to effectiveness appears in Asamoah-Gyadu's suggestion that among Pentecostals, "the effectiveness of a person's anointing depends on moral uprightness and enhanced spirituality achieved through fasting, Bible study and prayer."[36] He thus predicates the efficacy of ministry on clergy members' individual character and personal spiritual capability rather than attributing it to some perpetual supernatural essence conferred on the minister through the ordination ritual. In line with this position, Willimon challenges the medieval notion of "once a priest, always a priest" by arguing that "pastors are significant, not because of some inner, ontological essence they possess, but rather because of what needs to happen in the church. A functional rather than an ontological basis of the priesthood is essential."[37]

In an interview with Rev. Professor Chris Thomas on this subject, he intimated that we cannot call for absolute perfection in a priest before the priest's ordination and subsequent sustenance in ministry.[38] We can therefore respond to the constitutional stipulation of the Church of Pentecost described in chapter 1 demanding dismissal in cases of dishonesty and immorality by retorting that all the ministers would have to be dismissed, since none of them are perfect. Thus, there should probably be a clause of relativity on the magnitude of specific cases of immorality and dishonesty to guide the application of this constitutional provision. Thomas rightly argues that immoral conduct was discernible even among the Donatist priests, since priests, like all other human beings, are fallible. He is also convinced that God in his sovereignty can decide to use any human agent, so attempts to tie ministerial efficacy to character may not be valid in every context.[39] For instance, Judas Iscariot[40] had a "successful apostolic ministry" until he betrayed Jesus. Thomas also notes the crucial role Judas played in God's redemption plan, which generates the debate of how divine sovereignty relates to human responsibility and whether Judas should be held totally accountable for his actions. Thomas' perceptive conclusion that God can use

---

35. Ibid.
36. Asamoah-Gyadu, *African Charismatics*, 55.
37. Willimon, *Character and Calling*, 122.
38. Chris Thomas, Central University College, interview by Dela Quampah, Accra, Ghana, February 9, 2012.
39. Ibid.
40. For instance, in Luke 10:17, after the mission of the seventy, which did not exclude Judas, the disciples reported that even the demons were subject unto them in spite of Judas' moral failure.

everything, including evil, to accomplish his ultimate good purpose is instructional.[41] Responding to the question of what moral standard he would regard as acceptable for Christian ministry, Thomas explains that anyone who is committed to observing the Ten Commandments and is willing to study and improve themselves in moral philosophy and other disciplines relevant to ministry could be a good potential candidate for ministry.[42]

To my mind, the sacraments and the word of God have integrity of their own and cannot be defiled by the character quality of the human vessel handling them. It behooves the person receiving the religious facility to appropriate its efficacy by faith and integrity. This observation notwithstanding, I am convinced that character and charisma are complementary rather than competitive in ministry. This position is well articulated by Willimon: "But when it comes to pastors, smart or dumb, there is a link between character and competence that makes character and competence complementary." [43] The subsequent sections therefore explore the resilience of the polity, administrative structure, and constitutional provisions of select Pentecostal churches in responding to ministerial moral dynamics.

The Role of Moral Philosophy in Church Leadership

The responsibility of the clergy as moral guides to the church and society is obvious. According to Gyekye, "The role of the pastorate as moral leaders and shepherds is recognized in Christian, as well as non-Christian communities of all nations, including Ghana."[44] As he argues further, "Indeed, society expects them to lead exemplary moral lives; that is why people feel scandalized when a minister of religion is found guilty of moral or criminal offence."[45] This underscores the need to relate ethical theories to church polity in the application of principles and the examination of their effects—first, on the institutional structures, and secondly, on the individual stakeholders. Although one would think that church constitutions and their application should strictly reflect Christian or biblical moral theories, it is important to note that the Christian message has always incarnated in cultures that had already established their value systems.[46] And in many cases,

---

41. Chris Thomas, Central University College, interview by Dela Quampah, Accra, Ghana, February 9, 2012.

42. Ibid.

43. Willimon, *Character and Calling*, 41.

44. Gyekye, "Spiritual and Moral Leadership, 37.

45. Ibid.

46. If this observation of Gyekye's was anything to follow, then we would conclude

the interaction of the two value systems—traditional and Christian—reveal common grounds on the one hand and conflicting positions on the other. For instance, Ghanaian traditional ethics finds support for its rejection of murder in the Christian gospel, but the two systems do not necessarily agree on the issue of polygamy.

Consequently, it becomes necessary to relate moral theories that developed outside the Christian community to biblical ethics in order to find areas of agreement that will mutually reinforce each other. The underlying principle here is that there is a universal aspect to moral philosophy that may reveal obvious similarities that cannot be ignored. For example, the moral values referred to as "honesty" and "patience" carry the same meanings, whether in the Christian, Western secular, or traditional Ghanaian contexts. Obviously, the so-called secular approaches to moral philosophy can be valuable to ministerial ethics, although only with selective application. To illustrate this point, we see that the strict principle-based ethics of Kant, for example, shares many features in common with Divine Command theory. Similarly, although some Christians object to Utilitarianism as a hedonist philosophy, they might readily apply its cost-benefit approach in addressing moral dilemmas that the Bible does not directly address. And Fletcher's Situationist idea of Personalism—which argues that human experience rather than abstract concepts give meaning to moral principles, and hence that human beings come before principles—resonates well with New Testament ethics.

A close examination of Ghanaian Pentecostal church documents and their practices reveals a principled-based moral philosophy akin to Divine Command theory and its secular parallel in Kantian ethics. The ethical emphasis of many Pentecostal institutions seems to be deontological, which appears to confirm Fletcher's observation that Pentecostal morality is legalistic.[47] However, we cannot ignore the fact that beyond such documents, practical application of constitutional provisions would depend largely on the interpretation and focus of those in power.

It is also noteworthy that any worthwhile Christian ethical enterprise should contend not only with rules, regulations, and results, but must "go the extra mile" (Matt 5:41), in responding to human need and moral susceptibility. This is demonstrated in the magnanimity of forgiveness as well as the sacrificial service and support for the vulnerable without expectation of reciprocation. It is much to their credit that the institutional policies

---

that the integration of Christian moral values in Ghana would be an uphill task: "African leaders, whether political or otherwise, including our chiefs, are nurtured in a society whose morals are corrupt" (Gyekye, "Spiritual and Moral Leadership," 35).

47. Fletcher, *Situation Ethics*, 24.

and outreach undertakings of some of the Pentecostal churches in Ghana suggests an exemplary concern for the marginalized. In addition, some individual Pentecostal leaders personally demonstrate remarkable generosity and forgiveness in the face of deep provocation.[48] Nevertheless, there are instances when some of the leaders have deviated from such high ethical standards and demonstrated unprincipled subjective ethics to the detriment of their ministry and the public image of the churches they lead. This study has therefore set out to respond to this problem by examining the personal conduct of some such ministers in relation to their denominational ethical stipulations.

James Bridges observes that one significant feature of Christian ministry that sets it apart from other professions is its moral emphasis, and that therefore whoever cannot meet the moral demands of Christian ministry should avoid enlisting.[49] This resonates with Gula's idea that to uphold high moral standards in ministry, the structures of accountability assume the existence of stipulations in the form of admission requirements, the training program, the standards of competence for licensing, the methods of supervision and peer review mechanism, and the disciplinary procedures and sanctions for controlling deviant behavior.[50] Willimon also emphasizes the importance of institutional supervision in ministry: "Today, a singular mark of any 'profession' is that profession's ability internally to credential, examine, and police the members of the profession."[51] Willimon concludes that any church that neglects to maintain a structural method for the supervision of clergy by their fellows appears to invite an ethically dangerous ecclesiastical arrangement.[52]

The manifestation of ethical principles in the moral codes of churches reflects various approaches to moral philosophy. For instance, those who take a strict Kantian or Divine Command approach to ethics argue for rigid rule application in ministerial discipline. Willimon, who is of that persuasion, insists that any clergy member who is guilty of a severe moral lapse[53]

---

48. For instance, see Ntumy, *Struck Down But Not Killed*, which records the willingness of Apostle Michael K. Ntumy, Chairman of the Church of Pentecost, to forgive assailants who attempted to kill him with a machete.

49. Bridges, "Pastor's Personal Life," 105.

50. Gula, *Ethics in Pastoral Ministry*, 62.

51. Willimon, *Calling and Character*, 70.

52. Ibid., 71.

53. Unfortunately, Willimon does not define "severe moral lapse," which is always a problem for ethical systems that stress rules over results. In recognizing that the magnitude of offence or transgressions may vary with the situation, the deontologist approach may be challenged to demonstrate a certain level of in relativism.

should be removed from the ministry.[54] Churches whose polity leans towards deontology tend to dismiss ministers outright for a certain category of offences, and in certain cases, without any opportunity of restoration.[55]

It is important to note that the Pentecostal movement is characterized by a variety of approaches, not just in terms of theology, but also in its administration and ethics. This is confirmed by Mwaura's observation:

> Within the NPC [Neo-Pentecostal church] movement there are differences in doctrine, polity and ethics, in spite of a shared vision and vigorous liturgy. Among them are indigenous ministries, charismatic groups, interdenominational fellowships, Eucharistic ministries, deliverance, intercession, Bible distribution, children ministries and women's fellowship.[56]

Even within the Pentecostal movement, divisions prevail on key ethical concepts such as sanctification. It is clear that while some segments emphasize success prosperity and trendy fashion, others would eschew any form of ostentation.[57] While this variety in expression would suggest inconsistency to some students of the movement, I consider it to be a strength because Pentecostals can respond adequately to any critic who attempts to stereotype or overemphasize any one dimension of Pentecostalism. One of the strengths of Pentecostalism lies in its variety of expression. For instance, critics of the so-called prosperity gospel do not need to look far to find that some of the classical Pentecostal churches actually oppose the prosperity gospel. In addition, while some Pentecostal churches recognize the full range of women's ministry, others think it is unscriptural to ordain women. It is with this mindset of admirable diverse church arrangements that I proceed to examine the polity of selected Pentecostal churches in Ghana. It is also necessary at this stage to remind ourselves that all the churches selected for this survey fall within Gilkey's category of "the churches of the Spirit."

---

54. Willimon, *Calling and Character*, 74.

55. For instance, the Church of Pentecost, a classical Pentecostal Church that has been influenced by the entire sanctification doctrine, dismisses ministers for sexual immorality and fraud. Where a minister is clearly guilty of a sexual offence, they are never restored to ministry, but the situation is not very clear with regards to fraudulent behavior, since some pastors have been restored to ministry when they refunded the money they had misapplied or embezzled.

56. Mwaura, "New Religious Movements," 5.

57. For instance, the Deeper Christian Life Church proscribes members to wear jewelry to the extent of forbidding men to wear tiepins because the pins could attract the attention of ladies. Likewise, some members of the same denomination avoid the use of television and similar electronic gadgets.

Assemblies of God Ghana

Historical Background

Assemblies of God Ghana, was the first Pentecostal church to be introduced to the country through the efforts of American missionaries in 1931. The church is part of an international network of churches in 212 countries that registers about 53,000,000 members worldwide as of 2006, including 12,200,000 members in Africa.[58] In June 2007, the church had approximately three thousand branches in Ghana, but reliable membership figures were not readily available.[59]

Rev. Llyod and Margaret Shirrer, who were American Assemblies of God missionaries stationed in what was then Mosiland and is now Burkina Faso, crossed over to the northern region of the Gold Coast to plant the church. They settled at Yendi, Ghana, and were later joined by Miss Buelah Buchwalter and Guy Hickock, who both died in 1942. According to Thompson Yaw Ton-Laar, the Shirrers' success was attributable to their willingness to identify with the local Dagbons by learning their language and teaching literacy skills to the indigenes.[60] The first Ghanaian Mamprussi convert to the mission was Mba Mahama, who joined the church in 1936. The mission station at Tamale, Ghana, (which was the administrative capital of the Northern Territories) was established by Henry B. Garlocks in 1932. Walewale, another town in Ghana's Northern Territories, was evangelized by Eric Johnson in 1934. This is an excerpt from Ton Laar's report on the progress of mission work in Walewale and the outlying communities:

> The gospel found a firm foundation at Walewale, where the mission bungalow was built, and also at Gbimsi, where there was a good population of the Kasena people. Later on Wulungu and Kpansinkpe also received the gospel. These were typical Manprusi villages. Among the few converts were Brothers K. K. Kofi of Wulugu, Daniel Azundow of Kpasenkpe and Tia Yidana of Diani. These men later on answered the call of God on their lives [to be ministers] but suffered persecution from their families.[61]

58. Assemblies of God Ghana, *75th Anniversary Magazine*, August 6, 2006, 8.

59. Charles Appiah-Boachie, Assemblies of God Ghana, interview by Dela Quampah, Accra, Ghana, June 8, 2008.

60. Ton-Laar, *History*, 13.

61. Ibid. Reference to persecution in this passage carries both moral and historical lessons for students of church history. The moral dimension highlights the high price of oppression, rejection, and deprivation that pioneers of certain denominations had to endure. This calls for a sober reflection on the emphasis on success, prosperity, and creature comfort that characterizes a sizeable segment of the Pentecostal movement

The Shirrers were later joined by other missionaries who helped to spread the Christian message through community development, such as hosting literacy classes and organizing the men into work crews to learn carpentry and masonry skills. Concerns about health outreach saw the opening of the first AG Clinic at Saboba, Ghana, in 1948.

The southern phase of AG mission work began in 1945, when Mr. and Mrs. Burdette Wiles, two American missionaries, arrived in Kumasi, Ghana. Within a few years the Kumasi church became the base for outreach to major Ghanaian communities such as Sunyani, Nkawkaw, and Dorma-Ahenkro.[62] The Accra mission was initiated by Rev. Homer T. Goodwin on May 26, 1946, and the work progressed steadily, with other missionaries such as Rev. and Mrs. W. F. McCorkle and Rev. E. D. Davis adding their own contributions at various stages. The Evangel Assemblies of God chapel at Adabraka, being the first to be built in the city of Accra, Ghana, was completed and dedicated on October 19, 1959.[63]

The progress of this mission work compelled the 1949 inauguration of the Northern Ghana District Council headquartered in Tamale, which comprised of "national pastors and missionaries working in the Northern Sector of the country coming together annually to deliberate on matters pertaining to the work of God."[64] This was followed by a similar arrangement in 1950 to launch the Southern District Council site in Kumasi. To facilitate effective administration, the Southern District Council was divided in 1986 into the Mid-Ghana District Council and the Coastal District Council, headquartered in Kumasi and Accra, respectively. The Northern and the Southern District Councils met separately until 1964, when the first General Council Meeting was held at Kumbungu, Ghana, to synchronize administration by electing one General Superintendent, Harold Lehman, to head both the northern and southern sectors.

---

in Ghana today. Historical trends seem to suggest that Assemblies of God attracted a larger following and developed faster in the southern territories of Ghana than in the North. Many factors, such as harsh weather conditions, sparse population, and economic underdevelopment relative to the South could account for this; however, we cannot rule out the impact of persecution from family and communities of converts who were likely to emerge from either a Muslim or a traditional religious background.

62. Ibid., 33–34.
63. Ibid., 35–36.
64. Ibid., 56.

Leadership and Administrative Structure

The first AG Ghana Bible School started in 1950 at Kumbungu in the Northern Region and was headed by Rev. Fur Thomas, also an American missionary. The three Ghanaians who were the pioneer students of the Bible School graduated in 1951. Currently the church has two other Bible schools situated in Kumasi and Saltpond, Ghana, which have trained over two thousand pastors.[65]

The events and personalities that contributed to the progress and development of AG Ghana have not only defined the administrative structures of the church, they have also molded its ministerial ethics considerably. The long period of American missionary leadership from 1931 to 1970 significantly influenced the ethos of AG Ghana. The last American missionary to serve as General Superintendent of the Church was Rev. Harold Lehman, who handed the role over to the first Ghanaian General Superintendent, Rev. Elijah Nyamela Panka, in 1970. The latter held this position until Rev. Dr. S. B. Asore took over from him in 1986. Rev. Asore also served the AG, the nation, and the Christian community in various capacities as a member of the Council of State, Chairman of Bible Society of Ghana, and a member of the Board of Directors of the Ghana Institute of Linguistics, Literacy, and Bible Translation (GILLBT). The next General Superintendent, Rev. William Dontoh, succeeded Rev. Asore in 2002, but passed away in office in 2009. The current General Superintendent is Rev. Paul Y. Frimpong-Manso.

AG Ghana practices the congregational system of church governance,[66] which is largely a legacy of four decades of American missionary leadership. This kind of open democracy by which every action and decision of leadership is subjected to the examination of the whole church public seems to be foreign to Ghanaian culture. Traditional leadership, as discussed in chapter 2, was hardly subjected to the scrutiny, corrective measures, or majority consensus of the community. In an attempt to make the church more culturally relevant, AG Ghana has adopted a hybrid congregationalist approach to suit the Ghanaian context. According to General Secretary Rev. Appiah-Boachie, unlike the Baptist system of comprehensive congregationalism, which subjects the minister to the appraisal of the whole congregation at the Annual General Meeting, the church only demands that the local secretary fill out a questionnaire on the minister's performance.[67] The Ghanaian culture seems receptive to this arrangement since, as Rev. Appiah-Boachie

---

65. Assemblies of God Ghana, *75th Anniversary Magazine*, August 6, 2006, 11.

66. Charles Appiah-Boachie, Assemblies of God Ghana, interview by Dela Quampah, Accra, Ghana, June 8, 2008.

67. Ibid.

Leadership Structure in Select Ghanaian Pentecostal Churches

put it in his native Akan, "*abɔfra enka ɔpanyin asem*,"[68] that is, literally, "the child does not examine an adult's conduct." By implication, the followers should not openly evaluate their leader.

In terms of ecclesiastical titles, the American influence seems to dominate, for AG uses only two designations, "Pastor" and "the Reverend." The use of elaborate titles is one of the main features of Ghanaian traditional institutions and indeed a general cultural phenomenon.[69] This practice of using only a few church titles in such a large institution is foreign to traditional Ghanaian culture; other churches that appear to be more culturally relevant in this dimension have developed a hierarchy of elaborate titles. In an interview with Rev. Charles Appiah-Boachie,[70] it was revealed that AG also recognizes the functions of evangelists, who specialize in outreach programs to win converts; prophets, who possess peculiar spiritual insights to give direction to the church; and apostles, who have the unique authority to develop and institute policies that define church structure. However, AG does not encourage those who function in such offices to use them as official designations or titles.

The congregational leadership structure of AG makes up a local Church Board consisting of deacons and chaired by the pastor that constitutes the decision-implementation body of the congregation. The business meetings of the local church are held annually, with all adult members participating.[71] The local church is semi-autonomous and is supposed to send only 10 percent of its tithes[72] income to headquarters. The local Church Board is the policy-implementing rather than policy-making body, because policy-making is done by the whole congregation.

The corporate structure of AG Ghana is comprised of the General Council, the Regional Council, the District Council, and the local church. The highest decision-making body is the General Council, which consists of all AG Ghana ordained ministers, missionaries from a foreign sister church, approved personnel from para-church organizations, AG national departmental directors, and a voting delegate from each local church. Next in line is the Regional Council formed by all ordained ministers in the Region,

---

68. Ibid.

69. It is interesting to note that many Ghanaians introduce themselves to new acquaintances or on the phone by mentioning their titles first, as "I am Mr. or Pastor or Rev. Dr. Kweku Ananse," and insist that people should always address them as such.

70. Charles Appiah-Boachie, Assemblies of God Ghana, interview by Dela Quampah, Accra, Ghana, June 8, 2008.

71. *Constitution of Assemblies of God Ghana*, 12.

72. Tithes refer to 10 percent of congregants' income that is regularly paid to support the church.

Licentiates,[73] Exhorters,[74] expatriate missionaries, and a delegate with a voting right from each local church. Directly below and accountable to the Regional Council is the District Committee that serves as the immediate supervisory body above the local church, also comprising ordained ministers of all local churches within the district, Licentiates, Exhorters, lay pastors (part-time ministers), missionaries, Departmental Representatives, and a voting delegate from each local church.[75]

Position on Sanctification

Obviously, the level of emphasis any denomination lays on good character formation in its doctrines would be reflected in the moral conduct of its leaders and followers alike. It is therefore necessary to identify and discuss the doctrinal stance of AG Ghana on the concept of sanctification and examine its implications for ministerial ethics.

Article 6 of AG Ghana's constitution is its "Statement of Fundamental Truths," and the seventh item is entitled "Sanctification—A Holy Life":

a. Sanctification is an act of separation from that which is evil, and of dedication unto God—Rom 12:1–2; 1 Thess 5:23; 2 Cor 6:17.
b. God is holy and requires holiness in His people, for without holiness, no man shall see the Lord—Heb 12:14. By the power of the Holy Spirit, we are able to obey His command, "Be ye holy for I am holy."
c. Sanctification is attained through faith in the Word of God—John 17:17 and Eph 5:26, faith in the blood of Christ—Heb 10:10, 29, [and] through the work of the Holy Spirit in our lives—1 Pet 1:2 and Gal 5:16.
d. Sanctification is attained instantly—at conversion by union with Christ in His death and resurrection—1 Cor 6:11, [and] continually—by yielding of one's self to God—Rom 6:11–13.[76]

This particular article in the "Statement of Fundamental Truths" reveals that AG belongs to the Finished Work category of Pentecostals. This group of Pentecostals, as discussed in chapter 4, believes that sanctification

---

73. Licentiates are licensed to practice as ministers, but have yet to undergo ministerial training.
74. Exhorters are lay people who are certified to preach.
75. *Constitution of Assemblies of God Ghana*, 10.
76. *Constitution of Assemblies of God Ghana*, 3–4.

is given as part of conversion and later becomes a lifelong process—a position rejected by the Holiness Pentecostals. Consequently, this Finished Work group, which does not insist on the total eradication of sin from the believer's life, avoids strict and regimented ethics.

This category of Pentecostals emphasizes internal and attitudinal purity rather than the observance of external stipulations that are supposed to portray holiness. For instance, the Church of Pentecost and the Apostolic Church Ghana (which originated from the Holiness Pentecostal tradition) request that their womenfolk cover their hair at church and avoid the use of "ostentatious" cosmetics so that they might portray modesty and purity. Furthermore, these churches segregate the sexes in the pews as an external expression that the men and women in the church are not promiscuous. Although Assemblies of God is a classical Pentecostal church, its ladies are not obliged to cover their hair in church, the sexes are not segregated in seating or dancing arrangements, and the women are allowed to wear makeup.

Some of the prevailing moral restrictions in AG have to do with fornication, adultery, fraud, smoking, drinking alcohol, and the use of hard drugs.[77] The church takes the practice of substance abuse, which is injurious to health, seriously and sanctions any congregation member who indulges in it. The same level of concern is attached to any form of sexual misconduct or fraudulent behavior among the membership, and such transgressions are punished by suspension from full membership, or in extreme cases, excommunication.[78] This approach to regulating Christian conduct depicts a principle-based ethical system that stipulates institutional sanctions in response to moral lapses.

It is important to note that AG would sanction a member for "any moral or ethical failure, including sexual misconduct."[79] However, there are two clauses on discipline in its constitution that are ambiguous and may yield any kind of interpretation. These are: Section 60, Article 3b: "A failure to represent our Pentecostal testimony correctly," and Section 60, Article 3h:

---

77. Nana Agyapong, Assemblies of God Abofu, interview by Dela Quampah, Accra, Ghana, March 17, 2008. Rev. Agyapong reveals that if a member persists in these habits and in other open sins such as promiscuity, the offender would be allowed to attend church, but would not be permitted to enjoy full membership rights. For instance, the offender is debarred from taking Communion.

78. Stephen Kwefio-Okai, Assemblies of God Tesano, interview by Dela Quampah, Accra, Ghana, February 7, 2009. Kwefio-Okai suggests that, depending on the gravity of the offence, his Church Board could sanction members for a period of three months to two years or even excommunicate them altogether for offences such as polygamous marriage.

79. *Constitution of Assemblies of God Ghana*, 40.

"Any conduct that brings shame to the name of the Lord."[80] Although these clauses do not mention specific examples of conduct regarded as shameful or incorrect representations of Pentecostal testimony, it is believed that church leaders, guided by the Bible, would be able to identify such breaches and handle them appropriately.

Charity Projects

A comprehensive Christian ethical enterprise goes beyond just doing one's duty to include a compassionate and sacrificial response to human needs. As a corporate body, AG Ghana has risen to the occasion in responding to the crying social needs of the country. Currently, the church runs two hospitals at Saboba and Nyakpanduri, Ghana, while a third one is under construction in Kumasi. The church has also established numerous basic and secondary schools, while some local churches offer scholarships for needy students. In addition the church's homeless children rehabilitation project, called "Lifeline," at Agbogbloshie in Accra has rescued over 235 street boys and girls and provided them with vocational training.[81] Furthermore, AG has a disaster-alleviating department called Assemblies of God Relief and Development Agency (AGREDS) that has supported disaster victims in diverse ways.[82] The moral philosophy of AG in relation to its ministerial ethics is discussed more elaborately in the following chapter.

The Church of Pentecost

Historical Background

The Church of Pentecost has a registered membership of 1,586,590 people from 12,774 local congregations, with a total number of 704 fulltime ministers in Ghana.[83] By April 2006, the church had established sixty-five mission outposts in foreign lands. The church is noted for making Pentecostalism culturally relevant by adapting it to traditional Ghanaian forms of cultural expression, mainly in music, dance, and to some extent, theology and

---

80. Ibid.

81. Assemblies of God Ghana, *75th Anniversary Magazine*, August 6, 2006.

82. Ibid.

83. Ntumy, "State of the Church Address," presented at the Opening Ceremony of the Eleventh Session of the Extraordinary Council Meetings, Accra, Ghana, May 26, 2007.

administrative structure. The CoP is also associated with rigid discipline, which may have resulted from its checkered history of initial strives and dissentions.

The Church of Pentecost has its roots in the indigenous ministry of Apostle Peter Newman Anim (1890–1984), who later requested missionary support from the Apostolic Church headquartered in Bradford, England, to help develop the church.[84] The response to this appeal was to sponsor Pastor James McKeown to Ghana 1937. The efforts of Apostle Anim, who is regarded as the father of Ghanaian Pentecostalism, in alliance with Pastor James McKeown culminated in three major classical Pentecostal denominations: Christ Apostolic Church, the Apostolic Church Ghana, and the Church of Pentecost.

Anim was a Presbyterian from Anum Boso, Ghana, who experienced faith healing in 1917 while reading *Sword of the Spirit*, a Christian magazine from the Faith Tabernacle Church in Philadelphia.[85] This encounter motivated him to found a Faith Tabernacle Church in the same year at Asamankese in Ghana's Eastern Region and to establish links with the American church. Since Anim's church was birthed out of a direct spiritual healing encounter, he and his followers strictly adhered to a no-medication doctrine, forbidding converts from seeking medical attention when indisposed.[86]

Anim later switched allegiance from the American Faith Tabernacle Church to the UK Apostolic Church, because the former was evangelical but not Pentecostal. The Gold Coast Faith Tabernacle Church became affiliated with the Bradford Apostolic Church in 1935.

Barely three months after McKeown's arrival tension began to develop between he and his host concerning the ban on medication. According to Asamoah-Gyadu, "The mission partners, James McKeown and Anim, worked together for a while until they split up into separate apostolic churches, mainly over James McKeown's reluctance to observe a strict faith-healing stance adopted by the African movement headed by Anim."[87] As a result, in 1938 McKeown had to relocate to Winneba, Ghana, where he worked independently of Anim. The following year saw a permanent rift between McKeown and Anim's groups, and Anim's church later changed its name to Christ Apostolic Church in 1942.[88]

---

84. Larbi, *Pentecostalism*, 107.
85. Ibid., 99.
86. Leonard, *Giant in Ghana*, 22.
87. Asamoah-Gyadu, "Pentecostalism and the Missiological Significance, 30–57.
88. Larbi, *Pentecostalism*, 101.

After settling in Winneba, McKeown continued working as a missionary of the Bradford Apostolic Church until 1953, when certain developments led to his secession. McKeown attended the General Council Quadrennial Conference of the Apostolic Church at Bradford in 1953, where he was dismissed for failing to sign a constitutional amendment. The amendment sought to segregate the leadership of the church along racial lines; McKeown found this prospect objectionable and refused to sign, leading to his dismissal.[89]

When the Church in the Gold Coast heard the news of McKeown's dismissal, one faction rallied behind him and facilitated his return to the Gold Coast to lead the Gold Coast Apostolic Church. The other faction, which remained loyal to the Bradford Apostolic Mission, was called the Apostolic Church of the Gold Coast.[90] Thus, by 1953 tensions between McKeown, Anim, and the UK Apostolic Church had produced Anim's Christ Apostolic Church, McKeown's Gold Coast Apostolic Church, and the Bradford-allied Apostolic Church of the Gold Coast.

There was much conflict and litigation between the two churches, which caught the attention of the Convention People's Party government. As the head of state, Osagyefo Dr. Kwame Nkrumah intervened in 1962 to reconcile the existence of the two churches, but he requested that McKeown's group change its name.[91] Before this name change could be effected, the followers of the Bradford Apostolic Church wanted to compel the McKeown group to halt their efforts to secede. This prompted the General Secretary of the Ghana Apostolic Church (McKeown's group, the Gold Coast, was renamed as Ghana after independence) to write to the leader of the Apostolic Church of Ghana. Part of the original 1962 letter, titled "Agents of Bradford (England) Religious Institution Intrude Ghana Apostolic Church," is reproduced below:

> Since the Press release issued by the minister of Education on the Apostolic churches, against the implementation of which the Ghana Apostolic Church petitioned Osagyefo, the President of Ghana, Pastors, Overseers, elders and members of your Church have been forcing their way into our Church platforms to cause commotion in our chapels . . . By a copy of this letter I am hereby informing the Commissioner of Police, Ghana, of what you and the Apostolic Church are doing and asking him to assist our assemblies all over Ghana to thrust out any Pastor,

---

89. Leonard, *Giant in Ghana*, 138; Larbi, *Pentecostalism*, 212–13.
90. Asamoah-Gyadu, "Pentecostalism and the Missiological Significance" 37–38.
91. Larbi, *Pentecostalism*, 238–39.

> Overseer, Elder, or member of the Apostolic Church who makes an attempt to speak at any meeting of our assemblies without the permission of the Ghana Apostolic Church Pastor or Overseer in-charge of the Assembly. This also applies to any of your assemblies which moves as a whole body into our assemblies as the case has been in some places in Ghana.[92]

This letter seemed to have been effective and the Ghana Apostolic Church stabilized and consolidated its gains, changing its name in 1962 to the Church of Pentecost.

A particular internal leadership crisis that threatened the survival of the Ghana Apostolic Church is worth exploring here to help understand why the CoP maintains a rigid stance on ministerial ethics. When the ripple effects of 1957 political independence impacted the church, Pastor J. C. Anaman, who had risen to a position of trust as second in command after McKeown, saw an opportunity to oust the latter and replace him as Chairman. In 1960, when McKeown was out of the country on furlough, Anaman wrote him a letter suggesting that the President of the Republic of Ghana had written to demand that Ghanaians should take over and head all churches that had been planted by expatriates. McKeown consented and Anaman briefly became Chairman. A communiqué later issued by McKeown takes the story further:

> Later the Council learned that there is no letter from the Government on this matter, that the whole affair was a well-planned ecclesiastical coup d'état. The Council then demoted the man whom they had made Chairman. I was still on furlough; I could not understand what had taken place. I should have returned to Ghana about the end of 1960, but as I was told I would be arrested when I arrived in Ghana, I was advised to delay my coming. I arrived in March 1961, to find this confusion. The Council met at Kade prior to the Easter Convention. The case was opened and the plan of the Coup was uncovered. Pastor J. A. C. Anaman raised his hands to Heaven and called on God to witness that he had done no wrong. He was asked to produce the letter from the Government, there was no letter. Later he confessed his wrongdoing. He confessed but did not repent, he was the one who created the so-called working Committee to fight for him and work for all this confusion which we now find ourselves in.[93]

---

92. Egyir Paintsil to F. Johnson of the Apostolic Church, official letter, June 16, 1962, accessed at the Church of Pentecost archives in Accra, Ghana, May 5, 2006.

93. James McKweon, "Statement of the Facts," church communiqué, March 1962.

Events such as Anaman's unsuccessful attempt to overthrow McKeown demonstrate to any leader the need to demand the highest standard of loyalty and integrity from followers. As a result, McKeown instituted stringent measures to regulate behavior in the church, especially among its ministers, some of which are discussed below.

Leadership and Administrative Structure

After Pastor J. A. C. Anaman's foiled attempt to oust James McKeown, the latter resumed office as Chairman and worked until his retirement in 1982, having served the church forforty-four years. Apostle S. F. Safo took over from McKeown, but passed away in 1987. In April 1988, Prophet M. K. Yeboah was made Chairman of the CoP. Yeboah served two consecutive five-year terms, during which he was appointed to serve as a member of the Council of State to the National Democratic Congress government. He handed over the post to Apostle Micheal Kwabena Ntumy in 1998, who also served for two terms and was succeeded by the current Chairman, Apostle Dr. Opoku Onyinah.

The administrative structure of the CoP seems to be a blend of all three approaches to church governance, namely presbyterian, episcopalian, and congregational. It is best regarded as a dynamic approach that adopts a system when it is useful. What the Church of Pentecost refers to as Presbytery is actually a Session comprised of elders, deacons, and deaconesses—a more appropriate name might be local Church Board. Every local "Presbyter" thus becomes, in effect, a district Presbyter as well as an area Presbyter. The local churches are normally administered by a lay leader called a Presiding Elder who is supported by the elders, deacons, and deaconesses who comprise the local Presbytery. The Presiding Elder is directly responsible to the district pastor, who may be in charge of a number of local churches. The district pastor in turn reports to the Area Head (normally an apostle, evangelist, prophet, or a senior pastor), who supervises all the pastors and churches in the area with the help of an Area Executive Committee.

The highest decision-making body of the CoP is the General Council, comprising all apostles, prophets, evangelists, ordained pastors, elders' representatives from the areas, and National Heads (who may either be missionaries posted from Ghana or indigenous heads of external mission stations). The other members of the General Council are national deacons, trustees, chairmen of boards and committees, and the movement directors.[94]

---

94. These movements comprise of the Women's Movement, Children's Movement, Youth Ministry, Witness Movement, and Men's Fellowship.

In spite of its Presbyterian label, the CoP practices a highly centralized system of administration headed by an Executive Chairman who is supported by the General Secretary, the International Missions Director, and four other Executive Council members elected from Ghana, as well as one representative each from the Anglophone and Francophone mission outposts. The Executive Council has the prerogative to determine transfers, callings, appointments, and disciplinary action. About 70 percent of the income of the local church is forwarded to the headquarters, where the Finance Board, with the approval of the Executive Council, determines the disbursement of funds.

The Executive Council, depending on feedback from the Area Heads, decides on transfers, postings, callings, and appointments to which no one is allowed to raise objection. Some observers think that the administrative structure of the CoP reflects the traditional chieftaincy institution. After watching the numerous visitors to the CoP Area Head's home in Kumasi and the treatment they received there, Leonard reflects on McKeown's administrative legacy thus:

> In Ashanti Region, we sat for hours in the apostle's house as he received a constant stream of people. We did not understand the language but whether the visitor was a little child, the presbytery from a local assembly come to sort out some problem, or another apostle come to greet him, we noticed everyone was treated with the same attention and courtesy. I understood something David Mills said referring to James [McKeown]—in some ways he ran his administration like a tribal chief. This was how it must have been in the court of King David in the Bible—there was the same mixture of family accessibility and formal dignity. Again it was African—this model of apostleship fitted their culture.[95]

It cannot be denied that the CoP has contributed significantly to the use of ecclesiastical titles in Ghana. Titles such as deaconess, deacon, elder,[96] overseer, pastor, evangelist, prophet, and apostle (in ascending order) abound in the church. Among the clergy, these titles have hierarchical significance: The apostle is the ultimate title, followed in descending order

---

95. Leonard, *Giant in Ghana*, 125. It is noteworthy that one of McKeown's strengths as a missionary was his adaptability. He used to say that he would not plant an English oak in African soil; therefore, he studied the cultural context closely and reinforced whatever structures he thought would enhance his ministry. David Mills, whose opinion is captured in this quotation, was a missionary from Links International, a Pentecostal group from the UK who worked with the CoP.

96. These three categories of leaders are normally lay leaders who are not on the church payroll.

by prophet, evangelist, pastor, and overseer.[97] The calling and appointment to these offices is the preserve of the Executive Council. Unlike in the Assemblies of God, where duration of service and examination results are considered in promotions, the CoP does not have open and objective criteria for the purpose. This approach seems to have generated a lot of grumbling and murmuring, for some accuse those in charge of appointments of practicing favoritism with ecclesiastical offices. The church leadership may want to bring some level of objectivity and transparency to bear on these administrative procedures to help limit such allegations without eliminating the inspirational role of the Holy Spirit in such matters.

An examination of the status of women in the CoP reveals a case of institutional male domination. Ogbu Kalu argues that the beginnings of the Pentecostal movement produced prominent female functionaries who contributed significantly to the spread of the movement. This innovation, according to Kalu, "angered fundamentalists and fuelled their virulent attacks. This forced the restriction of women's ritual power that was installed based on some Pauline verses of terror. Exclusion of women consolidated a patriarchal ideology."[98] A similar trend seems to have characterized the contribution and position of women in the CoP. Leonard explains the influence of women in the origins of the church in the 1930s, saying, "Women were even opening assemblies at that time—Dunkwa on Offin, Kumasi, Sekondi, Takoradi—the women went to all the places from Saltpond . . . If James had his way, most of the human credit for the foundation of the Church of Pentecost would go to women like Mrs. Obo."[99] However Ernestina Quist, after recognizing the outstanding contribution of women in the early days of CoP laments their current relegation to insignificant roles in the church: "As the church [the Church of Pentecost] grew there were fewer opportunities for women to be leaders as society generally considers the woman's place to be essentially in the home. Women's role in the church is not very different from what pertains in the home."[100]

The CoP, which is the largest Pentecostal denomination in Ghana and boasts a total membership of 897,926 congregants,[101] cannot count a single woman among its 704 ordained ministers. Although women make up a two-thirds majority of church members (570,624 females against 327,302 male

97. In CoP terminology, an overseer is a minister on probation for ordination, and apart from a few exceptions, the probation period takes about four to five years.

98. Kalu, *African Pentecostalism*, 147–48.

99. Leonard, *Giant in Ghana*, 55.

100. Quist, "Roles of the Women," 62.

101. See "Church of Pentecost Council Meeting Report," June 2006, accessed at the Church of Pentecost archives in Accra, Ghana.

congregants), only two women, the Director of the Women's Movement and her assistant, participate in the annual General Council meetings that constitute the highest decision-making body of the church. They are allowed to preach on a few occasions, mainly when marking ceremonies relevant to women, but these few female leaders do not occupy significant administrative positions.

Position on Sanctification

The CoP appears to be regarded as one of the most disciplined churches in the country. This statement is supported by the opinion of the Honorable Shirley Ayorkor Botchwey, Deputy Minister of Trade, Industry, Private Sector Development, and President's Special Initiatives, who remarks, "One thing that we all need to note about the Church of Pentecost is that it is synonymous with discipline, tolerance, honesty, humility, hard work and pursuit of excellence."[102] Regardless of this appreciative stance, the church's strict response to moral failure reflects almost an absolutist approach to Divine Command theory, which has elicited criticism from some theologians. For instance, Asamoah-Gyadu argues that the way the CoP publicly exposes sinners is not pastoral, and they "are doing the same thing the Pharisees did,"[103] He also thinks it makes a section of the church consider themselves holier than those who are exposed to public shame.[104] Thus, the pendulum of public opinion swings between admiration for CoP's strict discipline and outright condemnation of its policies as Pharisaic.

In reality, the CoP does not have any elaborate documented statement on sanctification; however, the practical aspects of worship and church membership do emphasize holiness, sometimes to a fault. The Fifth Tenet of Faith of the CoP is entitled "Repentance, Justification and Sanctification." Under this heading there is a brief statement on sanctification: "We believe in sanctification of the believer through the working of the Holy Spirit (1 Cor 1:30; 6:11)."[105] Since the document does not expand the concept, it is difficult to analyze further. Suffice it to say, although the CoP emerged from the holiness tradition, observation shows that their position is shifting in practice towards the concept of progressive sanctification.

102. Address delivered by the said Deputy Minister at the Fourth Matriculation Ceremony of the Pentecost University College, September 29, 2007.

103. J. Kwabena Asamoah-Gyadu, Trinity Theological College, interview by Dela Quampah, Accra, Ghana, June 2, 2009.

104. Ibid.

105. *Constitution of the Church of Pentecost*, 2.

In terms of dress code and general behavior, the male leadership instructs the women to observe strict rules of conduct at church and at home. The women are charged to dress modestly by wearing long skirts and avoiding makeup or flamboyant fashion. They are also expected to cover their hair at church and sometimes even at home. This is reminiscent of Hollenweger's views on early Pentecostal attitudes toward fashion that suggests Christians should avoid fashionable clothes and women should reject trendy hairstyles and makeup. This position clearly has left its vestiges on classical Pentecostal denominations such as the CoP.

The CoP constitution appears to be deontological with strict applications, which sometimes raise issues of sensitivity to victims. For instance, Article 14 of the church's constitution details an elaborate approach to church discipline. The second item under Article 14 identifies the following punishable offences:

a. Habitually visiting questionable places
b. Falling into open sin
c. Embracing or spreading false doctrine
d. Divorcing a wife or husband
e. Marrying more than one wife
f. A sister getting married to a married man
g. Disobeying and showing disrespect to the church authority at any level
h. Practicing immorality[106]

A few of the offences captured here are highly detailed and specific, revealing a church that is extremely concerned about high moral standards. However, some of the items appear rather imprecise, such as "Habitually visiting questionable places" and "Falling into open sin." The key words in these statements, "questionable" and "open," are so vague that confusion can occur in their interpretation and application.

The attendant sanctions to these offences range from being publicly rebuked to the extreme of outright excommunication.[107] Sanctioning in the CoP can be stressful, for the offender is often called up front and exposed to the whole congregation. Some of the other moral issues captured in the church's constitution are discussed in the next chapter in direct relation to ministerial ethics.

---

106. Ibid., 75.
107. Ibid., 75–76.

Charity Projects

The CoP has demonstrated a high standard of social responsibility in undertaking numerous projects to provide essential social services such as education and healthcare delivery. The church also has a college situated in Sowutuom where students can access courses in Theology, Business Administration, and Information Technology. Pentecost Social Services is a semi-autonomous body of the church charged with oversight of the social outreach projects of the CoP. In the area of healthcare delivery, the church has a fully-fledged hospital, Alpha Medical Centre, located at Madina, Ghana, and clinics at Kpassa, Kassapim, and Twifo Agona, Ghana. The church has established sixty-one basic schools nationwide and boasts two senior high schools at Koforidua and Chinderi, Ghana, as well as five vocational schools nationwide. A special initiative worth mentioning is its Orphans and Young Widows Project, which provides financial assistance and skills training for these vulnerable members of society.[108]

Word Miracle Church International

Historical Background

WMCI was one of the charismatic churches that emerged entirely out of indigenous Ghanaian initiative as a result of the evangelical revival that hit the country in the 1970s and 1980s. Currently, the Word Miracle Church International has over eighty-three branches and more than fifty thousand members worldwide.[109] The church has a well-developed multimedia ministry that reaches millions of people by television, radio, audio tapes, and DVDs. WMCI has also developed a prominent international evangelistic program that enables the founder, Bishop Dr. Charles Agyin-Asare, to preach in over forty countries as diverse as Togo, Ukraine, Pakistan, Côte d'Ivoire, and India.

Bishop Agyin-Asare, founder and General Overseer of WMCI, was converted into the Church of Pentecost at Tamale in 1980 and lived with an employee of the church for two years under the oversight of the Regional Head, Apostle D. K. Arnan (this initial encounter with the Church of Pentecost would influence his church administration later). He was very active in

---

108. These statistics are made available in the "2008 PENTSOS Report" in the *2008 Church of Pentecost Annual Report* accessible at CoP headquarters in Accra, Ghana; see also http://acdep.org/wordpress/acdep-members/pentecost-social-services-pentsos/.

109. Akoto, *Ghana: Church Guide*, 62.

church and soon became a Sunday school teacher, secretary to the Women's Movement (due to the low level of literacy in the community, men were allowed to take leadership roles even in the Women's Movement), and an executive member of the youth wing.

Agyin-Asare's break with CoP occurred when he encountered the kind of authoritative leadership style that characterizes certain segments of the church. According to Agyin-Asare, when Apostle Arnan, his mentor, left Tamale, one Rev. S. A. Tetteh became his replacement. Agyin-Asare's encounter with Rev. Tetteh caused him to quit the Church of Pentecost. In Agyin-Asare's own words:

> Rev. Tetteh was informed by some of the young men in the church that I had taken over everything in the church. Without any investigation to ascertain the truth, he relieved me of my assignments in the church. With my zeal and enthusiasm to work, just being a pew warmer without any offence was not something I could stand a long time. After three months of that situation, I quit my job and decided to move down to Accra.[110]

So it was that in March of 1983 Agyin-Asare started an evangelistic ministry called Brother Charles Gospel Crusades. He had the opportunity to attend the Morris Cerullo School of Ministry in Accra in the same year. In 1984, he joined Brother Enoch Agbozo's Ghana Evangelical Society, where he was ordained as a missionary and sent to the hinterlands to preach. He later left the Ghana Evangelical Society to develop his own ministry. Agyin-Asare enrolled at Idahosa's All Nations for Christ Bible Institute in Benin City, Nigeria, in January 1986 to study Crusade Planning.

Upon his return from Nigeria, Agyin-Asare moved to Tamale and began WMCI in March of 1987. He visited England in 1991, where he was consecrated as a Pentecostal Bishop and awarded an honorary doctorate degree by the London-based Shiloh Apostolic Ecclesiastical College. WMCI headquarters were then relocated to Accra in 1994, and vigorous mission work commenced to plant branches of the church across the country and in many nations abroad.

In 1997, some of the pastors in the Eastern Region broke away from the church en masse after accusing Bishop Agyin-Asare of wickedness. According to Agyin Asare, the dissenting ministers had acknowledged publicly how much they had benefited from his leadership in material terms and from ministry opportunities only to turn around and attack him. This is how Agyin-Asare recalls the dissentions:

---

110. Agyin-Asare, *Celebrating the Pilgrimage*, 5.

However, the next month they said "the Bishop [Agyin-Asare] is a wicked man," [and] . . . I was also told that two of them had planned to take over their [churches] illegally. When I sent word to one of them asking him whether it was true, he denied, however a week later he took the church. I wrote to another asking him to take over the church because I realized that was what he was up to. He wrote back to say it was far from that. However, two weeks later he also took over that branch of the church.[111]

By "taking over," Agyin-Asare means these pastors broke affiliation with headquarters and took the affairs of the branch into their own hands. Agyin-Asare thinks these events taught him not to trust human beings, and the end result of these breakaways was the emergence of stronger and bigger WMCI branches in replacement.

Leadership and Administrative Structure

The administrative structure of WMCI is a hybrid of the various church governance approaches, similarly to the CoP. Aspects of its administration reflect a hierarchical approach, while other dimensions suggest a presbyterian system. Although the term "Church Board" associated with congregational governance is used, the administrative framework and functions seem to be more presbyterian than congregational. WMCI's hierarchical style is supported by the executive position reserved for the First Presiding Bishop, who, among other responsibilities, has the veto power to:

a. Appoint Executive Council without reference to the laid down procedure.
b. He shall have the right to nominate and appoint members to serve on the Executive Council.
c. He shall have the right to veto any decision of the Executive Council.[112]

The church leadership reflects a kind of blend of Assemblies of God congregational and the Church of Pentecost structure (which is reminiscent of the founder's CoP background). The highest policymaking body of WMCI is the General Council, with an Executive Council in charge of the implementation of such decisions and daily oversight of the church. For administrative purposes, the country has been demarcated into divisions that are headed by Divisional Church Councils. Below the Divisional Church

---

111. Agyin-Asare, *Celebrating the Pilgrimage*, 24–25.
112. Ibid., 13.

Council is a District Church Council that covers a smaller geographical area.

At the grassroots-level is the local Church Board, which comprises the branch pastor, church secretary, church accountant and three others chosen from among the elders, deacons, deaconesses, and members.[113] One function of the local Church Board that resonates with the subject matter of this study is in the area of discipline: "The Board shall serve as a disciplinary body for the Branch in respect of any other leaders of the Branch and Church members apart from Pastors, Elders, Deacons, and Deaconesses."[114] The local Church Board is therefore responsible for the maintenance of moral standards in the local church.

WMCI is one of the charismatic churches that holds women's ministry in high esteem. The church ordains women, and by May 22, 2007, had eleven female pastors.[115] Kalu is convinced that as a general rule, Pentecostal ministries give women the opportunity to minister their charismatic gifts at the ritual level, provided they do not challenge the patriarchal polity.[116] WMCI, however, permits female voices at the top echelons of administration, for the presiding bishop's wife is regarded as the co-founder of the church, and besides being the head of the Women's Ministry, she also deputizes for her husband to chair the Executive Council of the church. According to the church's constitution, "In the First Presiding Bishop's absence, the co-founder Rev. Mrs. Agyin-Asare shall chair the Executive Council."[117] According to Pastor Noah Twum-Asamoah, resident pastor of the headquarters branch in Dzorwulu, Ghana, the female ministers of WMCI are some of the most seasoned pastors the church boasts. There is ample evidence of women occupying significant leadership positions in the administrative structure of the church. The Secretary to the Presiding Bishop, the Registrar of Miracle Ministerial College, and the resident pastor of the Kwame Nkrumah Circle branch are all women.[118]

---

113. Ibid., 30.

114. Ibid. Although WMCI uses titles such as Elders, Deacons and Deaconesses, which are very popular in the Church of Pentecost (AG uses only Deacons), WMCI refers to the team of leaders in a local church as a Board rather than Presbytery, as in the CoP.

115. Michael Arhin, Secretary to the WMCI General Secretary, interview by Dela Quampah, Accra, Ghana, May 22, 2007.

116. Kalu, *African Pentecostalism*, 152.

117. Agyin-Asare, *Celebrating the Pilgrimage*, 12.

118. Noah Twum-Asamoah, Headquarters Church at Dzorwulu, interview by Dela Quampah, Accra, Ghana, May 22, 2007.

Position on Sanctification

WMCI's statement of faith does not directly mention the word "sanctification." Nevertheless, the ethical aspect of their tenets is captured under the heading, "The Fruit of the Spirit." The eighth item under Article 4 of the church's constitution declares, "We believe that every born again believer in the Lord Jesus Christ should produce the fruit of the Spirit: Love, Joy, Peace, Long-suffering, Gentleness, Goodness, Faith, Meekness and Temperance (Gal 5:22–23)."[119] As we have already discussed, there is a direct correlation between sanctification and the fruit of the Holy Spirit, since the attitudes referred to as the fruit of the Spirit represent the moral values that are expected of a Christian who is being sanctified.

However, through participant observation and my own interactions with some of the church's leaders, I have become convinced that WMCI belongs to the category of Pentecostals who believe in the doctrine of sanctification as a process. Unlike some Pentecostal groups who think certain forms of external expression denote holiness and high morals, the church does not insist on a rigid code of dress and the so-called Pentecostal "modesty." This does not mean WMCI has no concern for high moral standards. According to Rev. Noah Twum-Asamoah, their practice is to preach about decent dress and then leave such decisions up to the members, who they trust to make responsible choices. Furthermore, the church proscribes the consumption of alcoholic beverages in any form and would readily sanction members who are involved in promiscuous behavior such as adultery, and fornication. Such sanctions may range from suspension from full membership for a period of three to six months or, in some extreme cases, outright dismissal from the church.[120]

Furthermore, it is important to note that local church discipline features prominently in the church's constitution. The eighteenth item under Article 115 of the church's constitution addresses this important aspect of church life:

> a. If a person is accused of an offence of a nature that would affect the integrity, spiritual standard or testimony of the church, the person shall be brought before the Church Board (Matt 18:15–17). When a member is found guilty:
> b. The Church Board may write him a warning letter.

---

119. *Word Miracle Church International Constitution*, 73–74, accessed at the WMCI headquarters in Accra, Ghana, May 5, 2006. See also Perez Chapel International, "History," http://www.perezchapel.org/2/21/history.

120. Noah Twum-Asamoah, Headquarters Church at Dzorwulu, interview by Dela Quampah, Accra, Ghana, May 22, 2007.

c. He may be suspended from holding any office in the church, i.e., member of any church department, departmental head, treasurer, secretary, etc. During this time, he must be taken through counseling and the Word of God and prayer by the pastors of the church.
d. After a period of time, when the Church Board is satisfied that the accused has undergone adequate correction and discipline, he may be restored to his former position.
e. A church member who is dissatisfied shall have right of appeal to the District/Divisional/National and if possible General Council.[121]

Although this constitutional provision appears to be principle-based and "legalistic," to use Fletcher's words, it gives due consideration to the impact of any disciplinary action on the individual and directs that the process be monitored through to the point of restoration. This is discernible in the clause that provides for counseling and prayer support by the pastors to help the offending person reform. Moreover, the guilty person is graciously offered a second chance insofar as a member can be restored to his or her former position—unlike, for instance, the Church of Pentecost, where the suspended leader has no chance to ever take up his or her former leadership position again.

Redeem Evangel Church

Historical Background

The founder of REC, Rev. Christopher Atta Titriku, was converted to Christianity in 1977. According to K. K. Deh and E. L. Adjei, his co-biographers, Titriku "had a divine visitation of the Lord on three different occasions in regard to his divine calling and ministry."[122] It is significant to note that although this church was initially founded in Accra, the founder later decided to relocate his headquarters to the provincial town of Ho.

The church began in 1978 when Rev. Titriku started a prayer group known as Redeem Prayer Group in Achimota, Ghana, with eleven members who met regularly to pray and embark on evangelism. With time, the group expanded and the name was changed to Redeem Evangelism Incorporated. It is noteworthy that Rev. Titriku, and some of the charismatic church leaders did not have any significant level of theological education before

---

121. *Word Miracle Church International Constitution*, 73–74.
122. Deh and Adjei, *Rev. Christopher Atta Titriku*, 7.

embarking on ministry. The group later organized outreach programs to several towns in Ghana's Volta Region, including Worawora, Peki Dzake, Nsuta, and Kpedze. This group became the founding members of the Redeem Evangel Church. After this initial phase of ministry at Achimota, Titriku enrolled at Christ is the Same Training Institute of Evangelism and earned a certificate in Evangelism in 1978. Upon completion, he led a crusade in his hometown, Akoefe-Tokor, near Ho, which resulted in the planting of the Redeem Evangel branch.

Rev. Titriku again embarked on further studies in theology at All Nations for Christ Bible Institute in Benin City, Nigeria, where he graduated with a diploma in Christian Discipleship in 1980. All along, the main target and focus of Rev. Titriku's ministry has been the Eʋes in Ghana and Togo. This is attributable to a directive he claims to have received from God just before returning from Nigeria, when God told him to rejoin his own people, the Eʋes, and minister to them.[123] It was upon this instance that he left the Accra branch at Christian Village in the care of Rev. Essau K. Amezado to settle at Ho and take over fulltime oversight of the Akoefe-Tokor church.

In 1986, Rev. Titriku started another branch of the church at Ho, which was initially called Redeem Evangelism Incorporated. The Ho church grew rapidly and soon became the headquarters of the network of his churches. Eventually the name of the church was changed to REC in 1989. Currently, REC has a theological institute at Ho known as Evangel Ministerial Training Institute, which was inaugurated in 1999. By December 2006, the church had a total of twenty-two branches: fourteen in Ghana and eight in the Republic of Togo.

Administrative Structure

The administrative structure of REC does not readily suit the rigid classification of episcopal, presbyterian, or congregationalist patterns. The church, like the Church of Pentecost, seems to reflect a dimension of all three approaches in church governance. The local leaders of REC are elders, deacons, and deaconesses; however, the highest decision-making body in the local church is the pastor and elders board, which suggests a kind of representative or presbyterian approach. Nevertheless, REC also exhibits centralized or hierarchical trends, for much authority and power is vested

---

123. Ibid., 13.

in the General Overseer, who alone has the prerogative of ordaining new ministers of the church and assigning duties to all workers.[124]

Membership of the General Council of Elders includes the General Overseer, General Secretary, National Treasurer, all Regional Overseers, appointed district pastors and selected lay members. Next in line and directly responsible to the General Council is the Regional Council, which is made up of a Regional Overseer, Regional Secretary, Regional Treasurer, all district pastors in the region, and any such other members as the Regional Council shall direct.[125] Similar to the Assemblies of God structure, REC has District Councils that come between the local Church Boards and appropriate Regional Councils. The District Council of Elders consists of the District Pastor, all other Pastors or Presiding Elders in the District, District Secretary, District Treasurer, and one Elder from each local Church Board. Local church discipline and maintenance of moral standards is the responsibility of the local Church Board. The church's constitution stipulates that "in matters of punishment, it [the Board] shall, as much as possible, comply with the provisions contained in the Constitution."[126]

Position on Sanctification

REC offers a comprehensive declaration on sanctification. The presentation is so detailed that readers are left in no doubt that the church believes in progressive sanctification. Below is the relevant excerpt from the church constitution:

> Sanctification: We believe that without Christ we were in the world performing its sinful deeds, exercised by the lusts and craving, but at our conversion we were set apart from the tyranny of Satan, dominion of a sinful nature and contamination of a vile, worldly system unto a Holy and righteous God. Positionally, in Christ we were set apart unto God; presently we are progressively set apart unto God through the work of the Holy Spirit in the believer each day as he wars against the sinful nature; and futuristically, we will be glorified when our bodies will be resurrected and translated into the exact likeness of God,

---

124. *Constitution of the Redeem Evangel Church*, 32, corporate document dated 1998, accessed at REC headquarters in Ho, Ghana, May 5, 2006.

125. Ibid., 25.

126. Ibid., 30.

Christ's glorified body; separated unto God eternally (1 Cor 1, 2; 2 Cor 7; Heb 10:9, 10, 14; Thess 3:12, 13).[127]

This constitutional provision begins with a description of the sinful state of the believer before his or her conversion and the setting apart in devotion of the individual's life to God upon conversion, which is referred to as positional sanctification. It then proceeds to explain progressive sanctification, which is a daily exercise accomplished by the Holy Spirit in the believer's life.

In view of the level of attention REC gives to issues of morality, a significant portion of the church's constitution is devoted to discipline. The fourth item under Article 17, titled "The Administration of Punishment within the Church," deals with the various categories of offences, adjudication procedures, respective punishments, and the processes of restoration. For instance, the article declares:

> Some matters require Church punishments: Offences committed openly within the community leading to a scandal to the Church shall merit punishment as follows:
>
> a. Offences such as idolatry, partaking in fetish rituals, juju, sorcery, stealing, adultery, false swearing, suicide attempts, human exploitation, leaving husband or wife in search of wealth through dubious means, refusal to care for wife and children, cruelty, and similar offences.[128]

An elaborate system of adjudicating misconduct of members is outlined in the same constitutional provision. This involves investigation and arbitration by the Church Board to establish the guilt or innocence of the accused. Additionally, there are detailed pronouncements on sanctions for specific offences. Some such punishments include:

> 1. Suspension from the Lord's Supper [a symbolic congregational ritual meal] once or twice.
> 2. Indefinite suspension until the culprit shows signs of reform, which shall be announced to the congregation if necessary.[129]

In extreme cases, the Church Board is compelled to issue expulsion orders, and complete expulsion from the church shall be announced to the congregation. This is the severest punishment, to be applied to those who have ignored all warnings and rebukes.

127. Ibid., 6, art. 3, § 10, cl. h.
128. Ibid., 55, art. 17, § 4, cl. 1a.
129. Ibid., 62, art. 16, § 5.

1. Where the member voluntarily partakes of pagan rituals such as juju, sorcery, magic, soothsaying, spiritism, sacrifices, etc.
2. Acts that violate the Gospel and Christianity, such as polygamy and endogamy.
3. Other offences such as incest, fornication, adultery, sedition, stealing, and false swearing.
4. Taking the Church to a Court of Law.[130]

One notable feature of REC's constitution regarding church discipline is how it specifically and comprehensively spells out various misconducts and the appropriate responses from the church. This is a positive shift from other church constitutions that make only general and indefinite statements concerning moral issues. However, the mention of "endogamy" as a practice that violates the gospel needs to be reviewed, for endogamy only means marrying from within one's own tribe, which is acceptable to many Christian traditions.

Conclusion

A close examination of the leadership structure and constitutional provision of these select Pentecostal churches reveals a significant concern for high moral standards among congregation members, and more importantly, in the ranks of leadership. This concern demonstrates a bias towards deontological ethics under which constitutions spell out rules of conduct and attendant sanctions. Although we cannot deny the importance of such regulatory documents in the life of institutions, not least of all the church, with its extreme concern for moral rectitude, the interpretation and specific application of constitutional provisions should avoid a legalistic and oppressive ethical regime. It thus behooves the churches to provide institutional support and encouragement to promote exemplary moral behavior. By so doing, churches could give adequate attention to the result and impact of church discipline on individuals, thereby promoting self-worth and avoiding the tendency of using institutional structures to oppress the weak.

Although the relevant documents of almost all the churches under discussion focus on approximating high moral standards, the personal choices of individual Pentecostal leaders could be guided by a variety of ethical approaches. The next chapter therefore explores the realities of practical ministerial ethics that occur within some Pentecostal establishments as well as in the personal lives of church leaders.

130. Ibid.

6

Issues in Pentecostal Ministerial Ethics in Ghana

Introduction

THE ETHICAL PRINCIPLES OF Christianity we have discussed so far suggest that Christian leaders are expected to be moral icons. The author of James' Epistle admonishes, "Not many of you should presume to be teachers, my brothers, because you know that we who teach would be judged more harshly" (Jas 3:1). This assertion requires that the Christian leader, or "teacher," should know better, and as a result, excel in manifesting the values of the faith since his or her standard of behavior becomes a moral yardstick for his or her followers. It is also important to note that Christians are cautioned in the same text to avoid a presumptuous rush into leadership if they cannot live up to the exceptional moral demands of the office. No wonder church members, the general public, and the press in particular take pains to hold Christian leaders accountable for the moral values of the faith they profess.

In this chapter I have ventured to establish a biblical framework for ministerial ethics by interpreting and applying some of the relevant Bible passages to ministerial conduct. In addition, I have examined the impact of Ghanaian cultural values on the institutional structures and personal choices of Pentecostal churches and their ministers. Furthermore, institutional provisions in terms of ministerial ethical codes and disciplinary procedures in the selected churches will be explored to appreciate their adequacy in responding to ministerial ethical challenges. Beyond that, we will examine the contemporary situation in some Ghanaian Pentecostal ministries to discover how social norms, spiritual and institutional factors, and personal choices interact to shape church leaders' moral standards in ministry.

Ministerial Ethics: Biblical Standards

To reiterate, the Old Testament significantly projects the themes of holiness, righteousness, sanctity of life, fairness, justice, self-control, compassion for the vulnerable, and faithfulness, among others. Although Leviticus is appreciated as the priestly moral and clerical code of the Old Testament, Wenham has rightly observed that it is impossible to study the theology of Leviticus in isolation of other books of the Pentateuch, especially Exodus and Numbers.[1] For instance, Exodus captures the mediation of the Sinai Covenant and the erection of the tabernacle, which are all central to the functions of priests. Furthermore, Wenham is convinced that the theme of God's presence in Leviticus is not limited to worship, but permeates even the mundane duties of life, insisting that "the behavior of each member of the covenant people must mirror that of God himself (20:7)."[2] Focusing on God's demand for holiness, Wenham suggests, "'Be holy, for I am holy' (11:44–45; 19; 2; 20; 26) could be termed the motto of Leviticus. It was the duty of the priests to distinguish between the holy and the common and between the unclean and the clean (10:10)."[3] Wenham further intimates that anything given to God is holy—the sacrifices, the tabernacle and its equipment, as well as the Sabbath and the other religious festivals.[4] Furthermore, the sanctification of the priests is well-appreciated in Leviticus: "A person dedicated to the service of God is holy. Pre-eminently holy in this sense are the priests (Lev 21:6 ff.)."[5] However, it is noteworthy that the Old Testament priesthood was hereditary, and whether all the priests had the innate capacity to measure up to these exceptionally high moral demands remains debatable.

Consequently, the problem of moral failure among religious leaders became a prominent theme for the prophets who were inspired to call their colleagues in religious leadership to order. Jeremiah, for instance, exposes the false prophets and priests who abused authority in his day:

---

1. Wenham, *Book of Leviticus*, 16.
2. Ibid., 17.
3. Ibid., 22.
4. Ibid.
5. Ibid.

> The prophets prophesy lies,
> the priests rule by their own authority,
> and my people love it this way.
> But what will you do in the end? (Jer 5:31)

Commenting on this passage, Charles Feinberg explains, "Those who should have been the chief moral backbone of the nation had treacherously denied the Lord's commitment to them. The leaders have become misleaders. Foremost among the guilty were the false prophets . . . next to them were the spineless priests 'who ruled by their own authority.'"[6] Similar accusations directed at the priests occur in Ezek 22:26; Zeph 3: 34; Mal 1:6; and elsewhere.

In laying the foundation of the New Testament Christian ministry, Jesus established a contrast between his leadership and the shepherds of Israel; thus, Ezek 34 remains a foil to the good shepherd discourse in John 10:11–118. Jesus' declaration "I am the good shepherd" (John 10:11) becomes the benchmark for all Christian leaders. According to Merrill Tenney, the concept of a divine shepherd goes back to the Old Testament, as expressed allegorically in Psalm 23.[7] In addition, both Jeremiah (Jer 23:1–3) and Ezekiel (Ezek 34:12) regarded Israel as a flock of sheep and the political, social, and religious leaders as their shepherds.[8] In this instance, Jesus metaphorically compares the Christian minister's work to that of a shepherd whose lifestyle and activities are determined by the needs of the sheep. In Tenney's view, such shepherding "involved both protective concern and a sacrificial attitude. This is expressed in the words 'the good shepherd lays down his life for the sheep.'"[9] The good shepherd is expected to put the concerns of the sheep before his own and care for them to the point of risking his or her own life to defend the sheep. Jesus was so committed to this cause that he paid the ultimate price by dying for his followers and those yet to come (John 10:14–15).

Peter also expresses a similar perspective on Christian ministry: "Be shepherds of God's flock that is under your care, serving as overseers—not because you must, but because you are willing, as God wants you to be; not greedy for money, but eager to serve, not lording it over those entrusted to you, but being examples to the flock" (1 Pet 5:2). Here Peter identifies the key ethical issues of motive for becoming a minister and attitudes toward

---

6. Feinberg, *Jeremiah*, 418.
7. Tenney, *John*, 109.
8. Ibid.
9. Ibid.

money and power that have been perennial and controversial challenges in Christian leadership.

Paul wrote what may be regarded as the most systematic and thoroughly developed documents on Christian leadership in the New Testament in his epistles to Timothy and Titus. First and Second Timothy and Titus address various aspects of Christian ministry; however, the portions that are directly relevant to ministerial ethics occur in 1 Tim 3; 5:17–23 and Titus 1:6–8. In these passages, Paul delineates the timeless moral values and standards of conduct that are appropriate to a Christian leader: "Now the overseer must be above reproach, the husband of one wife, temperate, self-controlled, respectable, hospitable, able to teach, not given to drunkenness, not violent but gentle, not quarrelsome, not a lover of money. He must manage his own family well and see that his children obey him with proper respect" (1 Tim 3:2–5). Titus 1:6–8 echoes this message.

First Tim 3:2–5 reveals that the pastor's testimony is his greatest treasure, since the pastor is requested in the first instance to be above reproach, or ανεπιλημπτος. This, according to MacArthur, does not mean sinless perfection, for no human being could ever meet that prerequisite. He suggests it is "a high and mature standard that speaks of being a consistent example."[10] Stott also, in interpreting ανεπιλημπτος, rejects any suggestions of sinless perfection; he claims it refers to a blameless reputation that manifests in irreproachable conduct.[11] For lack of space, I would select from Paul's list of character prerequisites, "the minister's family life," "temperament," and "attitude to money" for further comment due to their significant and relevant moral import. Paul's insistence that the επισκοπος, or overseer, being "the husband of but one wife" has been variously interpreted. While some think it means "married only once," the most universally accepted interpretation is monogamy—that is, having only one wife at any given time.[12] MacArthur takes his interpretation beyond this marital arrangement to exclude those found guilty of marital infidelity from the ministry, reasoning that "we believe the Bible clearly teaches that once a man falls in the area of sexuality, he is unqualified for pastoral ministry any longer."[13] The next character

---

10. MacArthur, "Character of a Pastor," 68.
11. Stott, *1 Timothy and Titus*, 92.
12. Earle, *1, 2 Timothy*, 364.
13. MacArthur, "Character of a Pastor," 68. The biblical basis of this absolutist stance on excluding those guilty of marital infidelity from ministry is hard to find. One wonders why those who breach the other stipulations on Paul's list in 1 Tim 3:2–5, such as hospitality, self-control, and the right attitude to money, are not also dismissed. An argument from church history, which demonstrates that laxity toward sexual misconduct has bred persistently promiscuous ministers, appears more convincing.

quality for our consideration is νηφαλιον, which in classical Greek meant, "not mixed with wine,"[14] and later assumed the broader sense of "temperate" or "sober." In Anderson's view, the suggestion here is to be self-controlled, especially in the area of appetites, such that the pastor should avoid gluttony and ostentatious living.[15]

According to O'Meara, "history is not only the situation of the church; it is the church's mentor."[16] Therefore, no adequate exploration in ministerial ethics can be undertaken without a brief reference to church history. Two authors who have examined the ethical implications of Christian ministry over the generations are T. Burton Pierce's *Ministerial Ethics: A Guide for Spirit-Filled Leaders*,[17] and Stitzinger's "Pastoral Ministry in History."[18] Each identifies and attempts to explain some of the defining events and personalities that characterized the various significant epochs in the church's ministerial legacy. Stitzinger's five-epochal model seems easier to comprehend, compared to Pierce's eight-era demarcation. Stitzinger's segmented periods are comprised of the biblical period, the early Christian church (a.d. 100–476), the medieval period (a.d. 476–1500), the Reformation period (1500–1648), and the modern period (1649–present). One of the most influential documents on ministerial ethics, *The Rule of Saint Benedict*, emerged from the medieval era and still has an enduring impact on European Christian and social morality today.[19] Joan Chittister has accomplished a remarkable task in writing her commentary on *The Rule of Saint Benedict* and in making its application relevant to contemporary times. Chittister is deeply perceptive of the need to accept responsibility for one's faults and repent outlined in Saint Benedict's work: "If someone commits a fault while at any work . . . either by breaking or losing something or failing in any other way in any place, he must at once come before the abbot and community and of his own accord admit his fault and make satisfaction. If it is made known

---

14. Earle, *1, 2 Timothy*, 364.
15. Anderson, *Effective Pastor*, 7.
16. O' Meara, *Theology of Pastoral Ministry*, 83.
17. Pierce, *Ministerial Ethics*, 83–107.
18. Stitzinger, "Pastoral Ministry in History," 27–46.
19. In his preface to *Rule of Saint Benedict* (1982), Fry suggests that although Saint Benedict wrote his rule primarily for monks, his "sound principles of working and living together have proved relevant to people of all classes of society through fifteen hundred years" (Benedict, *Rule of Saint Benedict*, 9). The influence of the *Rule of Saint Benedict* on the European emotional expression of happiness in a gentle smile rather than garrulous laughter is attributable to rules fifty-two through fifty-four: "Prefer moderation in speech and speak no foolish chatter, nothing just to provoke laughter; do not love immoderate or boisterous laughter" (ibid., 28).

through another, he is to be subjected to a more severe correction."[20] Chittister's reflection on Saint Benedict's above rule is:

> Benedict clearly never supposes perfection in a Benedictine community ... what Benedict does require, however, is a sense of responsibility ... What everyone does affects all others and it is to everyone that we owe accounting and apology and reparation ... The notion that everything we do affects others and stands to be budged by them constitutes a concept of human community that is long lost.[21]

Chittister's application of the same rule to contemporary society is extremely revealing:

> In this world, corporations gut the center out of forests and say not one word of sorrow to the children of the world who will inherit the dry and eroded mountains on which the trees once grew. Bankers take profits that close business and say nothing to the people made homeless by the deal. Politicians make policies that rape the Third World and say not a thing to whole nations held hostage to greed. Individuals [pastors included] overheat, overconsume, and overbuy until the resources of the globe are wasted away to nothing and we think nothing of it.[22]

Scriptural stipulations and lessons from church history notwithstanding, the ability of certain Christian leaders to observe high ethical standards—which in turn accords them the moral authority to instruct others—has often been called to question. That is why we now turn to an examination of the practical realities of Pentecostal church leadership to find out how they compare to the biblical yardstick for ministerial ethics.

Institutional Provisions and Personal Standards

The Call and Philosophy of Ministry

The sovereignty of God's purpose for calling individuals into Christian ministry defies any objective, logical analysis. O'Meara ascribes the call to divine activity: "I am my vocation, for God who created my individuality out of finite potentials is the same God who has introduced me into his wider plan of meaning and life. It is out of this interweave of my personality

---

20. Ibid., 68.
21. Chittister, *Rule of Benedict*, 129–30.
22. Ibid., 130.

and promise that my vocation [and] God's various calls emerge."[23] By implication, the individuals who are called into Christian ministry have been created such that they can only fulfill their purpose for existence by serving in the ministry.

However, from the human perspective, the call to Christian ministry may normally be authenticated by three factors: personal inner conviction, the testimony of others, and the results or impact of demonstrated leadership ability. First, the dimension of one's personal conviction is extremely important because the ministry demands character, talent, and sacrifice, without necessarily promising financial reward. A strong inner conviction provides the necessary motivation and encouragement to withstand the pressures and psychological strains of Christian ministry. This aspect of ministerial calling can, however, be so subjective that its defining parameters may be difficult to identify. Secondly, in many cases, observations by mature Christians concerning a person's ability and potential for Christian leadership seem to be a useful guide in helping individuals to decide for the ministry. Evidently those who have experience in Christian leadership possess the capacity to detect latent ability and strength of character in others for the ministry.[24] According to Oden,

> The call to ministry requires not only a private, inward, intuitive feeling that one is called by God to ministry; if we had only that, we would invite the abuses of self-assertive, subjective, individualistic self-righteousness. To avoid these abuses, it also requires the affirmation of the visible, believing community. It is the church that outwardly confers the office of ministry.[25]

This kind of recommendation from a church context seems to serve as an expedient external confirmation of the inner conviction of the call to Christian leadership. Since many Christian leaders develop within a Christian church community, it is expected that the individual seeking ministry might have had some opportunities for service that may have afforded positive results. Such fruitful Christian duty offers another external proof and a source of confidence that the person has potential for the ministry.

At the heart of the issue of proper conduct in ministry is the fundamental concern of why a person decides to become a minister of the gospel. Alex Montoya is convinced that "The formulation of a statement of purpose is another way of referring to a philosophy of ministry. For a pastor, a

23. O'Meara, *Theology of Ministry*, 208.

24. This approach could be subject to human fallibility, for there are many instances of experienced ministers recommending or mentoring people who later fail in ministry.

25. Oden, *Pastoral Theology*, 20.

philosophy of ministry must come from the mandates addressed to Christ's Church."[26] In an attempt to discern motives for entering the ministry, I asked some Pentecostal pastors to disclose their personal philosophy of ministry and their ministry's basic guiding principle, and their responses are rather revealing. It is interesting to note that many of these respondents did not even think to articulate such a principle until the question was asked of them. I often had to allow some time for rumination before I was able to extract the following answers from some of these ministers: "To respond and obey to his [God's] divine call upon my life"[27]; "Preaching the gospel and healing the sick"[28]; "To serve my generation and advance God's kingdom"[29]; "I am in ministry because God has called me"[30]; "To know and fulfill God's will."[31]

The philosophy of ministry serves as a guide whose usefulness is underscored by Montoya: "It becomes the map to keep him on track, a guide for his course of action, to correct him when blown astray by the hazards of ministry, and an encouragement to his life when the weight of the task burdens and almost overcomes him."[32] Montoya further admonishes that if a minister has a flippant understanding of the purposes of the church, that minister may be tempted to use pragmatic, carnal, and even sinful approaches to accomplish personal goals in ministry.[33] Thus, developing a comprehensive philosophy of ministry and committing themselves to a consistent ethical system will continue to challenge Ghanaian Pentecostal ministers.

My suggested philosophy of ministry is that the minister is a person devoted to God who serves the best interest of God's people from God's perspective. This statement considers Christian ministry from three perspectives; the first being that those who engage in ministry consider themselves to be set apart for God and his purposes. Right from the outset, the

26. Montoya, "Approaching a Pastoral Ministry Scripturally," 48.

27. Karim Awuni, Church of Pentecost Ministry, interview by Dela Quampah, Accra, Ghana, May 22, 2008.

28. Duke Otoo, Chosen Vessels Ministry at North Kaneshie, interview by Dela Quampah Accra, Ghana, May 30, 2008.

29. J. C. Agbesi, Church of Pentecost, interview by Dela Quampah, Accra, Ghana, May 29, 2008.

30. M. Nana Banyin Arhin, Word Miracle Church International Headquarters Branch, interview by Dela Quampah, Accra, Ghana, June 1, 2008.

31. Stephen Kwefio-Okai, Assemblies of God Tesano, interview by Dela Quampah, Accra, Ghana, June 8, 2008.

32. Montoya, "Approaching a Pastoral Ministry Scripturally," 49.

33. Ibid.

Christian minister is aware that his life and service are regulated by divine principles rather than by personal agenda. Secondly, the church members receiving that service are identified with God, which implies that they belong to God; hence they cannot be abused or taken for granted. The third perspective, which is the most important, is to offer ministerial service from "God's perspective." The overriding concern that could help a Christian minister make responsible ethical choices is the awareness that ultimately he or she is accountable to God. There is therefore a need for ministers to consciously evaluate personal convictions as well as the social and institutional frameworks they operate within from God's perspective.[34]

Administrative Structure and Ministerial Ethics

The prevailing administrative structures in many Pentecostal churches suggest an appreciable concern for high ethical standards. In affirmation of Willimon's assertion that running a church without any structural clergy supervision is an ethically dangerous arrangement,[35] many of these churches have established ethically responsive supervisory structures. The procedures of calling, training, and supervising the individual in ministry demonstrate a commitment to impressive moral principles. The amount of attention a particular denomination gives to ethics in the various facets of ministry could arguably determine general standards of morality among its leaders.

As observed in the previous chapter, the ethical benchmark set by some of these churches' documents appears to be largely principle-based. However, the application of these principles against a cultural backdrop of patriarchal control could degenerate into a situational approach by which subjectivity interferes with objective and logical assessment. Furthermore, it becomes an issue of concern when the personal examples of some these

---

34. Institutions, including the church, sometimes make laws and engage in practices that serve the interests of the people in power. In modern times, stories of Pentecostal ministers who cause patients to deteriorate by detaining them instead of sending them to health facilities for treatment or who chain and maltreat lunatics at prayer camps are rife. In addition, abuses such as demonizing people and ruining their lives under the guise of revelation are common features of some Pentecostal ministers; Adwoa Konadu (whose name has been changed here) described a Pentecostal church she attended at Dansoman, Ghana, where women who failed to join their husbands in the church were branded as witches by the founder. The outcome of such accusations was to encourage such men to sue for divorce and marry someone else in the church.

35. Willimon, *Calling and Character*, 71.

church leaders reflect standards that differ from the principles they claim to uphold.

Qualifications for Ministry

In certain dimensions, the Ghanaian Pentecostal leadership scenario is hardly regulated. Institutional borders are difficult to establish, since new churches emerge frequently and older ones occasionally split to form different entities.[36] And since the Ghanaian Constitution upholds freedom of worship: "All persons shall have the right . . . freedom to practise any religion and to manifest such practice,"[37] practically no one can prevent the establishment of new churches unless their founders were to fall afoul of the law. In line with this, the concept of calling or vocation needs to be examined further, for some Pentecostal leaders enter ministry with little to no ministerial training. Some of the older Pentecostal churches, such as Assemblies of God, the Church of Pentecost, the Apostolic Church Ghana, and some of the structured charismatic churches such as WMCI, REC, and LIC have clearly defined procedures for engaging would-be church leaders into fulltime ministry.

For instance, in Assemblies of God, anyone who feels he or she has a call to become a minister must first discuss it with the local pastor, who would in turn present the candidate to the local Church Board for vetting. The next stage is to refer the candidate to the district pastor, whose recommendation would qualify the candidate to apply to any of the AG Theological Colleges. The candidate may then have to pass an entrance examination for admission to the college of his or her choice. Normally, after a two-year diploma training program, if the candidate is still focused on AG ministry, the candidate must interview with a panel consisting of the Regional Executive and both the dean and principal of the Theological College he or she attended.

After the individual has been accepted into the AG ministry, he or she is regarded as an exhorter who can preach and baptize, but cannot administer Holy Communion, bury the dead, or bless marriages. After a probation

---

36. Adesina explores the impact of this phenomenon on Ghanaian Christianity in his book, *Secession within the Charismatic Churches*. He identifies factors such as personal conviction, greed, lack of submission, and doctrinal differences as factors responsible for the frequent disaffiliations (Adesina, *Secession within the Charismatic Churches*, 33–35).

37. *Constitution of the Republic of Ghana*, art. 21, § 1c, http://www.judicial.gov.gh/constitution/chapter/chap_5.htm.

period of two years, the exhorter must pass an examination which, coupled with a favorable field appraisal from both the district pastor and Regional Superintendent, qualifies the exhorter for ordination as a licentiate. A licentiate can execute every ministerial duty except the blessing of marriage. After three years, the licentiate takes another examination, and supported by the recommendations of the district pastor and the Regional Superintendent, becomes fully ordained as a Reverend Minister.[38] This highly structured process of admission to the ministry is designed for quality assurance in terms of ministerial ethics and performance.

Many established Pentecostal churches have similar procedures leading to ordination. The Apostolic Church, however, calls ministers both on the recommendation of senior ministers and by prophecy,[39] and ordains them after a probation period of six years.[40] It is worth noting that the practice of calling ministers through prophecy is often abused in some church contexts. Nevertheless, the Apostolic Church Ghana has instituted the necessary check and balance of subjecting such prophecy to the scrutiny of the National Council of Apostles and Prophets for authentication.

I also discovered through fieldwork that in the REC, representatives of the General Council interview individuals who express interest in fulltime ministry. He (the church only allows male pastors) is then admitted to the church's training school for six months, and he subsequently goes on attachment with a senior minister for another six months. He is later posted and kept on probation for two years, and if his performance is satisfactory, he is ordained as an assistant pastor and allowed to work under the supervision of a senior pastor. Only when the assistant pastor maintains a good track record over a four-year period can he be ordained as a fully-fledged minister of the church.[41]

Word Miracle Church International's (WMCI) constitution makes equally robust demands in character quality and performance standards for prospective applicants to ministry with these prerequisites:

---

38. S. Wengam, Assemblies of God Ghana Headquarters, interview by Dela Quampah, Accra, Ghana, June 27, 2008.

39. This occurs when, under the claim of inspiration, someone mentions another person's name as a candidate for the ministry.

40. Kwadwo Baiden Denson, Apostolic Church Ghana, interview by Dela Quampah, Accra, Ghana, September 17, 2007.

41. Christopher Atta Titriku, Redeem Evangel Church, interview by Dela Quampah, Ho, Ghana, July 22, 2009.

1. In accordance with 1 Cor 12:2a and Eph 4:11, Ministers of the Church shall be those called into Office by revelation, prophecy or the recommendation of the Executive Council.
2. A Person may qualify for Admission into the Ministry if he is Born-Again and baptized in the Holy Spirit.
3. Qualifies in terms of 1 Tim 3:1–7 and Titus 1:6–8.
4. Willing to learn.
5. A mature person but not exceeding forty-two (42) years of age. This pertains to the fulltime ministry.
6. He is obedient to the General Church Council.
7. He has sound body and mind as shall be proved by medical examination.
8. He possesses a clear voice without impediment of speech.
9. He possesses such amount of education as shall be deemed satisfactory.[42]

This evidence of institutional demands to assess and regulate entry into some Pentecostal ministries reveals that the churches are concerned about moral standards and effectiveness in leadership. Nevertheless it is admissible that no human institution has absolute flawless and infallible systems that could totally prevent abuse; hence, in spite of these safeguards one cannot rule out the possibility of misfits entering the ministry. It is the awareness of this probability that has motivated many of the churches to institute disciplinary measures to check and correct misconduct in leadership, which would be discussed later.

Ministerial Formation

Cephas Narh Omenyo,[43] Leke Ogunewu,[44] Matthews Ojo,[45] and Emmanuel Kingsley Larbi have all observed that the Pentecostal movement was initially intolerant of theological education in an academic context. According to Omenyo, the response of the first generation Pentecostals to formal theological training was extremely negative, since they regarded theological seminaries as "theological cemeteries."[46] Omenyo, however, acknowledges that this trend has changed since the 1980s, when Pentecostals began ex-

---

42. *Word Miracle Church International Constitution*, 45, art. 74, § 1–2.
43. Omenyo, "Spirit-Filled Goes to School," 41–57.
44. Ogunewu, "Charismatic Movements and Theological Education," 58–82.
45. Ojo, *End-Time Army*, 236.
46. Omenyo, "Spirit-Filled Goes to School," 46.

pressing growing interest in theological education in Africa and some of the new churches established their own theological colleges.[47] However, a close study of the curricula of some of the colleges surveyed by Omenyo reveals little emphasis on ministerial ethics. Ogunewu laments that some Pentecostal leaders "abandoned their studies in order to engage in active evangelism" because they considered the call of God to be the only prerequisite for ministry.[48] Like Omenyo, Ogunewu acknowledges a current change in attitudes towards education and admonishes that Pentecostal theological education should be adequate both in quantity and quality.[49] Ogbu Kalu, Professor of World Christianity and Mission, at McCormick Theological Seminary in the United States, also lamented in an interview that when admitting people into the ministry, many Pentecostal churches use "apprenticeship and inbreeding," by which a potential minister just understudies a senior one instead of undergoing their own considerable period of rigorous ministerial education. This, according to Kalu, results in "ministerial mal-formation."[50]

Nevertheless, the link between success in ministry and education is not absolute, for many successful Pentecostal ministers did not have the benefit of any theological training before embarking on ministry. Donald Miller and Tetsunao Yamamori's observation on this issue is insightful: "We were surprised by how many of the highly successful pastors did not have seminary degrees. Some of them were well educated, but not in theological studies."[51] Such cases are, however, the exception rather than the norm, and no one can underestimate the value of education in theology and moral formation to successful ministry. The co-authors have identified some of the factors that hinder theological education among Pentecostal leaders as the high cost of college education and the lack of competent relievers for pas-

---

47. Ibid.

48. Ogunewu, "Charismatic Movements and Theological Education," 66.

49. Ibid., 74.

50. Ogbu Kalu, McCormick Theological Seminary, interview by Dela Quampah, Accra, Ghana, June 20, 2007.

51. Miller and Yamamori, *Global Pentecostalism*, 195. For instance, Bishop Dag Heward-Mills, founder of one of the largest Neo-Pentecostal denominations in Ghana, embarked on ministry without any theological education, although he was originally a medical doctor. This raises the problem of relating charisma to education in ministry. Quist likewise mentions women who, though illiterate, have been used by the Holy Spirit to lead famous prayer centers in the Church of Pentecost, such as Maame Dede of Kade and Maame Grace of Edumfa (Quist, "Roles of the Women," 67). Such examples make it difficult to demand education as a prerequisite to Christian leadership. Nevertheless, we cannot ignore the fact that some level of formal theological education would enhance performance and extend leaders' scope of influence to other segments of society.

tors while they are studying. Miller and Yamamori's response to this problem is: "Short courses in theology, practical ministry and biblical studies make more sense."[52] Professor Chris Thomas has also suggested that quality continued education for Pentecostal leaders already in ministry could help improve their ministerial conduct.[53]

The duration of training in many of the Pentecostal theological colleges is short, and in some cases, so inadequate that the curriculum on Christian and ministerial ethics receives little attention. This situation could be responsible for the inadequate knowledge of moral philosophy that seems prevalent among some Pentecostal ministers (see Table 4). In addition, scholars such a P. J. Nel, Peter Sarpong, and Samuel Waje Kunhiyop have demonstrated that the formal reflective approach used in Western Christian moral education seems foreign to Africa. Nel suggests that traditional African moral systems "may not necessarily be a philosophical or apprehensive system as text, but a system inductively construable from assumptions and actions of communities and individuals."[54] Kunhiyop claims it is a futile effort for anyone to attempt to study African ethics through abstract philosophical principles.[55] Sarpong is also convinced that studying virtues and vices in abstraction is alien to the Akan, "For it would appear that for the Akan, what a man is is less important than what he does. To put it more concretely, a person is what he is because of his deeds. He does not perform those deeds because of what he is . . . no man therefore is 'good' or 'evil' outside the context of what he does or omits to do."[56] Reconciling Sarpong's view with Gyekye's opinion poses a challenge to Ghanaian ethicists. Gyekye argues that the Greek pedagogical approach to morality is inadequate in making people ethical, and that therefore theological institutes should "put premium on spirituality and moral virtue" such that institutions "ought to teach virtue and how it can be cultivated." [57] Gyekye's emphasis on the concept of "virtue," which is normally an abstract character quality, conflicts with Sarpong's opinion, which discourages the intangible in the form of abstract ideas in Akan moral thought. With such conflicting voices emerging from African scholars on the correct approach to moral education, those

---

52. Miller and Yamamori, *Global Pentecostalism*, 196.

53. Chris Thomas, Central University College, interview by Dela Quampah, Accra, Ghana, February 9, 2012.

54. Nel, "Morality and Religion," 35.

55. Kunhiyop, *African Christian Ethics*, 8.

56. Sarpong, "Aspects of Akan Ethics," 40.

57. Gyekye, "Spiritual and Moral Leadership," 38–39.

engaged in the discipline are challenged to hold abstractions and concrete forms of moral education in a healthy balance.

The emphasis on a practical approach to morality advocated by some scholars seems to be responsible for the general impression of a lack of deep reflection on ethical ideas among Ghanaian Pentecostal ministers. Many of those I interacted with demonstrated little awareness of key theories and concepts in moral philosophy such as teleology and deontology, free will and human responsibility, Situationism, or ethical relativism. Those interviewed would readily submit that they were Christian moral absolutists but when exposed to an imaginary case of moral dilemma, they would suddenly shift position to respond as a Situationist. In certain cases, their Situationism had no philosophical grounding, which correlates with Fletcher's concepts. Their idea of "Situationism" is one that makes a decision when they find themselves in a particular situation, rather than following Fletcher's principle of doing what love demands in the situation. Some of the more prominent Ghanaian Pentecostal ministers interviewed seem to suggest that their ethics were duty-based when the issue was clearly stated in the Bible, but they would consider a teleological or Situationist approach in the case of an ethical dilemma.[58]

With regard to duration and intensity of training, Pentecostals can take a cue from the African traditional religions discussed in chapter 2, in which acolytes undergo intensive training from six months to four years. According to Ekem, "Akan traditional religion trainee priests, priestesses and shrine devotees are expected to so discipline themselves that they would be transformed into persons who are awake and spiritually sensitive to the promptings of the deities as well as the needs of communities where their priesthood will be exercised."[59] From the Eυe context, Dawubo Gavɔ, the priest in charge of Anyigbatɔ Shrine in Denu, Ghana, explains that a prospective priesthood candidate is normally observed for six months before admission, then trained for a further three years.[60] I want to suggest that to help improve the moral formation of their ministers, Pentecostal

58. The said ministers include: Oko Bortei-Doku, Pastoral Care Department of Lighthouse Chapel International, interview by Dela Quampah, Accra, Ghana, June 13, 2007; Noah Twum Asamoah, interview by Dela Quampah, Accra, Ghana, May 22, 2007; Micheal Kwabena Ntumy, Church of Pentecost, interview by Dela Quampah, Accra, Ghana, February 21, 2007. However, Rev. Charles Appiah-Boachie, General Secretary of Assemblies of God Churches in Ghana, thinks his church's ethics is strictly and consistently duty-based (Charles Appiah-Boachie, Assemblies of God Church, interview by Dela Quampah, Accra, Ghana, June 22, 2007).

59. Ekem, "Fulfilling Your Ministry," 28.

60. Dawubo Gavɔ, Anyigbatɔ Shrine at Denu, interview by Dela Quampah, Denu, Ghana, April 2, 2012.

churches could set a target of between two to three years of training for new ministers; this suggestion is informed by both the Bible and the secular academy. Jesus' disciples followed him for three years before they were left on their own as leaders of the early church. In addition, many college programs in the humanities require a period of at least three years for the student to adequately grasp the rudiments of any discipline enough to earn a Bachelor's degree.

The low level of formal theological education among some church leaders has not escaped the attention of prominent academicians and other keen observers of the Christian community. Professor Andam, Vice-Chancellor of Kwame Nkrumah University of Science and Technology, is reported to have insisted that there was a crying need to extend the training period of pastors, saying, "the situation where students graduate from some Bible training schools after three-months' training was wrong, since those graduates lacked the right training in the Scriptures."[61] Similarly, Rev. W. W. Marfo, on a religious program dubbed "Open Doors" that aired on Unique FM on October 26, 2008, lamented the practice of people who think they have been called rushing into ministry without training and thus have little knowledge of the dynamics and ethics of ministry. Marfo also identified the period of three years of training as necessary for those who aspire to Christian ministry.

Application of Ministerial Ethical Codes and Constitutional Provisions

Since each Pentecostal denomination has an identifiable administrative structure, the stipulations of its ministerial code of ethics may be designed to suit the particular context. For instance, those who practice the centralized system of administration, such as the Church of Pentecost, request that their ministers comply with postings and transfers without raising any objections. On the other hand, in many cases congregational churches, including Assemblies of God, allow their ministers to settle in congregations of their own choice.

In certain instances, some churches' approach to ethics appears rigid, with little sensitivity to the impact of policies on the individuals involved. This is often revealed in the application of church discipline. For example, while some of centralized churches like the Church of Pentecost would

---

61. Maximus Attah, "Extend Time for Training of Pastors—Prof. Andam," *Daily Graphic*, October 6, 2005, 30.

punish cases of immorality such as embezzlement of funds or sexual misconduct with outright dismissal without possibility of restoration, others such as Assemblies of God, Redeem Evangel, Word Miracle Church International, and Lighthouse Chapel International would rather rehabilitate the offender and encourage the transgressor to continue or return to ministry after complying with the sanction.

One major problem with some Pentecostal ministries is that they have no clearly defined or documented code of ethics for their ministers, although these same institutions nevertheless hold individuals accountable for unethical behavior. The churches that could not provide a documented ministerial ethical code when I visited their offices included the Apostolic Church Ghana, Assemblies of God, the Church of Pentecost, Redeem Evangel Church, and Christian Mission Dunamis. WMCI is one of the few with a ministerial ethical code that the founder had developed into a book, *Pastoral Protocol: A Guide to Ministerial Ethics*. Beyond the moral standards applied to the ministry this book, the WMCI's constitution also makes provision for disciplinary action against ministers who breach the code of conduct. Article 87 of the WMCI's constitution is titled "Ministerial Discipline" and offers the following stipulations:

> Disciplinary action shall be taken against a Minister in respect of the following actions:
>
> 1. Unfaithfulness
> 2. Disobedience to his calling
> 3. Refusal to fellowship with fellow Ministers
> 4. Preaching erroneous doctrine
> 5. Negligence of duty
> 6. Insubordination
> 7. Drunkenness or smoking
> 8. Absence from duty without permission
> 9. Fraud
> 10. Dishonesty
> 11. Immorality[62]
> 12. Use of indecent language or disorderly behavior
> 13. Refusing access to a Church building, mission house or pastor's residence.
> 14. Failure to honor financial obligations, including the payment of tithes, payment of local Church amalgamation

---

62. Identifying "immorality" as a separate item in this list is superfluous, since almost all the vices captured in the list, such as fraud, dishonesty, etc., all happen to be immoral acts. This reflects a Ghanaian attitude of classifying sexual misconduct only as immorality.

and failure to pay for Church stationery and materials sold for the Church, etc.
15. Any other conduct or behavior that in the opinion of the General Church Council directly or indirectly brings the name of the Church into disrepute.[63]

The WMCI's constitution further outlines the procedure for investigation by the Ministerial Disciplinary Committee and the adjudicating system, including the right to appeal. The appropriate disciplinary measures are also clearly stated in the constitution, which include caution, suspension, demotion, termination, summary dismissal, and excommunication.[64] Offences for which a minister may suffer summary dismissal are theft, fraud, dishonesty, immorality, and gross insubordination.[65]

In seeking to discover the practical application of the constitutional provision related to ministerial discipline, I accessed church records detailing the dismissals of ministers. According to these records, five WMCI ministers were dismissed between 2005 and 2007 for offences such as sexual misconduct, non-performance, insubordination, and for getting involved in visa fraud.[66]

Lighthouse Chapel International, one of the prominent charismatic churches in Ghana, was founded in 1988 by Bishop Dag Heward-Mills, a professional medical doctor at Korle Bu Teaching Hospital. Known as the Mega Church, it has developed into a network of over four hundred branches. According to Dorothy Akoto, "Bishop Heward-Mills oversees this charismatic denomination, which now operates in thirty-four different countries in Africa, Europe, the Caribbean, Australia, the United States and South America."[67] LCI happens to be one of the few Pentecostal churches with a documented code of ethics, which was authored by Heward-Mills himself and published as *Ministerial Ethics: Practical Wisdom for Christian Ministers*.[68] In his opinion, the causes of misconduct are traceable to societal pressure felt by contemporary ministers:

> The challenges and realities of modern-day ministry are fraught with all sorts of pressures. The pressures of finances, the

---

63. *Word Miracle Church International Constitution*, 51.

64. Ibid., 52.

65. Ibid., 53.

66. Records obtained courtesy of Michael Arhin, Secretary to the WMCI General Secretary, interview by Dela Quampah, Accra, Ghana, May 22, 2007.

67. Akoto, *Ghana: Church Guide*, 75.

68. Heward-Mills, *Ministerial Ethics*. There was, however, no access to the church's constitution, which is not available to the general public.

pressures of family and the pressures of human expectations are just a few of the many demands of ministry; these pressures in the Lord's work are often the causes of improper behaviour in a minister's relations with others.[69]

The book has various sections that address moral standards in ministry from the perspectives of both the founder and associate pastor. The first section, which addresses ethical standards from the founder's perspective, is entitled "Ethics for the Head" and reflects a consciousness of the leader's duties and responsibilities. He instructs founders to "Let everyone know that you are the Head, and that you 'know' that you are the Head."[70] Such a statement reveals a mindset of a leader who is aware of the position's responsibility, which corroborates Willimon's idea that "power ought to be owned, admitted and used responsibly and critiqued publicly."[71] However, the possibility of public criticism of the use of ecclesiastical power is a challenge to Pentecostals leaders in Ghana. The other sections of the book address issues relevant to the moral responsibilities of associate or assistant pastors and also respond to various aspects of ministerial morality, covering areas such as the minister's relationship to family, superiors, subordinates, colleagues, wider society, and financial management.

Although REC does not have an exclusive document detailing a ministerial ethical code, I was able to access a manual entitled "Rules and Conditions of Service for the Pastoral and Non-Pastoral Staff of Redeem Evangel Church" that details the types of offences that warrant punishment: "Disciplinary action will be taken against an employee in respect of inefficiency or misconduct, e.g., willful disregard of instructions, neglect of duty, absenteeism, stealing, drunkenness and immorality, etc."[72] The disciplinary process varies with the magnitude of the offence, but ranges from verbal to written warning to interdiction and ultimately to dismissal. Though there is no clause on restoration, during my interview with Rev. Titriku, the church founder, he intimated that if a minister is dismissed, the person is offered the opportunity for re-engagement upon demonstrating genuine repentance and reformation. Rev. Titriku further stated that REC has so far dismissed one minister who could not be restored because he did not appear to have

---

69. Ibid., 1.

70. Ibid., 7.

71. Willimon, *Calling and Character*, 109.

72. "Rules and Regulations of Service for the Pastoral and Non-Pastoral Staff of Redeem Evangel Church," 3, art. 3, § 1, unpublished document accessed at REM headquarters in Ho, Ghana.

reformed.[73] I was privileged to read the dismissal letter, which was signed by General Secretary B. M. Degboe and specified the minister's offences as alcoholism and sexual misconduct.[74]

Among the classical Pentecostals, the Assemblies of God and the Church of Pentecost have highly developed administrative structures; however, neither church has an appreciable documented ministerial ethical code. What I was able to obtain from the AG is a book that presents general theories on ministerial conduct from an American perspective; consequently, some of the concepts do not appear to be directly relevant to the Ghanaian situation. The book, *The Spirit-Filled Pastor's Guide*,[75] which is more like a manual for ministry than an ethical code, covers a wide range of topics such as pastoral theology, organization, evangelism, and ritual, among others. Only one chapter is devoted to ministerial ethics, in which the author examines the minister's relationship with his or her predecessor, successor, visiting ministers, and other pastors.[76] Beyond that, the author also discusses pastoral theology and limits the discourse to the acquisition of knowledge in homiletics, church history, personal evangelism, and apologetics.[77]

To supplement the content of this book, AG Ghana's constitution features a section intended to control its ministers' behavior and guide their sense of ethical responsibility. The constitution stipulates that a Credentials Committee of the General Council shall be the final authority in matters of doctrine and personal conduct of all ministers.[78] The causes for which AG would take disciplinary action against a minister include:

   a. Any moral or ethical failure, including sexual misconduct;
   b. A failure to represent our Pentecostal testimony correctly;
   c. A contentious or non-cooperative spirit;
   d. A declared open change in doctrinal views;
   e. A habit of incurring debt which brings reproach;
   f. Contracting any form of marriage contrary to the principles of the Church;
   g. Violation of ministerial ethics;
   h. Any conduct that brings shame to the name of the Lord;

---

73. Christopher Atta Titriku, Redeem Evangel Church, interview by Dela Quampah, Ho, Ghana, July 22, 2009.

74. B. M. Degboe, General Secretary, to Kpedze, Ghana, Redeem Evangel Church branch minister, dismissal letter REC/HQ/P.3/33, March 8, 2005.

75. Riggs, *Spirit-Filled Pastor's Guide*.

76. Ibid., 248–64.

77. Ibid., 42–44.

78. *Constitution of Assemblies of God Ghana*, 40.

i. Failure to honor financial obligations, including the payment of tithes;
j. Barricading a Church building, Mission House or Pastor's abode;
k. A minister or his/her spouse engaging in active partisan politics.[79]

The disciplinary procedure of AG allows for appeal until a clear and significant case of misconduct is established, at which time the dismissal or other corrective measures are published to notify the general church public.

The Church of Pentecost is known for its strictness in matters of discipline; internal evidence made available in a recently published history confirms this:

> The Church [CoP] does not compromise with sin in any form. It is frowned upon and treated with seriousness, though out of love. Leaders who misconduct themselves and, thereby, bring into disrepute the Church and their own lives are suspended from active Church activities or any office they might be holding at the time.[80]

The *Church of Pentecost Minister's Handbook* contains some material on ministerial ethics, for the document deals with discipline by identifying the following forms of misconduct as causes for the dismissal of a minister:

i. Theft
ii. Fraud
iii. Dishonesty
iv. Immorality
v. Adultery
vi. Insubordination
vii. Drunkenness
viii. Serious dereliction of duty
ix. Unfaithfulness to the Church
x. Disobedience to his calling
xi. Refusal to fellowship with fellow ministers after attempts have been made to settle the misunderstanding
xii. Preaching erroneous doctrine
xiii. Living a questionable life
xiv. Conduct which, in the opinion of the General Council, may directly or indirectly bring the Church into disrepute.[81]

---

79. Ibid., 40.
80. Asem, *History of the Church of Pentecost*, 158.
81. *Church of Pentecost Minister's Handbook*, 20, § 10, unpublished document available at Church of Pentecost archives in, Accra, Ghana.

The rigidity of this moral code becomes clear in that stipulations like "dishonesty," "unfaithfulness to the Church," and "living a questionable life" attract outright dismissal without any attempt to define the degree, for example, of the "dishonesty" that would warrant dismissal.

A practical application of these rules occurred when disciplinary action against certain CoP ministers was announced in circular letters. One pastor from Offinso West District, New Tafo Area, was demoted from "Pastor" to "Overseer" for gross indiscretion in the handling of a disciplinary case involving his immediate family member.[82] In another incident, a pastor from Ho North District[83] was dismissed outright for misapplying church income. This approach to ministerial discipline has yielded some benefits, for CoP ministers do not often appear in the press in connection to scandalous ministerial behavior. In an interview with Apostle Dr. Opoku Onyinah, Rector of Pentecost University College[84] and International Executive Council member of the CoP, he indicated that because the church was proactive in applying the rules for misconduct, there would be little newsworthy information for the press to report.[85]

According to the *Church of Pentecost Minister's Handbook*, "A dismissed minister may be suspended and later reinstated to full membership by the lifting of the suspension administered by the Executive Council, *but he shall not be restored into the ministry*."[86] That a *dismissed* minister may be *suspended* might not be meaningful to the lay person, for one might ask how a dismissed person could be suspended at the same time, but this distinction is very meaningful in the CoP context. "Dismissed" here refers to being sacked from the ministry, while "suspend" denotes a milder disciplinary action such as being debarred from taking Holy Communion or taking up any other leadership roles in the church. Thus, a minister who is dismissed from the CoP's service may continue to worship in the church, but will be suspended for some time.

---

82. J. E. Ameyaw, Acting Chairman of the Church of Pentecost, to all CoP Assemblies worldwide, circular letter accessed at CoP headquarters in Accra, Ghana, July 18, 2007. The use of real names here is justified by the fact that the circular letters are all public documents.

83. Michael Kwabena Ntumy, Chairman of the Church of Pentecost, to all CoP Assemblies worldwide, circular letter accessed at CoP headquarters in Accra, Ghana, August 16, 2007.

84. While this research was underway, Apostle Dr. Opoku Onyinah became Chairman of the Church in August of 2008.

85. Opoku Onyinah, Pentecost University College, interview by Dela Quampah, Accra, Ghana, March 24, 2007, emphasis mine.

86. *Church of Pentecost Minister's Handbook*, 21, emphasis mine.

Although this extreme concern for high ministerial moral standards is commendable, certain dimensions, such as the impact of sanctions on individuals and families, need to be revisited. The CoP may do better to show more concern for a dismissed pastor's wife and so reconsider its approach to calculating the financial entitlements of a dismissed minister. If a minister is dismissed for misconduct such as adultery, his wife—who may have given up a lucrative job to support her husband in ministry and might not have any hand in the immoral act—receives no financial aid. The church may find it necessary to offer some kind of support to such innocents in appreciation of their service and sacrifice, and more importantly, in compassion for their plight.

In addition, the *Church of Pentecost Minister's Handbook* specifically states, "a minister who resigns without blemish from the service of the General Council shall be entitled to 'A' and 'B' contributions after deductions there from any indebtedness to the Church."[87] However, it is a different case with dismissed ministers: "A minister summarily dismissed on grounds of gross misconduct shall be entitled to 'A' contribution only, after deducting there from any indebtedness to the Church."[88] The "A" contribution is the individual's contribution towards their pension fund, while "B" constitutes the employer's part, thus the *Church of Pentecost Minister's Handbook* stipulates that if ministers are dismissed, they are entitled to only their own contributions to the fund and must forfeit the rest. Church leadership may wish to consider that since this pension is something the employee has earned it should not be subjected to institutional discretion.

Modes of Assessment

In an attempt to maintain admirable standards of moral conduct among their ministers, some Pentecostal churches have developed methods of assessment to evaluate individual performance. Assessment forms from the Apostolic Church and the Church of Pentecost, for instance, identify specific areas of ministerial conduct. Among other categories of assessment, the Apostolic Church form appraises ministers on human relations and team spirit (see Appendix 1). The Church of Pentecost Ministers' Appraisal Form also evaluates ministers on issues of integrity, cooperation, conduct, how well they manage relationships, leadership ability, etc. (see Appendix 2).

---

87. Ibid., 30.
88. Ibid.

In surveying some of the emerging Pentecostal churches—including Rev. Emmanuel Ofosu-Akuamoah's Redemption Faith Ministry in Kwashieman, Rev. Francis Yeboah's Living Praise Sanctuary Ministries in Kwashiebu, and Apostle Waye Onyinah's Christian Mission Dunamis, Sakaman—it became evident that their institutional structures were being developed progressively. As a result, no policy document relevant to ministerial ethics was readily available. This situation does not imply that such churches do not give any attention to moral concerns in ministry. On the contrary, some have highly responsible pastors whose concern for decent ministerial conduct has inspired them to develop creative ways of addressing moral challenges in ministry.

One such approach, which can be presented as a useful model to other Pentecostal church leaders, is the establishment of voluntary associations of ministers. Apostle Waye Onyinah has initiated a group called the Association of Pentecostal Pastors whose headquarters are in Sakaman, Ghana. This group, which had a total membership of seventy pastors as of January 21, 2008,[89] is a voluntary association with the following aims and objectives:

a. To promote mutual fraternity among Pastors of Pentecostal churches
b. To help young Pastors through counselling
c. To organise periodic seminars and/or conferences for the members
d. To encourage and motivate members who face difficulties, and
e. To exchange pulpits by her members.[90]

Apostle Waye Onyinah is convinced that there are many pastors who are talented on their own, but lack adequate education and training for ministry. In his view, such ministers could be trained through similar associations to develop character qualities and resources worthy of their vocation.[91] Apostle Onyinah describes his method as a peer review approach by which members hold each other responsible for ethical conduct. During our interview, the process of developing a disciplinary code for APP was underway; however, they were forced to annul one minister's membership in December 2006 for expressing excessive anger at a public gathering.[92]

---

89. Data courtesy of Waye Onyinah, founder of the Association of Pentecostal Ministers, interview by Dela Quampah, Accra, Ghana, June 21, 2008.

90. *Constitution of the Association of Pentecostal Pastors*, 1.

91. Waye Onyinah, founder of the Association of Pentecostal Ministers, interview by Dela Quampah, Accra, Ghana, June 21, 2008.

92. Ibid.

He also cited promiscuity and drunkenness among pastors as some of the major moral issues the Association had to often grapple with.

Specific Ethical Issues

Relationships

One area of ethical concern that deserves extra attention from Pentecostal ministers is the issue of relationships. The extreme tests of character all people experience in interacting with family, friends, colleagues, and supervisors has in certain cases exposed unethical behavior in some Pentecostal ministers. Clergy marriage and sexuality have received copious attention in much of the available literature on ministerial ethics. Willimon claims sexual immorality among clergy is a "sin against the Christian community, and a fundamental reproach to the communitarian vocation of pastors."[93] Willimon strongly advocates the dismissal of pastors "who can only sometimes be counted upon to keep their marriage vows."[94] Miles is also convinced that "of all clergy misconduct, sexual misconduct is especially reprehensible."[95] She offers rather sobering statistics from a study of sexual affairs among the clergy: 12.7 percent of pastors admitted to having sexual intercourse with a parishioner; 38.6 percent admitted to some "sexual contact," and more than 75 percent of the clergy reported that they know a pastor who has had sexual intercourse with a parishioner.[96] Gula suggests that pastoral sexual misconduct has a devastating impact because of pastors' symbolic representation of the church, and ultimately, God. Gula concludes with this telling observation: "Moreover, in the public's eye, nothing quite makes for sensational news the way a sex scandal in ministry does."[97]

Pierce responds to the problem by suggesting some precautionary measures such as taking extra caution when a male minister is counseling a female parishoner, avoid taking advantage of the love and trust of a female counselee, and discouraging vigorous frontal hugging and kissing. [98] Mile's list of precautionary measures also include self-awareness, watching

---

93. Willimon, *Calling and Character*, 77.
94. Ibid.
95. Miles, *Pastor as Moral Guide*, 103.
96. Ibid.
97. Gula, *Ethics in Pastoral Ministry*, 92.
98. Pierce, *Ministerial Ethics*, 223–24.

for signs that the opposite sex might be attracted to the minister, and being conscious of the minister's responsibility to maintain proper boundaries.[99]

Divorce and remarriage are thorny issues in Christian ministry, and Miles has perceptively observed that many books on pastoral ministry avoid any attempt to pass judgment about divorce.[100] Pierce is one of the few authors who insist that the prohibition of divorce is clear and categorical in the Scriptures.[101] Furthermore, Pierce identifies some of the problems associated with divorce, saying, "Almost invariably, divorce reflects alienated affections in one or more lives. Divorce flouts the marriage ordinance of God. Divorce destroys a home and the relationships that make it a haven in a troubled world."[102] Although Pierce's position may appear laudable, taking an absolutist stance against divorce ignores certain harsh realities of the marital relationship. Miles thinks taking such a strict view of the marriage vow can be abused to make the weak spouse a sacrificial lamb to the stronger partner. Such a situation, she argues, provides "an excuse for sadistic abuse and control on one side and passive masochism on the other."[103] This implies that each problematic marriage should be assessed on its own merit, rather than maintaining inflexible positions that might be more detrimental than beneficial. Although this position might appear to some as Situationist and "unbiblical," at least it has the strength of realism.

From 2005 to 2007, the domestic life of Archbishop Nicholas Duncan-Williams, founder of CAFM, became a prominent topic in the Ghanaian media when he went through divorce proceedings with his wife Francisca.[104] The whole of the Christian community and wider society wondered how a leader and model of such high standing could have become estranged from his wife. In her book, *Reflections: The Untold Story*, Mrs. Francisca Duncan-Williams reveals some of the tensions behind the divorce: "In my marriage, I found loneliness in another form. This time around, the loneliness was worse than first because it constituted a greater disappointment."[105] Mrs. Duncan-Williams' loneliness had to do with neglect by her husband, whose ministerial duties kept him away from home for long stretches of time. Eventually, she sued for divorce and it was granted.

99. Miles, *Pastor as Moral Guide*, 111–12.

100. Ibid., 82.

101. Pierce, *Ministerial Ethics*, 142.

102. Ibid.

103. Miles, *Pastor as Moral Guide*, 82.

104. "Archbishop's Divorce Shocks Action Chapel," *Ghana Web*, June 30, 2005, http://www.ghanaweb.com/GhanaHomePage/NewsArchive/artikel.php?ID=84859.

105. Duncan-Williams, *Reflections*, 34–35.

Exegetes such as Stott argue that Paul's single wife clause for Christian leaders in 1 Tim 3:2 is an exclusion clause for those who have divorced and remarried.[106] Pierce also suggests that divorce undermines the minster's moral authority as a guide for family relationships, for "Having been divorced, even the most gifted minister cannot be respected and accepted as the pastoral role model for family relationships in the congregation."[107] Debate surrounding the acceptance of the leadership of a divorced and remarried minister was triggered when the report of Archbishop Duncan-Williams's remarriage hit the headlines.[108] Responding to this issue, Apostle Ekow Badu Wood, General Secretary of the GPC, intimated that the GPC did not approve of the remarriage and had therefore decided to send a letter of reprimand to the Archbishop.[109] Apostle Ekow Badu Wood claims the GPC resorted to this course of action because Archbishop Duncan-Williams was not forthcoming with information on the cause of his unstable marriage when they attempted to help restore the relationship.

To some Christians, the Archbishop had broken the biblical injunction that proscribes divorce. This transgression, critics reasoned, could lead the church towards a position of subjective ethics, wherein individuals would determine their own family values instead of living by standard biblical principles. For instance, we must wonder how Archbishop Duncan-Williams would respond to requests for divorce from members of his congregation—that is, whether he would have the moral authority to counsel against it. However, although it is clear that principle-based ethics would fault the Archbishop's divorce, we do not know every dimension to the case. Supposing his marriage to Francisca had degenerated to a situation that was life-threatening, then guided by the principle of utility, we could argue that the divorce procedure, although seemingly unethical, was a reasonable decision.

In an extremely disturbing case of sibling relationship management, an Assemblies of God minister was provoked to commit the ultimate crime of killing his own blood brother. I visited Nsawam Medium Security Prison on November 14, 2008, to interview Pastor John Tekpertey, who had been remanded to the prison's custody for three years.[110] Pastor Tekpertey, who

---

106. Stott, *1 Timothy and Titus*, 93.

107. Pierce, *Ministerial Ethics*, 145.

108. C. B. Okine, "Rosa: I'm Happy with What the Lord Has Done," *The Mirror*, May 6, 2008, 19.

109. Ekow Badu Wood, General Secretary of the Ghana Pentecostal Council, interview by Dela Quampah, Accra, Ghans, June 28, 2008.

110. John Tekpertey, interview by Dela Quampah, Nsawam, Ghana, November 14, 2008.

was fifty-six years old at the time, had a wife and three children and had served as an exhorter in AG for five years in Asesewa, Ghana, before being ordained and posted to Kpong, Ghana, as a pastor for three years. In all, he had been in AG ministry for eight years before committing the crime that would land him in prison. According to Pastor Tekpertey, he had a misunderstanding with his younger brother, Tetteh Tekpertey, over property rights, since the latter wanted to mortgage a portion of their late father's cocoa farm without the rest of the family's approval.

When John confronted Tetteh and asked him to stop the mortgage procedure, Tetteh had John arrested for threatening his life. After the pastor was granted bail, he appealed to a traditional ruler to intervene and settle the case out of court. Tetteh, however, went ahead and mortgaged the land without waiting for an amicable settlement. This action provoked Pastor Tekpertey to visit his brother's house to discuss the issue. A quarrel ensued, and John struck Tetteh with a stick, killing him instantly. John was arrested and taken to Asamankese Circuit Court, which had remanded him to prison for the past three years awaiting trial. The pastor attributed his actions to extreme provocation and admitted, upon reflection, that he should have behaved otherwise and let go of the property. Rev. Superintendent James Tetteh, the prison chaplain, gave a good testimony of Pastor Tekpertey's conduct in prison and said he was helpful in leading worship and offering Christian service to fellow prisoners.

Although we may try to understand Pastor Tekpertey's motives, it is still worthwhile to examine this rather outrageous act of fratricide in light of some of the ethical concepts discussed earlier. According to Tekpertey, his intention was to hit his brother in order to teach him a lesson, but not to kill him. All the same, we must wonder how a pastor could ever resort to violence in seeking redress for an offence. This reveals a situation of an extremely subjective response to an event that proved to be a severe test of character. In addition to breaking God's moral law, Tekpertey's use of brute force reveals an ethical relativity that fails the test of Kant's categorical imperative, since Tekpertey ignored the rights of others in making a crucial moral decision.

The second pastor I encountered at Nsawam Medium Security Prison that day was Pastor David Tetteh, an associate pastor at God's Divine Tabernacle Ministry, a charismatic church headquartered in Nungua, Ghana.[111] Pastor Tetteh was twenty-eight years old and had a three-year-old child by a woman with whom he had been cohabitating. According to Tetteh, his

---

111. David Tetteh, interview by Dela Quampah, Nsawam, Ghana, November 14, 2008.

call to ministry came in a series of dreams in which he saw himself preaching and healing people. This call was further confirmed by the testimony of senior ministers of his church.

However, because of financial difficulties, he was compelled to continue living with this woman even though he was not married to her. This lady and her mother together provided for his needs and also took care of their three-year-old child. According to Tetteh, the relationship turned sour when he began to suspect the lady of having an affair with another man. Tetteh confessed that he had physically abused his partner on several occasions in the past, culminating in an incident in July of 2008 when the lady told him over the phone that she had lost interest in their relationship. In reaction, Tetteh picked up a knife, went to the lady's house, and assaulted her. Consequently, he was brought to court and sentenced to six years in prison. When I met Tetteh, he had spent four months of his jail term at Nsawam Prison. My interaction with him revealed that he was still struggling to come to terms with his situation, preferring to blame demons than accept responsibility for his violent conduct. However, Rev. Superintendent James Tetteh spoke well of him as one of the useful Christian leaders in the prison.

Pastor David Tetteh's case, when examined closely, suggests a laxity in attitude to family values that manifested in his common-law marriage and failure to uphold the principle of respect for the sanctity of life. The ethical principles behind this crime are difficult to understand, and we can only ascribe Tetteh's behavior to a subjective morality that rejects societal norms and Christian principles guiding marriage and the preservation of life.

The relationship between some Pentecostal ministers and their colleagues, supervisors, and followers sometimes generates so much conflict that we must struggle to reconcile their attitudes with Christianity's love-your-neighbor message. Some of these conflicts go beyond the church context, going so far as to seek out secular courts for redress. Such cases have at times become so rampant that Ghana's Attorney General could not avoid making a public statement during a visit by ministers of Christ Apostolic Church. According to one media report,

> Attorney General and Minister of Justice, Mr. Joe Ghartey, has decried the increasing levels of litigation in the church, saying it contravened the Holy Bible and the work of Christ. He said there was the need for Christians to show tolerance and compromise and resolve their disputes internally, using alternative dispute resolution mechanisms instead of resorting to the courts.[112]

---

112. M. A. Dabbu, "A-G Decries Increasing Litigation in the Church," *Daily Graphic*, June 29, 2007, 3.

It is interesting to observe from this report that Ghartey was playing the role of a preacher in admonishing clergy members who ought to have known better. Responding to the Attorney General's comment in the same news report, Rev. Amponsah Frimpong, Head of the Legal Department of CAC, confirmed that the church was involved in "unbridled litigation" but was making efforts to withdraw all cases from the courts to be settled internally.[113] Rev. Amponsah Frimpong confirmed in an interview that since their meeting with the Attorney General, CAC had reconciled two litigating factions in Kumasi's Old Bantama area without recourse to secular courts.[114]

Attitude to Power

Another area of great diversity in Pentecostal leadership manifests in attitudes toward power. Globally, the movement has produced both heroes and villains, depending on leaders' use or abuse of power. From a positive perspective, Miller and Yamamori intimate that many successful Pentecostal churches have developed a flat organizational structure by which the senior pastor's creative vision is supported and implemented by associates, staff, and the laity.[115] The co-authors pay tribute to exemplary Pentecostal leadership, saying, "Some of the wisest senior pastors we interviewed had made replication and expansion of their ministers their primary goal rather than making themselves indispensable."[116] In contrast, Miller and Yamamori's research also revealed a cult-like attachment to certain founding pastors. In one case, a commentator told the co-authors "about a successful young minister that for many of his members the question would not be whether to jump at his requests, but to ask, 'How high?'"[117] Reflecting on this state of affairs, Miller and Yamamori observe, "this style of leadership has many potential pathologies, both for the individual leaders who starts to mistake ambitions for the will of God, and also for the congregation whose growth is stunted so long as membership is based on attraction to a person rather than a transcendent vision."[118]

A general observation of the Ghanaian Pentecostal scene reveals some exemplary leadership; the late Prophet M. K. Yeboah and Rev. Asore, for

---

113. Ibid.

114. Amponsah Frimpong, interview by Dela Quampah, Kumasi, Ghana, July 4, 2008.

115. Miller and Yamamori, *Global Pentecostalism*, 186–87.

116. Ibid., 187.

117. Ibid.

118. Ibid., 187–88.

example, have demonstrated humility and an appreciable immunity to the intoxicating effects power. Many pastors lead unassuming lives and are willing to accept postings to remote areas and deprivation of modern amenities. They readily identify with their congregation members and survive on the modest income their denominations provide as well as congregation members' humble generosity.[119]

Nevertheless, in certain circles, the problem of power abuse is often identified as one of the difficulties that plague the Pentecostal movement in Ghana. Relevant to this viewpoint, Asamoah-Gyadu argues that any movement that emphasizes spiritual manifestation normally generates autocracy, since anyone who is "closer to the Spirit" is revered to the extent that even his or her personal opinions are regarded as coming from a divine source.[120] This observation seems to support my thesis that traditional leadership styles are reflected in Ghanaian Pentecostal leadership. Since matters of the spirit are not readily verifiable, those regarded as more in tune with the spirit world, be they traditional priests or chieftains (who are supposed to be closely affiliated to the ancestors), are revered such that no one challenges their opinions. There seems to be a parallel tendency among Pentecostal leaders to develop similar personality cults. In an attempt to cover up their lack of accountability and transparency, congregation members are advised to "touch not the Lord's anointed." This resonates with Waruta's notion that some Christian leaders have exploited the African cultural heritage of reverence to their spiritual leaders for their own personal glory and enrichment.[121] Kalu is also convinced that the church derives its character and sources its ideals from the interior of the African worldview.[122] He argues that the manifestation of power abuse in modern institutions is rooted in traditional values:

> This is why rulers in Africa act as chiefs and wield symbols such as the fly whisk, the leopard skin and the "big man's" walking stick. The effort is a form of villagization, the transfer of patriarchal ethics from the village to the town and to the modern state, a deliberate manipulation of public space . . . so as to escape the accountability which the modern state demands.[123]

---

119. These observations have their source in my personal experience and interactions with colleagues when I served as a District Minister of the Church of Pentecost for three years (1996–1999) at Kpedze, a provincial town near Ho, Ghana.

120. J. Kwabena Asamoah-Gyadu, Trinity Theological College, interview by Dela Quampah, Accra, Ghana, June 2, 2009.

121. Waruta, "Jesus Christ for Africans Today?" 63.

122. Kalu, "Shape and Identity," 1–22.

123. Ibid., 2.

An appeal by Mrs. Gifty Afenyi-Dadzie, a former member of the Council of State who stopped worshipping at Word Miracle Church International to return to her former Wesleyan Methodist congregation, called for accountability from church leaders to their members:

> A Member of Council State . . . has appealed to Church leaders to appreciate the demand to be accountable to their congregation and not hide behind spiritualism of being accountable to only God . . . The leadership should therefore appreciate that those whose sweat and toil keeps the wheels of the Church going must be given information, even if it's through their representatives, so as to help maintain integrity of leadership.[124]

Rev. Professor Emmanuel Kingsley Larbi also blames the Pentecostal church leadership's lack of democratic transparency for the degree of tension and relationship problems that seem to be emerging in their fold. He finds it objectionable that an autocratic leadership approach seems to be surfacing in some Pentecostal churches under which the leader's view is never challenged, thereby undermining accountability and fostering abuse of authority.[125]

On occasion, internal denominational power struggles occur when there is a chance for one among a group of Pentecostal ministers to rise to a higher office. In certain instances, the situation becomes so explosive that it leads to dissension, church splits, and open litigation at the law courts, which tends to receive much media attention. One prominent example is seen in the Christ Apostolic Church's (CAC) July 2003 church split. Chairman Rev. Dr. Augustine Annor Yeboah was voted out of power and replaced by Rev. Michael Nimo. As a result, the former broke away to found a new church, taking several members with him.[126] Winners' Chapel also experienced a leadership crisis that resulted in a break when the former Ghanaian leader, Bishop George Adjeman, led one faction to form a new church that he initially called Life Assembly, only to change the name a few weeks afterwards to Winners' Chapel Ghana.[127]

---

124. Gifty Afenyi-Dadzie, quoted in M. Oppong and M. A. Paintsil, "Church Leaders Must Be Accountable to Members," *The Spectator*, May 1, 2008, 23.

125. Emmanuel Kingsley Larbi, founder of Regents University College of Science and Technology, Dansoman, interview by Dela Quampah, Accra, Ghana, June 21, 2007.

126. Edward Mingle, "Annor Yeboah's Move to Split CAC," *Ghanaian Times*, July 26, 2003, 3.

127. Breda Atta-Quayson, "Winners' Church Falling Apart," *Daily Graphic*, June 22, 2004. This crisis featured in the Ghanaian media for a considerable length of time as the two factions issued press releases to defend their positions. The immediate cause of the split was the decision to transfer George Adjeman from Ghana to Nigeria. According

O'Meara intimates that titles in the early church were functionary;[128] however, it appears the intoxicating effect of power has influenced some Pentecostal leaders to become preoccupied with trappings of position such as titles, expensive regalia, flashy vehicles, and palatial residences. This penchant for impressive titles and accolades among Pentecostal leaders has often attracted the attention of some opinion leaders and social commentators. According to the *Ghanaian Observer*, Professor Kwesi Yankah, Pro-Vice Chancellor of the University of Ghana, has expressed "grave concern about the gross misuse or abuse and sometimes the fraudulent uses of academic titles . . . by impostors and academic charlatans."[129] The eminent scholar discerned a local love for "pomp and pageantry," especially in the form of awards ceremonies, as the underlying factor motivating politicians and other public figures who engage in this practice. Although we might think pastors would earn no censure under such moral scrutiny, to the contrary, the press report reads:

> Disputed titles used in Ghana include religious honorifics . . . without due process, lay preachers, perhaps in the name of free expression, have elevated themselves overnight as pastors, reverend ministers, bishops and archbishops, bypassing laid down procedure . . . Of late the title "Reverend" soon after its use, has quickly attracted the [additional title of] Doctor, Dr. to render the honoree a "Reverend Dr." . . . A close look would sometimes reveal that none of the titles have been properly earned.[130]

Reflecting on this situation, Ogbu Kalu thinks that despite their original egalitarian stance, "African Pentecostals changed from puritan anti-establishment to pomp, pageantry and episcopacy."[131] By implication, the Pentecostal movement—which started on the margins and upheld a holiness code of economically prudent living with equal opportunities to everyone to contribute his or her talents and ideas—appears to have become

---

to a press release from the Nigeria mission, Adjeman "was transferred because of misappropriation of funds," (Yaw Boadu-Ayeboafu, "The Winners' Chapel Saga: Reasons for Transfer of Bishop Adjeman to Lagos," *Daily Graphic*, July 10, 2004). See also Yaw Boadu-Ayeboafu, "Winners' Chapel," advertiser's announcement, *Daily Graphic*, August 9, 2004.

128. O'Meara, *Theology of Ministry*, 75.

129. Kwesi Yankah, quoted in Jonathan Adams, "Academic Titles on Sale," *The Ghanaian Observer*, November 30, 2009, 2.

130. Ibid.

131. Ogbu Kalu, McCormick Theological Seminary, interview by Dela Quampah, Accra, Ghana, August 29, 2007.

hierarchically structured and worldly, having at least partially compromised its initial spiritual focus for social recognition and economic power.

Women's Liberation

Gender discrimination against women appears to be a universal phenomenon, and Stott explains the rather unfortunate, if realistic, male views on the issue:

> For there is no doubt that in many cultures women have habitually been despised and demeaned by men. They have often been treated as mere playthings and sex objects, as unpaid cooks, housekeepers and child minders, and as brainless simpletons incapable of engaging in rational discussion. Their gifts have been unappreciated, their personality smothered, their freedom curtailed, and their service in some areas exploited, in others refused.[132]

This misguided global perspective on females notwithstanding, the magnitude of the problem varies from community to community. As stated in chapter 2, women have been traditionally marginalized in Ghana and are often only seen as useful in carrying out domestic chores. As a result of this cultural misconception, women are often allowed to play only the most insignificant roles in the leadership structure of social institutions, including the church. Quist, reflecting on a native Akan myth, has observed that much like the creation narrative in Genesis, women are often branded as the cause of problems of the world.[133]

Considering the liberationist message of the gospel, we would expect the church to spearhead the freedom charter for women, but unfortunately the church seems to be the last social institution willing to accord full recognition to women's leadership potential. Stott, in appraising this problem in Britain observes, "By the 1960s only two professions were still closed to them [women], the London Stock Exchange and the ordained ministry of the historic churches. In 1973, however the Stock Exchange capitulated. Now it is only ordination which, in some churches, is denied to women."[134]

The roles and recognition of women among Pentecostals is another area that highlights the diverse nature of the movement. While some churches have lifted every limitation to women's leadership role in their

---

132. Stott, *New Issues Facing Christians*, 285.
133. Quist, "Roles of the Women," 47.
134. Stott, *New Issues Facing Christians*, 287.

denominations, others refuse. Kalu, in analyzing the attitude of Pentecostal churches toward women, explains that "there are four prominent categories of female discourses within African Pentecostalism: founders, sisters, first ladies, and jezebels."[135] The founders are women who demonstrate outstanding charisma to establish and lead a denomination or healing ministry, as have ladies such as Pastor Christy Doe Tetteh, founder of Solid Rock Chapel in Accra and Maame Grace Mensah of CoP Edumfa Prayer Centre in Ghana's Central Region. The "sisters" Kalu identifies are women who are allowed to exercise their charismatic gifts at the ritual level without confronting the patriarchal base of church polity. By "first lady," Kalu refers of the pastor's wife, who in some churches serves as the focal point for mobilizing the women for evangelism. Cast in a negative light are those women referred to as jezebels, who are accused of targeting Pentecostal ministers to sexually entrap them.[136]

Generally, a handful of Ghana's Pentecostal churches are receptive to the idea of women's ministry. For instance, the Assemblies of God Church has ordained twenty female pastors.[137] There is also an emerging trend in some charismatic churches that, apart from ordaining women in their own right, also elevate the founder's wife, by default, to the level of minister. For example, Mrs. Viviane Agyin-Asare, wife of the founder of WMCI, is ordained and regarded as the co-founder of the church. As to whether such women develop their leadership potential by creating their own sphere of influence or merely operate in the shadow of their husbands' charisma is a debatable issue.

As noted above, the Church of Pentecost, as the largest Pentecostal denomination in Ghana, cannot count even a single woman among the ranks of its 704 ordained ministers.[138] Although women make up a two-thirds majority of the congregation, only two women—the Director of the Women's Movement and her female assistant—participate in the annual General Council meetings (gatherings of more than five hundred church leaders) that constitute the highest decision-making body of the church. After exploring women's contributions to the church and recognition of their roles in the CoP, Quist's conviction is that although women in CoP are not devoid of charisma, they are restricted in its use by the patriarchal structure.[139]

135. Kalu, *African Pentecostalism*, 148.

136. Ibid., 148–53.

137. See Assemblies of God ordination records accessed at AG archives in Accra, Ghana, March 21, 2007.

138. See "Church of Pentecost Council Meeting Report," June 2006, accessed at the CoP archives in Accra, Ghana.

139. Quist, "Roles of the Women," 68.

Generally, the dominant male Pentecostal church leadership has defined roles and stereotypes for women. The influence of women, no matter how resourceful they may be, is normally restricted to women's ministry. In an interview with Apostle Dr. Micheal Kwabena Ntumy,[140] he suggested that the CoP could not ordain women ministers in the foreseeable future, since many of churches led by female ministers seemed to be suffering problems. Although Apostle Dr. Ntumy did not state the specifics of these problems, his view contrasts with the opinion of Pastor Noah Twum[141] of WMCI, who freely admitted that many of their female ministers ranked among the church's most seasoned leaders.

To Rev. Christopher Titriku, founder of REC, the whole idea of women's ordination came down to doctrine; he argued that since the Bible proscribes it—citing the examples of Jesus calling only male disciples and of Paul forbidding women to teach or rule over men (1 Cor 14:34–35; 1 Tim 2:11–14)—anyone who ordains women would be breaking a divine injunction.[142]

Other arguments against women's ministry include the challenges of maternity leave and domestic responsibilities, which may compete with ministerial duties. However, we might argue that since other institutions in commerce, industry, and academia as well as sister churches engage women in significant leadership roles, the rejection of women's ministry in some churches is ascribable only to the choice of those in authority. It is noteworthy that apart from Assemblies of God, almost all of the other classical Pentecostal churches, including the CoP, Christ Apostolic Church, and the Apostolic Church Ghana, refuse to practice female ordination.

Interestingly, one of the factors responsible for this attitude of male dominance in Pentecostal churches is the fact that even female congregants in many of these churches seem to prefer the ministry of male pastors to female pastors. This viewpoint was attested to by two female ministers in WMCI: Rev. Millicent Nana Atsu, the headquarters minister in charge of outreach, and Rev. Cecilia Adzo Dickens, Registrar of Miracle Ministerial College, the theological training establishment of the church.[143] Both

---

140. Micheal Kwabena Ntumy, Church of Pentecost, interview by Dela Quampah, Accra, Ghana, February 27, 2001.

141. Noah Twum Asamoah, interview by Dela Quampah, Accra, Ghana, May 22, 2007.

142. Christopher Atta Titriku, Redeem Evangel Church, interview by Dela Quampah, Ho, Ghana, July 22, 2009.

143. Millicent Atsu, Word Miracle International Church, interview by Dela Quampah in Accra, April 3, 2009.

lamented that this situation is partly attributable to Ghana's traditional culture, which normally accords women little recognition.

Undermining the Virtue of Responsibility

Reflecting on O'Meara's discerning observation that "if history is the church's life situation, it is also its cross,"[144] we can likewise infer that if culture is the vehicle of the gospel, it is also its cross. Theologians such as Bediako,[145] Asamoah-Gyadu,[146] Larbi,[147] and Mwuara[148] acclaim the contextualization and relevance of the Pentecostal churches in "successfully" engaging with the African worldview. Larbi thinks "the significant factor that has given rise to a boom in Pentecostal activities in the country [Ghana] is that Pentecostalism has found a fertile ground in the all-pervasive primal religious traditions, especially in its cosmology and in its concept of salvation."[149] This is confirmed by Mwuara's opinion:

> Pneumatic experiences resonate well with indigenous African spirituality, with its belief in the existence of spiritual forces. But whereas in indigenous spirituality people are subject to the capriciousness of spirit forces, in classical/spiritual AICs [African-Initiated Churches], liberation is experienced through the salvific death of Christ and the power of the Holy Spirit, which it made possible.[150]

Mwuara, however, proceeds to identify the inherent pitfalls in this situation of extreme consciousness of spiritual experience. She explains:

> Some prophet-healers capitalise on the fear of people, who believe that their problems arise from witchcraft and sorcery . . . This reinforcement of the belief in witchcraft and sorcery (much as we accept it is a reality in Africa) has entrenched this belief. There are people who are unwilling to look beyond these beliefs for the sources of their problems, even when there is a logical explanation to them.[151]

144. O'Meara, *Theology of Ministry*, 85.
145. Bediako, *Jesus in Africa*, 22.
146. Asamoah-Gyadu, *African Charismatics*, 17.
147. Larbi, *Pentecostalism*, 31.
148. Mwuara, "New Religious Movements," 8.
149. Larbi, *Pentecostalism*, 31.
150. Mwuara, "New Religious Movements," 8.
151. Ibid., 16.

The ethical problem that emerges from this situation is that the obsession with superstition tends to weaken congregation members' sense of responsibility. As discussed in chapter 2, the Ghanaian worldview projects a high level of consciousness of spiritual reality; it is often claimed that evil spirits operate variously through witchcraft, dwarfs, ghosts, mermaids, and ancestral curses that work to harm people or impede their progress. In traditional society, it fell to the priests to identify and exorcise people burdened by evil spirits to prevent them from harming the community. Some Pentecostal ministers seem to have taken advantage of these traditional beliefs by specializing in handling the demonic through witchcraft accusations and what is termed "deliverance."

On September 16, 2009, I visited Achimota Forest Reserve to participate in a prayer meeting with a group led by "Prophetess" Lydia Selorm, a member of the Presbyterian Church of Ghana. The manifestation of such a Pentecostal phenomenon in a group led by a lady from one of the Western mission-oriented churches appears to confirm my concerns that both positive and negative trends in Pentecostalism would invariably influence other persuasions of the Christian faith.[152]

During the opening prayer session, "Prophetess" Selorm directed the members to invoke the fire of God to consume every enemy of their families who might militate against their success in life. Afterwards, Brother Okoe, who was also a lay member of PCG, preached a sermon on "How Demons enter People." He introduced his sermon by saying that many people were praying all over the nation because they suffered existential problems. These problems, he said, were attributable to demonic activity. Brother Okoe then proceeded to identify and explain the various means of demonic influence. The first to be identified was a person's family line. In his view, one of the basic ways of contracting evil spirits is through one's lineage. He developed this theme further by advising his hearers to be hesitant in inheriting any dead relative's property, because the dead person's ghost could then possess the beneficiary. Brother Okoe went on to mention child naming rituals, excessive ambition, greed, participating in traditional festivals, and some food items as other means by which a demon could possess his listeners. Obviously, the ethical implication of such demonology is to shift blame for human choices and attitudes to the activities of evil spirits.

152. See Omenyo, *Pentecost outside Pentecostalism*. This is confirmed further by the views expressed by almost all the participants at the Lausanne Theology Working Group Africa Chapter, "Seminar on Prosperity Teaching," Akropong, Ghana, September 3–4, 2009. Many of them were of the opinion that, contrary to popular thinking, the prosperity gospel is no longer the preserve of Pentecostal churches, for it has taken root in all the Christian denominations in Ghana.

On May 29, 2009, an event took place in Ghana that, if given adequate attention by academics and church leaders, could make a positive impact on the religious and socio-economic life of the nation. A seminar was organized by the Centre for Inquiry in collaboration with the Ghanaian chapter of Society for Women and AIDS in Africa on the theme of "Witchcraft and Superstition: Impact on African Development." Mr. Leo Igwe, Chairman of the Centre for Inquiry, a transnational organization, rightly "stressed the need to fight against superstitious beliefs that had the tendency of undermining development, creating fear, hatred and confusion, which oppressed women and undermined their ability to succeed."[153] In my view, a seminar of this nature had been long overdue, but it is notable that it was organized by a civil society group rather than the church, which should have taken the lead in fighting superstition in Africa. To aggravate matters, many presenters at the conference accused those churches referred to as "spiritual" of actually promoting witchcraft and superstition. According to the *Daily Graphic* report, Mrs. Bernice Heloo, President of the Society for Women and AIDS in Africa, said such churches are responsible for the perpetuation of superstition and witchcraft beliefs in Africa.[154]

We might suppose that with the benefit of formal education and exposure to science and technology, current African Christian leaders would be equipped to respond to these prehistoric societal problems with a balanced spiritual perspective. But the grip of witchcraft and superstition on the consciousness of many Pentecostal leaders directs their ministry to engage in pre-science age practices such as witch-hunting—a worrisome development. As Gifford observes, "Concerned Ghanaians themselves speculate on the modern spread of belief in witchcraft, and its baneful influence."[155] Onyinah is one of the concerned Ghanaians who thinks the preoccupation with the demonic by Pentecostals generates tension within cultures and other religions, as well as causing harm to candidates of exorcism.[156] He laments, "Additionally, in some ways, exorcism was found to be an instrument for oppressing the poor."[157] Asamoah-Gyadu is also convinced that some deliverance ministers are merely capitalizing on people's fear of tragedy to manipulate and abuse them.[158]

153. L. Igwe, quoted in Jennifer Dornoo, "Superstitious Belief: Its Impact on Development," *Daily Graphic*, May 30, 2009, 11.

154. B. Heloo, quoted in ibid.

155. Gifford, *Ghana's New Christianity*, 88.

156. Onyinah, "Akan Witchcraft," 392.

157. Ibid., 393.

158. J. Kwabena Asamoah-Gyadu, Trinity Theological College, interview by Dela Quampah, Accra, Ghana, June 2, 2009.

Asamoah-Gyadu identifies an important moral implication of the deliverance ministry in observing that some Pentecostals leaders ascribe moral failure to demonic activity. In a similar vein, Onyinah examines the practices of deliverance and exorcism by which sinful behavior is ascribed to evil spirits, and concludes by insisting that the Bible seldom identifies demons as the source of sinful behavior.[159] George Folarin also reflects on the demonization practice prevailing in Nigeria and concludes, "this wrongly relieves men of responsibility for their sins, and their problems. All the blame is now shifted to the devil and his agents."[160] Asamoah-Gyadu further insists that when pastoral care attributes moral failure to demons, it becomes impossible to hold people accountable for their behavior.[161] Evidently, this superstition-driven approach tends to limit people's sense of responsibility, misleading them to abandon personal efforts at moral reformation and try to cast out "the demon of lying" instead.

Ganusah also contributes to the witchcraft debate in her insightful research on puberty rites among the centrally-located Eʋes. She argues from the premise that demonic and witchcraft-related issues defy empirical examination, but that since epistemology is possible without scientific proof, we cannot dismiss such claims as invalid. That is, knowledge can be acquired through means such as dreams and intuition and not only through our physical senses. Ganusah further argues that in spite of the various psychological and sociological theories that may attempt to explain the witchcraft phenomenon away, the average Ghanaian is convinced of its reality.[162] To quote Ganusah, "beliefs and practices about witchcraft are so embedded in the life situation of the people that they could not be laughed out of existence."[163] She also points out that the existence of the demonic has some biblical basis, and consequently advocates prayer that invokes the power of the Holy Spirit to overcome the manifestation of evil spirits.

Whatever our view on the existence of demons, it cannot be denied that the Bible recognizes their manifestation in terms of such adversities as sickness. Jesus performed many exorcisms and healed several invalids by first casting out the evil spirit behind the condition (Matt 17:14–18, Mark 5:1–16, Luke 8: 26–35). We can therefore logically conclude that dealing with evil supernatural forces is an integral part of Christian theology. Nevertheless, the approach some Ghanaians ministers take seems to suggest a

---

159. Onyinah, "Akan Witchcraft," 356.
160. Folarin, "Prosperity Gospel in Nigeria," 95.
161. Asamoah-Gyadu, *African Charismatics*, 197.
162. Ganusah, *Christ Meets the Ewe-Dome*, 109.
163. Ibid., 111.

deviation from biblical standards. Jesus' strategy of dealing with demon-possessed people was to invoke the power of God to cast the oppressive spirit out of the person's life. The practice of identifying "flesh and blood" witches behind a suffering parishioner's crisis so as to invoke a curse upon the "demonic agent," a practice popular among deliverance ministers, seems alien to scriptural norms.

In Onyinah's opinion, the Christian community needs a doctrinal reconstruction that responds to the tension between traditional ideas on demonology and Christian concepts to rebuild what he calls "the framework of biblical theology."[164] In the church context, education can be useful in developing a robust and revolutionary theology that instills courage in Christians to face the vicissitudes of life boldly, rather than laying their troubles at other people's door. Onyinah is one theologian who has made this attempt by suggesting that the eschatological tension of a redeemed people living in a fallen world would inevitably expose them to certain tragic events: "Misfortune does not mean that the devil has attacked; neither does it mean that the person has sinned. It may simply be the result of our fallen world."[165] Examining the deliverance and demonic phenomena from a pastoral perspective, Emmanuel Lartey rejects the reductionist approach that explains every difficulty in terms of spiritual causation, thereby turning Christianity into a formulaic model of "fear and faith."[166] His suggested solution advocates a constructive and critical engagement with these practices in order to develop an effective pastoral response.

Conclusion

I have attempted to establish in this chapter that church polity and the character quality of individual ministers interact to define ministerial ethics in every denominational context. An assessment of the administrative structures and constitutional provisions of some of the Pentecostal churches reveals that these organizations demonstrate concern for high moral standards among their ministers. Some of these ministers have complemented this institutional concern by emerging as moral models for both the church and wider society.

This constructive ministerial ethical outlook notwithstanding, some level of moral laxity in relationships, power abuse, denial of women rights, and counterproductive demonology appears to be casting a slur on the

164. Onyinah, "Akan Witchcraft," 358.
165. Ibid., *Spiritual Warfare*, 35.
166. Lartey, "Of Formulae, Fear and Faith," 5–13.

image of the church leaders in question. Despite the high moral principles captured in the church documents cited, some of the pastors' conduct reveals a significant deviation from such stipulations to the detriment of both church and society. The next chapter therefore examines responses by relevant segments of society to this problem.

7

Analysis of Information on Pentecostal Ministers

Introduction

So far, I have attempted to establish that there seems to be a level of tension between what *is* and what *ought to be* in the moral standard of Pentecostal church leaders in Ghana. We have discovered that although some church leaders maintain the high standard of moral conduct that their conscience, Christian faith, and society demand of them, some serious cases of moral infractions have also been registered in their fold. The events and personalities involved in this sad state of affairs often feature prominently in news stories, creative works, public opinion, and in the public pronouncements of church leaders themselves.

However, it would be remiss of any objective observer of the Ghanaian Pentecostal scene to accept these reports without making any effort to verify their accuracy. Furthermore, all stakeholders ought to reflect upon these issues in order to develop a constructive and adequate response to such practices. Consequently, I have explored the role of the media in shaping public opinion on Ghanaian Pentecostal ministerial ethics by investigating relevant news stories—a process that involved talking directly with many of the people identified in such stories. Interviews, questionnaire responses, and relevant primary literature are also examined here to help understand the prevailing moral standards in Pentecostal leadership in Ghana.

Public Opinion

Public opinion, to a large extent, seems to be replete with a barrage of criticism directed at Pentecostal leaders in an attempt to hold them accountable to the ethical standards of their faith. Besides news reports and statements from public opinion leaders, misconduct by the clergy provides a ready theme for creative works in the arts. For instance, Wole Soyinka's *The Trials of Brother Jero*,[1] although set in Nigeria, resonates strongly with the Ghanaian context. The play reveals Brother Jero as a charlatan of a prophet who takes advantage of Chume, his faithful acolyte, and his wife, Amope. Brother Jero buys goods on credit from Amope and defaults on the payment, so the lady decides to lay siege near the prophet's residence to recover her money. When Brother Jero discovers that his creditor is Chume's wife, he advises Chume to take Amope home and beat her—although hitherto Brother Jero had forbidden wife-beating. The timelessness of Soyinka's theme of hypocrisy manifests in its relevance and resonance with contemporary developments on the Christian scene.

Dr. Ephraim Amu (1899–1995) also engages with the theme of clergy morality in his song "*Esrɔm Miele*." The lyrics, which are in the Eʋe language, capture the high moral expectations society has for Christian leaders in general. According to the songwriter's daughter, Misonu Amu, this song was composed to mark the ordination of Amu's bosom friend and colleague, the late Rev. Professor Baeta in 1935 into the ministry of the Evangelical Presbyterian Church Ghana:

> "*Esrɔm miele, bɛ miadi Yesu*"
>
> *Esrɔm miele, esrɔm miele, esrɔm meile*
> *Bɛ miadįi, mia dįi, mia dįi Yesu tutuutu*
> *O! Mawu dowɔla dįi wu, dįi wu*
> *dį Yesu afetɔwu*
> *L'ame dokuibɔbɔ danyi kpoo me*
> *dįi wu, dįi wu, dį Yesu afetɔwu*
> *Lɛ havi subɔsubɔ vivie mɛ*
> *dįi wu, dįi wu, dį Yesu afetɔwu*
> *Lɛ sesed'ame ti de too me*
> *dįi wu, dįi wu, dį Yesu afetɔ wu*
> *O! Mawu dowɔla dįi wu, dįi wu, dį Yesu afetɔ wu loo.*[2]

The English translation, which seeks to approximate the original intended meaning appears rather literal than idiomatic, follows:

---

1. Soyinka, *Jero Plays*, 8–44.

2. This song is printed here with the express permission of Misonu Amu, the custodian of the Ephraim Amu estate.

"We Are Learning to Be Like Jesus"

We are learning, we are learning, we are learning
to be like him, absolutely like Jesus.
O! You, God's servant, be more like him, be more like him, be more like
him, be more like Jesus.
In quiet humility,
be more like him, be more like Jesus.
In sacrificial service to mankind,
be more like Him, be more like Jesus.
In deep sympathy with fellow humans,
be more like him, be more like Jesus.
O! You, God's servant, be more like him,
be more like Jesus.

The subject of this composition is the need for "God's servant," or the Christian leader, to stand out as a stellar moral example for the rest of humankind. The song further identifies specific virtues that such leaders should symbolize in listing humility, sacrificial service, and compassion for the vulnerable. The composer emphasizes the need for the Christian leader to set enviable moral standards by repeating the refrain, dii wu (that is, "be more like Christ," in comparison with other people).

Public Opinion: Laity Survey

I used a questionnaire (see Appendix 4) to undertake a survey of the opinion of 177 lay people concerning Pentecostal ministerial moral standards. Since the issues explored have implications beyond the scope of the churches I have chosen for my case study—namely, the Church of Pentecost, Assemblies of God Church Ghana, and REC—the questionnaire was administered beyond that context. Forty-two people from the CoP responded, while thirteen respondents came from AG, thirty-two came from WMCI, and twenty-two people from REC responded. Respondents from all other Pentecostal churches numbered fifty-seven and respondents from the historically Western mission-oriented churches totaled eleven. The disparity in the total number of respondents to specific questions came about because respondents did not necessarily answer every question. This questionnaire is made up of two sections: Section A requests that respondents select one Pentecostal minister and evaluate the impact of his or her ministry and moral life, while Section B is designed to gather information on all Pentecostal ministers in general. Table 2 below illustrates the responses to Section A on specific ministers.

Table 2: Assessment of the Moral Standards of Specific Pentecostal Ministers[3]

No.	Issue	Yes	%	No	%	Not Sure	%	Total
1	Ministry has benefited me.	156	88%	2	1%	19	11%	177
2	Ministry changed my behavior.	112	63%	1	0.5%	64	36%	177
3	Minister is demon-conscious.	34	19%	101	57%	42	23%	177
4	He accuses people of witchcraft.	4	2%	116	69%	47	28%	167
5	He is a respectful leader.	154	87%	2	1%	21	11%	177
6	He is confidential.	139	78%	3	2%	35	20%	177
7	He is decent with the opposite sex.	143	81%	4	2%	30	17%	177
8	He is democratic.	135	76%	8	5%	34	19%	177
9	He is ostentatious.	31	18%	100	56%	46	26%	177
10	Tricks for money.	2	1%	136	77%	39	22%	177

The general impression Table 2 yields is that those who sought the ministry of the leaders in question tended to give these ministers an overwhelming endorsement. The first question sought to find out whether the ministry of the specific pastor selected by the respondent has been beneficial to the respondent. A significant number of 156 respondents (88 percent) answered in the affirmative. The second item is a derivative of the first question and attempted to discover whether the specified minister had helped to improve the respondent's behavior. In response, a majority of 112 people (63 percent) responded with "Yes." It is noteworthy that a significant number of sixty-four respondents (36 percent) were not sure of the ethical impact of the specified pastor's ministry on their lives, indicating the need for increased moral education for ministers so that they may transmit its benefit to their congregations.

The third question revealed that 101 people (57 percent) thought their pastor was not demon-conscious. This can be considered as a positive development, especially when coupled with fourth question, which found that

---

3. The numbering of these categories corresponds to questions 9–20 listed under the "Assessment" section of Appendix 4. Please note that the use of the masculine pronoun here is in the generic, universal sense, due to space considerations.

116 of respondents (69 percent) claim the minister under scrutiny did not accuse people of witchcraft. In terms of the minister having respect for other people (question five), a significant number of 154 (87 percent) thought the minister in question respected people. In response to the sixth question, I discovered that 139 people (78 percent) were convinced that the minister they were evaluating respected confidentiality. A total of 143 respondents were sure that the minister treated the opposite sex with decency according to question seven, implying that they were not promiscuous. In response to the eighth question, 135 respondents (76 percent) reported that their minister was democratic, while thirty-four people (19 percent) were not sure.

In the ninth question, I explored the suggestion that some of the ministers were extravagant or had expensive habits. In response, thirty-one people (18 percent) chose "Yes," while one hundred people (56 percent) responded with "No," and forty-six people (26 percent) were not sure. The final question sought to discover whether the selected ministers used tricks to extort money from their followers. Only two people answered in the affirmative, while 136 people (77 percent) said "No," and thirty-nine respondents (22 percent) were not sure. Although this field data appears to show an impressive degree of approval of the morality of a majority of the ministers evaluated, the numbers indicating certain negative attitudes are also significant and merit reflection. For instance, 19 percent of respondents said the ministers they evaluated were too demon-conscious, while 17 percent of respondents claimed their pastors were extravagant.

The second part of the same questionnaire, reproduced in Section B of Appendix 4, was designed to sample respondents' views on general information and certain general perceptions of all Pentecostal ministers. These responses are illustrated in Table 3 below.

Table 3: General Information on Moral Standards among Pentecostal Ministers[4]

No.	Issue	Yes	%	No	%	Not Sure	%	Remarks
1	Knows a tribalistic minister.	21	11%	124	70%	32	18%	177
2	Knows a promiscuous minister.	50	28%	91	51%	36	20%	177
3	Knows a fraudulent minister.	43	24%	100	56%	34	19%	177
4	Knows a charlatan prophet.	55	31%	82	46%	40	23%	177
5	Supports women's ordination.	117	66%	27	15%	33	18%	177

4. The numbering of these categories corresponds to questions 21–25 listed under the "General Information" section of Appendix 4.

The first question recorded in Table 3 asked respondents if they knew any Pentecostal minister who practiced tribalism; twenty-one people (11 percent) said "Yes," while 124 respondents (70 percent) said "No," and thirty-two people (18 percent) said they were not sure. Concerning sexual misconduct, the second question sought to find out whether respondents knew any Pentecostal ministers who were promiscuous; fifty of them (28 percent) said "Yes," while ninety-one respondents (51 percent) answered "No," and the remaining thirty-six people (20 percent) were not sure. The third question asked respondents if they knew any Pentecostal minister who had embezzled money; forty-three people (24 percent) were positive that they knew one, while one hundred respondents (56 percent) said "No," and thirty-four people (19 percent) said they were not sure. To find out how widespread false prophecy had become, question four asked respondents to indicate whether they knew any prophet that had misled somebody; fifty-five people (31 percent) knew a false prophet, while eighty-two people (46 percent) did not know any, and forty people reported being unsure. The final question examined the respondent's attitude towards women's ordination. There seems to be an overwhelming support for it, since 117 respondents (66 percent) answered in the affirmative, while twenty-seven (15 percent) were opposed to the idea, and thirty-three respondents (18 percent) chose not to take any stand on the issue. This shows how far Ghanaian society has shifted from a male chauvinist position towards advocating support for women in church leadership.

Unlike Table 2, Table 3 does not indicate such tremendous acclaim for Pentecostal ministerial ethics in Ghana. Although all of the indicators appear to be generally positive—70 percent of respondents did not know a tribalistic minister, 51 percent were not aware of any promiscuous minister, 56 percent could not point to a case of ministerial embezzlement, 46 percent had not personally encountered any case of a misleading prophet, and 66 percent supported women's ordination—the level of approval given on some of these issues seems to have been rather thin. It therefore becomes an issue of concern if, for instance, 28 percent of respondents knew sexually incontinent pastors, while 24 percent were personally aware of ministerial embezzlement cases, and 31 percent could point out misleading prophets.

Some of the respondents went further to explain their understanding of certain aspects of Pentecostal ministerial morality and provided me with elaborate responses in their own words, the more revealing of which I have recorded below.

Under witchcraft accusations, the following replies seem noteworthy: "It [witchcraft accusations] is not necessary because it brings about hatred in most families"; "It's awful"; "It is real, I can testify of someone I know";

"There is nothing wrong if they [the so-called witches] are accused publicly. They should be prayed for"; "Witchcraft accusations should be treated with maximum care"; "I don't think people should be accused of witchcraft. The pastors should be confidential about it"; and "It scares me and makes me wonder if it really exists." The tone of these answers suggest a polarization of positions, for one group is convinced of the reality of witchcraft and supports its public exposure, while the other group is skeptical about its existence and would rather have it handled as a private matter.

Another item in the questionnaire that also prompted engaging answers inquired whether the individual had received a prophetic message from a Pentecostal minister. Of note here is that this item offers a follow-up question that asked how meaningful and relevant the message was to the respondent. The following responses to both questions are presented verbatim: "It was prophesied to me that I will one day be a great person"; according to the respondent, the message was "so much meaningful." Another respondent reported, "That I will be filled with the Holy Spirit and in six months I will find my beloved"; this respondent also claimed that she found the message meaningful. A third person said, "It was prophesied that I will one day be a great person"; this respondent also found this message useful. One of the particularly poetic prophetic messages relayed reads: "As stars don't struggle to shine and rivers don't struggle to flow, so shall you also not struggle to succeed in life"; this message was also relevant to the person who received it. Another respondent stated that she encountered a man of God who revealed "things that go on in households," and although she did not report the specific message, she claimed, "I find the message meaningful because I remember that was the same situation that goes on in our house. I took the message and the guidelines and it has really helped us." These responses offer ample evidence that some churchgoers find prophetic messages useful and encouraging. However, we also need to explore the opinions of those who think otherwise.

Other respondents were not so enthusiastic about the impact of the prophetic messages they had encountered. One person who thought he was deceived outright by a prophet wrote, "I received a message that somebody wanted to kill me with a food poisoning and it was not true." A few others who were also unimpressed by "the oracle" responded by saying they found the messages "somehow meaningful," and three of such prophesies are captured here: "I see that you are a prophet and a teacher so go and work on it"; "I was told that someone was going to give me a car as a gift and at the same time take me to the USA"; and "I will be a great man, I will be head of my family. Satan has seen it so they have planned evil against me." These answers further reveal that the Pentecostal ministries host both genuine prophets and charlatans, and anyone dealing with them may have to be discerning in choosing whether or not to take their insights seriously. One category of prophets that needs to be avoided is the group that frequently instills fear in people by predicting disaster in order to exploit their followers' sense of insecurity.

In response to the questionnaire's request for general comments on Pentecostal ministers, some respondents had this to say: "Some are good leaders, God fearing, loving and caring"; "They [Pentecostal ministers] make a lot of sacrifices to cater for others at the expense of their own families"; "They [Pentecostal ministers] are righteous men and holy men who are training other people in the kingdom life." A rather interesting response to this question reads, "Some of them are being deceived by the devil, while most of them are on guard against him." Another person wrote of Pentecostal ministers, "Most of them are able to exhibit what they preach and also comport themselves well in society." Someone else shared the opinion that "some [Pentecostal ministers] are too judgmental; even when they have only met you for the very first time." Yet another person was convinced that "some are good and others are bad influences on the society. Some manipulate innocent people to either take money from them or sleep with them, which is a disgrace to the church."

By and large, those who seek out the services of Pentecostal ministers seem to register a positive impression of their ethics. On many specific issues of moral relevance, the respondents seem to have afforded the said ministers a positive evaluation. Nevertheless, some of the indicators record significant numbers that speak critically of the conduct of ministers, which we must view as a call for redress. Compared to the largely negative assessment of the press, the followers of the ministers under discussion have a more constructive opinion about their moral impact. Let us now examine some of these media reports.

Evaluation of Media Reports

It is necessary at this point to recognize that the Ghanaian press is not only preoccupied with publishing unsavory stories about the category of churches under discussion. Indeed, there seems to be a significant level of positive reportage on the activities of Pentecostal churches. Almost all Ghanaian television stations frequently broadcast their sermons, and both the electronic and print media cover church and para-church activities, which sometimes teaches audiences constructive moral principles. Furthermore, Pentecostal church projects that support the socio-economic infrastructure and extend aid to the underprivileged often attract positive attention from Ghanaian journalists.

Some instances of appreciative reporting on Pentecostal churches are presented here. A three-part feature article by Rev. Professor Asamoah-Gyadu targeted at educating the general public on the distinguishing features of Pentecostal churches was carried by *The Spectator* in April 2008. In the last article of the series, he described their ethical standards thus: "The main distinguishing characteristic of classical Pentecostal churches is that they usually have a stronger holiness ethic and several of them have established as fully-fledged denominations, with very well-defined doctrinal positions, clearly established administrative structures and succession plans."[5] In another news item, the *Ghanaian Times* reported on a camp meeting organized by the Greater Accra branch of the Assemblies of God Church for female junior high school graduates in May of 2008. The Minister of Women and Children's Affairs, Hajia Alimah Mahama, who served as a guest speaker, commended the church by stating that "the innovative effort of the Assemblies of God Church in bringing together young girls from their churches to instill in them religious and moral values clearly demonstrates the church's readiness to empower its future leaders."[6]

Another constructive media report in the *Ghanaian Times* on Pentecostal churches covered a social outreach project. The event captured in this news item was the inauguration of the Church of Pentecost School Complex at Akyem Oda by the Chairman, Apostle Dr. Micheal Kwabena Ntumy. The function, which was attended by the Hon. Yaw Osafo-Marfo, Member of Parliament for Akyem Oda, and Mr. Frank Kwame Busumtwi, Birim South District Chief Executive, marked the formal opening of a GH₵45,000 (US$22,500) structure to house a primary and secondary school.[7]

This positive image in the press notwithstanding, there is a wide suggestion that there may be more coverage of unethical conduct than constructive representations of the ministers under discussion. To reiterate a point from chapter 1, the Centre for Media Analysis published research revealing that of the stories carried in the Ghana's print media on charismatic churches between July 1 and September 30, 2005, 49 percent of the news items were negative, 29 percent were written in a neutral tone, and

---

5. J. Kwabena Asamoah-Gyadu, "Who Are Pentecostals? Who Are Charismatics? Part III," *The Spectator*, April 19, 2008, 23.

6. Hajia Alima Mahama, quoted in L. Kwesi Akpalu, "Religious Leaders Urged to Help Eliminate Outmoded Customs," *Ghanaian Times*, May 20, 2008, 11.

7. C. Neequaye, "Inauguration of Church of Pentecost School Complex at Oda," *Ghanaian Times*, May 16, 2007.

only 22 percent were positive.[8] This implies that although church members overwhelmingly endorse the moral conduct of their own ministers, at least according to the survey results detailed above, the press appears to portray a less impressive opinion of such leaders. For instance, the media often carries stories and opinion pieces by influential people that seem to suggest that Pentecostal leaders do not only preach prosperity, but also extort money, misapply church funds, live ostentatiously, and seek to establish personality cults.

In an attempt to ascertain the authenticity of one such report I sat through a court session that involved Rev. Prince Adeblorh-Dugah, founder of the Gateway Chapel at Nungua, who was arrested for allegedly duping members of his congregation out of GH₵250,000 ($120,000). According to the reporter covering the proceedings, the money was first raised from church members through a scheme dubbed "Help Your Neighbour Welfare Scheme," only for the pastor to end up "using the money to purchase three vehicles."[9]

The court session I attended was held at Accra High Street Cocoa Affairs Circuit Court 8 on July 23, 2006. I listened as the defense counsel, Rev. Adeblor-Dugah's lawyer, cross-examined the prosecutor, Inspector J. Kwaku Lodonu. The lawyer for the defense insisted that contrary to Lodonu's assertion, the actual name of the welfare scheme was "Aid Your Neighbour Missions" rather than "Help Your Neighbour Welfare Scheme." The defense counsel further claimed that Rev. Adeblor-Dugah was on trial for leading a church that was pursuing the second of its two objectives, which were first, to preach the gospel of Jesus Christ all over the world, and second, to seek the financial welfare of its members.

The charge proffered against the pastor was the unlawful establishment of a financial company that was taking deposits and granting loans. When the defense counsel asked Inspector Lodonu whether he had seen the constitution of the welfare scheme, his answer was in the negative. Although the prosecutor reported that Rev. Adeblor-Dugah was accepting deposits from both outsiders (which was unlawful) and his own church members, the defense Counsel said that was not the case.

---

8. Ben Ephson, "Research Reveals Negative Media on Charismatic Churches," *Daily Dispatch*, October 25, 2005. The newspapers covered in this research included the *Daily Graphic, Ghanaian Times, Daily Dispatch, Daily Guide, The Crusading Guide, The Independent, Network Herald, Public Agenda, The Insight, The Searchlight, The Statesman, The Chronicle, Free Press, The Lens,* and *Accra Daily Mail*.

9. M. A. Baneseh, "Man of God in the Dock over ₵2.5 Billion Fraud," *Daily Graphic*, March 23, 2006, 1, 3.

My request for an interview with Rev. Adeblor-Dugah after the court hearing was declined. However, I was able to gather from an investigator that the church had collapsed, for the members who fell victim to the ill-fated welfare scheme had revolted against the pastor. This investigator, who brought about the pastor's arrest, intimated that he had posed as an outsider applying to become a member of the welfare scheme, and his application was about to be processed when the arrest took place. Rev. Adeblor-Dugah's readiness to register a complete outsider to the church into the so-called welfare scheme implicated him as running an illegitimate financial organization. The investigator has since submitted the application form, which would have been used to register him on the so-called welfare scheme, into court evidence.

In May 2011, Bishop Vaglas Kanco, General Overseer of the Vineyard Chapel International (headquartered in Madina with other branches in Ghana), was jailed for eighteen years for duping a British woman out of £120,000 under the pretense of praying to sanctify the check she had issued in the name of her former partner.[10] In another instance, *The New Punch* headline for March 30, 2007 read, "Revolt at CAC [Christ Apostolic Church]: Chairman Thrown out, Spends ₵2.2Bn on Lincoln Navigator." The story purports that Apostle Michael Nimo, who was Chairman of the church for four years, had been voted out of power and replaced by Apostle Stephen Amoaning. There is a slight twist in this particular report that attempts to link this development to the exit of Apostle Nimo's immediate predecessor, Rev. Annor-Yeboah, who seceded from the church after he was voted out of the chairmanship in July 2003.[11] Part of the *New Punch* story reads:

> Nearly four years after initiating a palace coup to sweep Rev. Dr. Augustus Annor Yeboah, the then-National Chairman of the CAC, off his feet under inexplicable reasons, members of the General Council of the church, by a decision taken at their last General Meeting at the Bunso Cocoa College in the Eastern Region, have also handed Rev. Apostle Micheal Nimo the same bitter pill he and others administered to Rev. Annor Yeboah about four years ago.[12]

---

10. Seth J. Bokpe, "Clergy under Fire for Acts Unbecoming of Men of God," *Daily Graphic*, August 15, 2011, 1, 3.

11. See E. Mingle, "Annor-Yeboah's Move Splits CAC," *Ghanaian Times*, July 26, 2003, 1.

12. Ebenezer Ato Sam, "Revolt at CAC: Chairman Thrown Out," *New Punch*, March 30–April 2, 2008, 1, 8.

The report ascribes this turn of events to "the opulent and profligate (extravagant) lifestyles of the current executives." The reporter specifically accused Apostle Nimo of spending church funds to purchase a Lincoln Navigator, an expensive cross-country vehicle.[13] A June 29, 2007 follow-up report in *The New Punch* added to the allegations that former Chairman Apostle Nimo took huge amounts of money for warm clothing allowances and a per diem when travelling abroad; in addition, he owned numerous cars in addition to the two official vehicles allocated to him.

My interaction with Apostle Stephen Amoaning, current Chairman of CAC, Apostle Michael Nimo, and the editor of *The New Punch*, Ebenezer Ato Sam, concerning these accusations revealed that the storyline may not have been as factual as the reporter would lead us to believe. Responding to these allegations, current Chairman Apostle Stephen Amoaning said they were all unfounded.[14] According to him, the ousting of Apostle Nimo from the chairmanship carried no indication of revolt as *The New Punch* report suggested; rather it occurred through the due process of balloting. He further intimated that the allegations of misappropriation of church funds were all baseless and said they had invited *The New Punch*'s editor, Ato Sam, to apologize for defamation of character. According to Apostle Amoaning, the editor had been using his paper to settle a personal score, for he was part of the faction that broke away to follow Rev. Annor-Yeboah in 2003.

Apostle Michael Nimo, who is at the center of all these allegations, is now stationed at Takoradi, Ghana, as the Western Region Head of the church. In an interview, he also confirmed the current Chairman's point that the assertions in the *New Punch* were fictitious and that the editor had formally apologized to him and to the church for dragging their names in the mud.[15] When I inquired whether the newspaper had retracted the story, Apostle Nimo's answer was negative. A further inquiry to find out why no action had been taken to set the record straight garnered the answer that since CAC had featured in so many negative press reports, church leaders had thought it wise to spare members from another round of unsavory media coverage and so Apostle Nimo chose not to file a defamation case in court.[16]

I was able to interview the editor of *The New Punch*, Ebenezer Ato Sam, on the reports in question and he acknowledged that there actually was no

---

13. Ibid., 1, 12.

14. Stephen Amoaning, Chairman of Christ Apostolic Church, interview by Dela Quampah, Accra, Ghana, October 8, 2008.

15. Michael Nimo, Western Region Head of Christ Apostolic Church, interview by Dela Quampah, Takoradi, Ghana, October 13, 2008.

16. Ibid.

revolt at CAC, as his story had purported. He also admitted that the change in leadership was attributable to a credible democratic process of voting. Concerning his allegations about ex-Chairman Apostle Nimo's numerous vehicles, Ato Sam said the church had explained to him that some of the vehicles were personal gifts from individuals. The editor, however, insisted that he would not retract the story until he had received documented proof that the vehicles were given to Apostle Nimo as presents.[17]

My research has thus refuted *The New Punch* report of a revolt at CAC. The veracity or otherwise of the allegations concerning misappropriation of church funds by Apostle Nimo to buy vehicles could not be conclusively determined, since documentary proof of transfer of ownership was not provided. The implication of such unsubstantiated media allegations does irreparable damage to the public image of the institution or individual concerned. We might therefore think that any form of legislation that would prevent the publication of such unfounded allegations before full investigation was undertaken would be welcomed.

Such occurrences may have influenced Rev. Professor Emeritus Kwesi Dickson's reported accusations against exploitation by charismatic churches in his 2005 presentation in Adabraka, Accra at the annual Dunwell-Acquah-Grant Memorial Lectures. To the eminent professor (who appears to be risking over-generalization), these churches are "a machinery for money-making; the pastors are cheats and a liability to our society."[18] Editor Ben Ephson also expressed a similar conviction in an interview by saying some Pentecostal ministers are fraudulent; in spite of that, he concedes that they still offer valuable services to society.[19] Apostle George Ofori-Atta, founder of Peculiar People's Chapel, is also reported to have "blamed leaders of the Pentecostal and charismatic churches for breeding social vices such as personal aggrandizement, greed and a false notion of the theory of prosperity, which he said has constituted the foundation of the charismatic movement."[20] He further stated that as a result of the misguided "understanding of prosperity doctrine, some leaders and followers of charismatic churches had found themselves in jail because of greed and criminal

---

17. Ebenezer Ato Sam, *New Punch* editor, interview by Dela Quampah, Accra, Ghana, October 21, 2008.

18. K. A. Dickson, quoted in M. N. Torgbor, "Charismatic Churches Exploiting the Poor," *Daily Dispatch*, September 7, 2005, 8.

19. Ben Ephson, *Daily Dispatch* editor, interview by Dela Quampah, Accra, Ghana, July 23, 2008.

20. R. Kwei, "Pastor Stirs Controversy: Blames Church Leaders for False Theory of Prosperity," *Daily Graphic*, December 27, 2005, 1.

activities."[21] This opinion seems to be confirmed by the observation of Rev. Superintendent James Tetteh, who said that in the five years of his chaplaincy at Nsawam Medium Security Prison, no minister from the mainline churches had been incarcerated there—the only Christian ministers who were jailed there happened to be four Pentecostal pastors.[22] Two of them were imprisoned for defrauding people, one for murder, and the fourth for criminal assault.

As much as we cannot deny that many of the stories published on the immoral conduct of Pentecostal ministers are factual, it is also suggested that there is evidence of a degree of subjectivity to such reports. This subjectivity seems to be due to several concerns, not least of all among them commercial interest. It appears some of the damaging headlines on Pentecostal pastors are mere sensationalist allegations. For instance, I contacted *Daily Graphic* reporter M. A. Baneseh to establish the guilt or otherwise of Pastor Emmanuel Kofi Tei, a Pentecostal minister and founder of Mispa Miracle Church at Dodowa, Ghana, who she reported as having abducted and seduced a seventeen-year-old girl.[23] To my surprise, the reporter casually said that she had lost trace of the case.[24] In such a situation, if the pastor had been later acquitted, his reputation would have been irredeemably tarnished. Consequently, it would be advisable for the media to delay the publication of such potentially libelous stories until the guilt of the individual had been established beyond reasonable doubt in court. Alternatively, reporters could follow the story through to the conclusion, covering developments at every stage. Otherwise, the credibility of the media itself will be significantly undermined. It is therefore advisable for the reading public to try and ascertain the facts behind some of these sensationalist headlines before drawing any conclusions.

As stated earlier, media and public opinion on Pentecostal ministers is not unrelentingly negative. Sections of Ghanaian society appreciate their contribution to the spiritual and socio-economic progress of the nation. For instance, after reading a rather scathing article in *The Spectator* titled "Where Is the Church: As Streetism, Child Prostitution Overwhelm

---

21. Ibid., 1, 3.

22. Supt Tetteh, Prison Chaplain, interview by Dela Quampah, Nsawam, Ghana, November 14, 2012. Tetteh, however, made the positive statement that none of the pastors who were jailed at Nsawam Prison ever came back as a repeat offender. By implication, the time served in jail may have helped to reform them.

23. M. A. Baneseh, "Pastor in Court for Abducting Girl, 17," *Daily Graphic*, April 23, 2006, 34.

24. Ibid., *Daily Graphic* reporter, interview by Dela Quampah, Accra, Ghana, June 17, 2008.

Society?" written by a columnist dubbed "Watchwoman" (whose real name is Doris Dartey), one Ignatius Acheampong was moved to write a rejoinder. Acheampong offers these insights:

> These things [Christian charity projects] will never be seen by our social commentators. They see only what a few pastors and misguided prophets are doing wrong . . . For the sins of a few, Christianity is castigated so cruelly by people who should know better . . . It is just fashionable to bash Christians, because it is the only religion that will not visit violence on its critics. Television plays, films, social commentary, etc., are all filled with criticism of Christians. It is the only religion against whom anybody can take liberties and expect to sleep soundly.[25]

In an interview with Rev. Father Raphael Osei Soadwah of Saint Paul's Catholic Seminary in Sowutuom, he also expressed the opinion that majority of Pentecostal ministers live morally upright lives and make positive contributions to Christianity and society as a whole. He thought it was unfair to use the misguided conducts of a few of such leaders to brand all the others.[26] A similar opinion is held by Daniel Abugah, a reporter for *Gospel Advocate*, who said the persistent negative reporting on Pentecostal churches by the media came from unfounded impressions rather than facts in many instances. According to Abugah, this sensationalist coverage, which seems to be motivated by commercial interests, contributes to the promotion of negative public perceptions of such ministers. Abugah is also convinced that the positive contributions of Pentecostal ministers to the overall welfare and progress of the Ghanaian society far outweighs their negative impact.[27]

Response to the "Prosperity Gospel"

Media sensationalism notwithstanding, it cannot be denied that the ostentatious lifestyles of some Pentecostal church leaders call for serious self-assessment on their part. As models in a developing economy, one would think that leadership in every facet of society would exemplify thrift and the prudent investment of limited resources. Nevertheless, some of the expensive outfits, flashy vehicles, and palatial accommodations enjoyed by some

---

25. Ignatius Acheampong, "Re: Watchwoman—Where Is the Church?" *The Spectator*, March 15, 2008, 4.

26. Raphael Osei Soadwah, Saint Paul's Catholic Seminary Sowutuom, interview by Dela Quampah, Accra, Ghana, June 22, 2009.

27. Daniel Abugah, *Gospel Advocate* reporter, interview by Dela Quampah, Accra, Ghana, March 11, 2008.

of such church leaders reflect an uneconomical application of resources at the very least. Among these church leaders, it seems the flaunting of wealth has become the benchmark of success and God's blessing, rather than the fruit of prudent investment and the judicious application of resources. It is rather revealing to observe that this unproductive attitude toward wealth is often endorsed using Scripture passages and preached as "prosperity gospel" from many Pentecostal pulpits. The presentation of such prosperity and success concepts give the impression that Christians have an automatic right to success and that prosperity is so much a part of the salvation package that if a Christian is poor, then there must be something wrong with that person's faith.

Anderson's attempt to identify some of the major tenets of the prosperity message is instructive: "The will of God is for people to prosper or succeed in every area of life (Psalm 1, 3; John 2)"; "The atonement of Christ includes provision for deliverance from sickness and poverty as well as from sin"; "God's covenant with Abraham, inherited by the Christian believer, includes a promise of material prosperity (Gen 12:1–3; 13:1–2)"; and "The means by which prosperity and health are appropriated is by faith alone."[28] On many occasions, worshippers are motivated to exhibit their faith in generous offerings to enable them access these blessings. Asamoah-Gyadu,[29] Gifford,[30] and Anim[31] have all demonstrated that the strand of prosperity message prevalent in charismatic churches in Ghana is the product of the fertile interaction of American televangelist concepts and traditional Ghanaian ideas of success and fulfillment.

In extreme cases, this success motif becomes susceptible to a kind of triumphalism that takes presumption over faith and claims control of all spiritual and natural phenomena. This approach to Christianity is what O'Meara refers to as "sacral religion," which according to him, "brings the perennial temptation to encapsulate the divine. Sacral religion is a phenomenon of extremes: it parades exaggerated claims and it achieves nothing."[32] Indeed, such an approach can even be downright destructive, as was made evident by Apostle K. K. C. Gadzekpo of the Church of Pentecost, who claimed he could drive through a flooded river at Kparekpare in Ghana's Volta Region on the strength of faith. Despite bystanders' ardent attempts to

28. Anderson, "The Prosperity Message," 75–76.
29. Asamoah-Gyadu, *African Charismatics*, 204–6.
30. Gifford, *Ghana's New Christianity*, 47–56.
31. Anim, "Prosperity Gospel in Ghana," 1.
32. O'Meara, *Theology of Ministry*, 44.

dissuade him, he died along with one of his subordinate pastors, while his wife and driver were rescued from drowning.[33]

As observed earlier, the Pentecostal phenomenon defies stereotyping, since a more comprehensive view of the prosperity teaching admits a certain level of positive impact. For instance, although Asamoah-Gyadu raises issues with the prosperity message, he admits that the concept has contributed to making charismatic churches financially independent and suggests they might offer lessons to older churches that are still dependent on Western mission donors.[34] Michael Okyerefo also appreciates the fact that the activities and messages of Pentecostal churches are the creating communities of resourceful people that will be necessary to generating development.[35] Anim postulates that the primal concept of wealth and success served as *praeparatio evangelica*, or advance preparation, for the gospel to the concept of prosperity. His perspective reveals a liberationist impact by which the prosperity message frees the mind from the fear of witchcraft and releases adherents to pursue an unhindered wealth-creation agenda.[36] Kalu engages with Giffords' depiction of Neo-Pentecostals in his *Ghana's New Christianity* as lacking a sound work ethic in waiting for a miracle to propel believers to success, yet Kalu claims adherents appear to be ostentatious. Kalu goes on to wonder, "If these Christians sit back and wait on God to supply their needs, where do they get the money that the pastors may demand? Where do the fancy cars and material signs of success, described by Gifford, come from?"[37]

Ministers' Response to Ethical Issues

At this stage, I would like to consider how some Pentecostal leaders have responded themselves to the problem of unethical ministerial conduct. There is a suggestion that if the media seems to have a preoccupation for ministerial scandals, such reporters are supported by certain members of the ministerial fraternity who consciously encouraged them in their investigations. A case in point is when *The Spectator* reported that Apostle John Anan Adotey, President of the Apostolic Church Ghana, encouraged the media to "expose corrupt pastors and church leaders who have compromised Christian

33. M. Azure Awuni, "Two Church of Pentecost Pastors Drown in Test of Faith," *Daily Graphic*, August 30, 2010, 3.
34. Asamoah-Gyadu, *African Charismatics*, 227.
35. Okyerefo, "Promotion of Human Capital," 58.
36. Anim, "Prosperity Gospel in Ghana," 42.
37. Kalu, "Yabbing the Pentecostals," 11.

values and ethics for worldly possessions."[38] This notwithstanding, the accusations of unethical behavior leveled against Pentecostal ministers have received various responses from the ministers themselves, many of which are discussed in this chapter.

I think it important to point out that the generalizations that purport that Pentecostal church leaders show little concern for high moral standards cannot be further from the truth. Many ministers model admirable ethical principles and couple them with sermons and literature that promote high Christian moral value formation. Bishop Emmanuel Sackey, second-in-command at LCI, treated the topic in a sermon titled "Types of a Good Heart."[39] He based his sermon on Proverbs 4:23, "Keep your heart with all diligence for, out of it spring the *issues* of life" (NKJV). Bishop Emmanuel Sackey identified a "good heart" as first, "the true heart," second, "the sprinkled heart," and third, "the honest heart."[40] Bishop Sackey intimated that a true heart is one that does not harbor hypocrisy; such a person does not come to church on Sunday morning behaving like an angel but behave during weekdays like "the devil's nephew."[41] The bishop explained that a sprinkled heart is a heart that allows God to purge it of sin, evil, and wickedness. The third kind of heart he spoke of was the "honest heart," which accepts God's word in all honesty and applies it to his or her life for moral transformation.

In another instance, although Prophet Emmanuel Dodzi of WMCI preached on "Building a Strong Church through the Home Cell," a topic that had no direct moral focus, he was quick to slot in the fact that the cell provides a place for conflict resolution and facilitates disciplinary action against members who engage in various kinds of misconduct.[42]

In the Church of Pentecost, a message of emphatic moral import is expressed in statements that the church regards as its collective covenant declaration: "the Church [CoP] should remember not to harbour sins, evil

---

38. John Anan Adotey, quoted in I. Motey, "Expose Corrupt Pastors, Church Leaders: Apostle Adotey Urges the Media," *The Spectator*, June 16, 2007, 23. Whether it is acceptable for a minister of the gospel to appeal to the press to report on the failings of his colleagues is debatable, considering it that may be inappropriate to wash dirty linen in public. We must wonder whether it would be more proper for the ecclesiastical authorities to help sanitize the pastorate rather than submitting such a sacred assignment to the press.

39. Emmanuel Sackey, "Types of a Good Heart," sermon delivered to Lighthouse Chapel International Headquaters, Sunday June 6, 2008, North Kaneshie, Ghana.

40. Ibid.

41. Ibid.

42. Emmanuel Dodzi, "Building a Strong Church through the Home Cell," sermon delivered to WMCI Headquarters, July 13, 2008, Dzorwulu, Ghana.

deeds and evil people among her membership, but rebuke, discipline and restore backsliders in the spirit of love, compassion and patience."[43]

I undertook a survey to discover the functional implications of certain ministerial and ethical concepts relevant to the Ghanaian Pentecostal leadership context by using a question guide to personally interact with fifty such leaders. Although administering this series of directed questions demanded more effort and time than a questionnaire, it has the advantage of approximating accurate answers, since the researcher is on hand to explain difficult concepts. The choice of respondents intentionally went beyond my case study churches because the issues explored have implications for the wider Pentecostal leadership. In addition, I interacted only with the rank and file of ministers in order to examine the leadership styles of those in higher offices from the perspective of their subordinates. From the case study churches, I spoke with twelve ministers from Word Miracle Church International, five from Redeem Evangel Church, thirteen from the Church of Pentecost, and nine from Assemblies of God Church. Respondents from other churches totaled eleven.

Table 4: Ministers' Responses to Some Ministerial and Ethical Issues

S/N	Concept	Yes	%	No	%	Not Sure	%
1	Minister had adequate theological education.	14	28%	36	72%	0	0%
2	Existence of a code of ethics.	22	44%	28	56%	0	0%
3	Minister's familiarity with ethics.	16	32%	31	62%	3	6%
4	Minister has a respectful supervisor.	46	92%	0	0%	4	8%
5	Minister's supervisor is democratic.	37	74%	4	8%	9	18%
6	Church administration is transparent.	20	40%	23	46%	7	14%
7	Church has audited accounts.	31	62%	18	36%	1	2%
8	Aware of controversial fundraising methods.	42	84%	4	8%	4	8%
9	Knows extravagant ministers.	39	78%	2	4%	9	18%
10	Ministerial discipline acceptable.	32	64%	12	24%	6	12%
11	Preaches prosperity gospel.	28	56	20	40%	2	4%
12	Preaches sanctification.	50	100%	0	0%	0	0%
13	Undertakes witch hunting.	22	44%	27	54%	1	2%

---

43. *The Church of Pentecost Minister's Handbook*, 54.

The first question sought to find out whether the initial theological education the minister received before embarking on ministry was adequate, and a significant number of thirty-six ministers (72 percent) responded in the negative. This finding reinforces an earlier concern I we discussed about the need to increase the period of training for the Pentecostal ministers. The second question inquired about the existence of a documented ministerial code of ethics in the respondent's church, and twenty-eight respondents (56 percent) said "No." The third item tested the ministers' familiarity with some key terminology in moral philosophy such as "Deontology," "Utility," "Situationism," and "Absolutism." Three respondents (6 percent) were not sure, thirty-one of them (62 percent) responded with "No," signifying the low level of awareness of moral philosophy among the ministers. With the fourth question, I sought to find out whether the immediate supervisor of the respondent respected his subordinates, and a remarkable number of forty-six ministers (92 percent) responded in the affirmative, with a low number of four ministers surveyed (8 percent) claiming they were not sure. This implies that unlike the traditional context, in which juniors may receive little respect from their superiors, senior Pentecostal ministers tend to behave well toward their subordinates.

The fifth question assessed the level of democracy demonstrated by respondents' immediate supervisors.[44] Thirty-seven ministers (74 percent) said their supervisors were democratic, while four of them (8 percent) said they were not, and nine (18 percent) were not sure. This is also a demonstration of a departure from traditional Ghanaian leadership, which hardly reflects any level of appreciable democracy. The sixth question was framed to find out whether administrative procedures such as appointments, transfers, and promotions were transparent to respondents, to which twenty-three of them (46 percent) said "No," twenty of them (40 percent) said "Yes," and the remaining seven (14 percent) reported that they were not sure. Answers to the seventh question reveal that about thirty-one of the fifty ministers surveyed (62 percent) have access to externally audited accounts of their establishment—a situation that suggests these churches maintain an appreciable standard of accountability. The responses I received to reveal that an overwhelming majority of forty-two people (84 percent) were aware of some Pentecostal ministers who used controversial fundraising methods, while four people (8 percent) said they did not know of the use of any such questionable fundraising methods and another four people claimed they

---

44. These supervisors, who are mostly ministers, carry various titles such as District Pastor in Assemblies of God Church, or Area Head in the Church of Pentecost, etc.

were not sure.[45] There also seems to have been a general impression even among the ministers that some Pentecostal leaders live extravagantly, for a significant total of thirty-nine of them (78 percent) were convinced that some of their colleagues did not use resources judiciously.

Concerning disciplinary actions against offenders, an appreciable number of thirty-two ministers (64 percent) approved of the disciplinary codes and their implementation in their respective churches. During my interaction with the ministers, twenty-eight of them (56 percent) admitted that they had been preaching the so-called "prosperity gospel," while twenty ministers (40 percent) did not. The fact that each of the Pentecostal ministers is concerned with issues of morality is confirmed by the claim of all fifty respondents that they do preach regularly on sanctification. The last question yielded revealing data on the concept of witchcraft, for a slim majority of twenty-seven ministers (54 percent) said they had never identified a witch or wizard in their ministry. Nevertheless, twenty-two of them (44 percent) confirmed that they had identified witches in their ministry, making this an issue of concern in Pentecostal theology.

Beyond the itemized issues illustrated in Table 4, some respondents provided further insights on a handful of the topics under examination, which I have recorded here. One respondent reported that some Pentecostal leaders have built heavy protocol and a troop of bodyguards and personal assistants that made them inaccessible to congregation members. Another minister was convinced that some of his colleagues practiced tribalism in appointing people to church offices and also in promoting them.

Concerning ostentatious lifestyles among ministers, a few of the respondents thought that some of the public perceptions of extravagance were wrong. Such ministers are convinced that "ostentation" and "extravagance" are relative terms, and depending on a person's background and training, these words should be applied differently. One response, which I found rather fascinating, came from two respondents who insisted that to set a public example of thrift and economical use of resources, ministers should reject gifts that might reflect opulence or promote waste.

Many of the respondents suggested strategies that could help improve the negative press image of Ghanaian Pentecostal leaders. To some of them, more emphasis on education was necessary, especially in moral philosophy, which could help ministers make informed and constructive ethical choices. Such education, they suggested, could come in the form of seminars, conferences, symposia, mentoring, counseling, etc., throughout ministers'

---

45. Some of the popular examples cited included the selling of prophylactics, charging consultation fees, and coercive methods such as making an offering in order to curse one's enemy.

working lives. It was also intimated that those who admit others into the ministry might have to do more rigorous screening in order to select people of character and high moral standards. Others suggested that the formation of umbrella organizations that hold individual ministers accountable for their behavior would help control unethical conduct in ministry. One respondent was of the opinion that since human beings are fallible, ministerial misconduct cannot be totally eradicated; therefore, the churches should make provision for the correction, reformation, and reinstatement of offending ministers.

A handful of respondents were convinced that the press, motivated by commercial interest, was exaggerating some of the alleged ministerial scandals. They thought journalists had to be better educated in checking the authenticity and accuracy of such stories before publishing them. An interesting answer from one respondent suggested that the media exposure had a positive dimension to it, since it might help check unethical conduct among ministers.

It is also noteworthy and much to be appreciated that some of the Pentecostal churches are self-critical—that is, their ministers evaluate themselves and also allow their conduct to be examined by their colleagues and the church public alike as a control measure in ministerial ethics. It was also observed that the public revelation of ministerial offences could serve as a deterrent to potential offenders and also help the culprit reform. Thus, we can conclude that approaches to ministerial discipline vary from one denomination to the other, and depending on who is implementing the code of conduct and the level of public exposure given to the case, immoral behavior may be either flushed out or tolerated within ecclesiastical structures. In this light, we may even conclude that the frequent media reports on the unethical conduct of Pentecostal ministers can be productive in terms of institutional accountability, provided such reports are based on facts.

Rev. Professor Asamoah-Gyadu also thinks that the media seems to be demonstrating a penchant for Pentecostal leadership scandals because such ministers present themselves as paragons of virtue and brand leaders of other Christian denominations as "sinners."[46] Thus, the media publishes such stories with enthusiasm to reveal to the public that Pentecostal ministers are also human and fallible. I think there is much valuable insight in Asamoah-Gyadu's observation. Pentecostal leaders can learn from it and be humble enough to admit that, like other Christians and the rest of mankind,

---

46. Asamoah-Gyadu, Trinity Theological College, interview by Dela Quampah, Accra, Ghana, June 2, 2009.

we are all on pilgrimage towards perfection. Indeed, we are all seekers, groping after the redemption of our corruptible nature.

It has also been suggested that Pentecostal leaders do not give character development and ethical issues the deserved attention in their ministry (although my survey results in Table 4 reveals that all of those surveyed claim to preach on sanctification). Among those who express concern over the need for Pentecostal ministers to give more attention to moral and ethical issues is Rev. Opoku-Acheampong, who is convinced that "if publishers of religious books can dwell on morality, it will go a long way to impact positively on society."[47] It cannot be denied that sometimes the Pentecostal wing of the Christian faith concentrates on matters of prosperity and the attainment of material success or social recognition at the expense of character-building and moral uprightness. They must strike a balance between their focus on charisma and character for a more holistic Christianity.

The falling standards in Pentecostal ministerial ethics have engaged the attention of the ministers themselves, and some have directly responded to the accusations leveled at them via sermons, press releases, and interviews. Reacting to the decision of the West African Examinations Council to ban pastors from endorsing examination application forms, Apostle Micheal Kwabena Ntumy observes that the fact that the West African Examinations Council could not trust pastors is an indictment on such ministers.[48] To reiterate, Apostle John Anan Adotey, President of the Apostolic Church Ghana, thinks exposure in the media can contribute to solving the problem of ministerial misconduct.[49] Another minister, Rev. Dr. Joseph Kweku Asante, General Overseer of Full Gospel Centre and Director of King of Kings Bible College and Seminary, thinks the intervention of GPC and Christian Council of Ghana could "help develop discipline among pastors in the country to safeguard the image of the clergy."[50] Rev. Noah Twum agrees that problems exist in the Pentecostal ministries concerning moral standards, which he also thinks could be controlled by more education on ethical issues.[51]

---

47. Quoted in Adjoa Yeboah Afari, "Produce Books to Transform Lives of People," *Ghanaian Times*, October 24, 2007, 14.

48. Quoted in A. Cobba-Biney, "No Pastors Please!" *The Spectator*, April 21–27, 2007, 3.

49. Quoted in I. Motey, "Expose Corrupt Pastors, Church Leaders: Apostle Adotey Urges the Media," *The Spectator*, June 16, 2007, 23.

50. Quoted in D. Abugah, "'Arrest' Indiscipline among Pastors," *The Gospel Advocate*, October 28–November 10, 2007, 1.

51. Noah Twum Asamoah, interview by Dela Quampah, Accra, Ghana, May 22, 2007.

One area of criticism that Pentecostal ministers often react to is that of financial accountability and extravagant living. In a media report, Apostle Ekow Badu-Woode, General Secretary of the GPC, is said to have rejected any notions that the Pentecostal ministers are gold diggers: "The GPC has strongly refused the increasing criticism and perception among the media and the general public that charismatic churches are in church business for money."[52] Rev. Noah Twum is convinced that a minister is at liberty to enjoy genuinely acquired wealth.[53] Addressing the same issue from another perspective, Rev. Divine Nortey, National Crusade Director and Radio Pastor of Gospel Light International Church in Accra, insisted that ministers need strong four-wheel-drive vehicles to travel across the country and must maintain an appreciable living standard that would be respected by all people, including the wealthy.[54]

In an interview with Apostle Ekow Badu-Wood, he lamented that the challenges of unstable ministerial marriage, flamboyant dressing, and obsession with prosperity in general are undermining moral standards among Pentecostal ministers. According to Apostle Ekow Badu-Wood, the GPC has an Ethics Arbitration and Development Committee that addresses concerns surrounding the unethical conduct of ministers. However, he pointed out that this organization only deals with churches as a corporate body and does not get involved with individual ministers. As a result, the Ethics Arbitration and Development Committee is unable to take any action against pastors unless their denominations refer disciplinary cases to them.[55]

In response to the issue of negative media reports on Pentecostal leaders, Apostle Wood thinks although some of these reports may be true, the media frenzy seems to be characterized by sensationalism, so audiences should read these stories critically. He did admit that since the churches are divine-human institutions, we cannot rule out imperfection among church leaders. In his opinion, "the pastors come in various shades and colors—trained and untrained, called and uncalled."[56] He promised that the GPC

---

52. Daniel Abugah, "Church Business, Not Money Business, Says GPC Secretary," *The Gospel Advocate*, October 28–November 10, 2007, 1.

53. Noah Twum Asamoah, interview by Dela Quampah, Accra, Ghana, May 22, 2007.

54. Divine Nortey, Gospel Light International Church, interview by Dela Quampah, Accra, Ghana, May 3, 2008.

55. Ekow Badu-Wood, General Secretary, Ghana Pentecostal Council, interview by Dela Quampah, Accra, Ghana, on December 8, 2005.

56. Ibid.

is making efforts to educate and train its pastors in all aspects of ministry, including ministerial ethics.[57]

Among the many responses to the problem of ministerial misconduct is the strong suggestion from certain sections of society that the formation of churches should be regulated. Rev. Abamfo Atiemo, a minister of the Presbyterian Church of Ghana and lecturer at the Department for the Study of Religions at the University of Ghana, is of a different opinion. He thinks the church scene should not be regulated and is convinced that because secular institutions are not informed on religious matters, "Government should not be trusted with basic freedoms like the right of worship."[58] Rev. Atiemo is convinced that although religious faith should logically inform good behavior, this does not always happen. In his opinion, "Ethics and religious faith do not always converge."[59] He also rejects the idea of subjecting the control of the founding of new churches to existing denominational leaders.[60] Rev. Atiemo is convinced that such leaders would use their theological mindsets and denominational parameters to restrict fresh approaches to the expression of authentic Christian spirituality, thus undermining the essential principles of freedom of worship.

I am supportive of Rev. Atiemo's position, since attempts to regulate the Christian landscape would inevitably infringe on the constitutional provision of freedom of religion. Unless the emerging churches violate the Constitution of Ghana, they should be left alone to be self-critical, trusting that their internalization of moral values and their followers' moral assessments will help them keep up an appreciable standard of institutional regulation in ministerial ethics.

Conclusion

It is obvious that Pentecostal leaders have made a positive impact on Christianity and the wider Ghanaian society. Their sermons have rescued many youths and adults from profligate lifestyles and empowered them to pursue moral uprightness in channeling their resources into constructive ventures. The Christian education programs of such churches produce literature and messages that apply Christian principles to every dimension of life,

---

57. Ibid.

58. Abamfo Atiemo, Presbyterian Church of Ghana and University of Ghana Department for the Study of Religions, interview by Dela Quampah, Accra, Ghana, August 27, 2008.

59. Ibid.

60. J. Ackom Asante, "Maintaining Pastors Image," *The Spectator*, May 26, 2007, 4.

including family values that promote coherence and stability in society. The upwardly mobile youth among their following are encouraged to develop their talents and take advantage of opportunities for self-growth and community development. Furthermore, these churches have partnered with government to create jobs, build socio-economic infrastructure, and donate generously to alleviate the plight of vulnerable and marginalized members of society.

All these positive contributions notwithstanding, public opinion and media reports are fraught with accounts of unethical behavior of Pentecostal ministers. Church leaders are often presented as compromising on Christian moral standards by demonstrating greed and opulence, abusing power, trampling on human rights, assaulting those who provoke them, and sexually harassing women. Although some of these allegations have been proven to be true, in other cases, the stories seemed to have been published either out of sensationalism, commercial interest, or to settle personal scores.

I have also tried to establish that some Pentecostal ministers, operating within various institutional structures, have made efforts to address the issue of declining moral standards among their fold. Furthermore, it is gratifying to note that my fieldwork has generated data that reveals a high level of awareness of the practical moral problems among Pentecostal leaders. Some of the prominent leaders among them who engage with moral issues have responded by commenting on these problems in various forums and suggesting practical solutions. It is heartwarming to know that some of the ministers surveyed have also demonstrated a certain level of self-criticism. However, there appears to be an urgent need for such churches to give more attention to education on moral issues and to feature concerns for integrity and Christian character development in their sermons and literature more than they have ever done.

8

Summary, Conclusions, and Recommendations

Summary

THE SPHERE OF INFLUENCE of Pentecostal churches in shaping the future of Christianity in Ghana has become so significant that, beyond theological investigations, the phenomenon has attracted the attention of sociologists, historians, journalists, and even politicians. The movement has produced outstanding leaders, some of whose churches have become huge institutions of considerable international repute. However, public opinion, press reports, and insightful responses gathered from some church leaders and academicians seem to suggest that although the Pentecostal movement has made a general positive impact on Ghanaian society, serious concerns remain about low ethical standards among some church leaders.

I have examined the traditional domestic, communal, and religious institutions that provide the social context for the development of Ghanaian Pentecostal leadership in order to appreciate how indigenous value systems have influenced their ministerial ethics. Some of the concerns identified include issues of autocracy, human rights abuse, lack of equal opportunity, the promotion of superstition, and the injudicious use of material resources—problems that are reflected among Pentecostal ministers to various degrees.

The key concepts in moral philosophy, as well as the various theories that guide moral decision-making have been evaluated here for a more objective and logical assessment of the various value systems that Pentecostal ministers may express. It was, however, discovered that the level of awareness of key ethical concepts among the ministers surveyed seems to be rather limited. There appears to be a link between this low level of awareness of moral philosophy in traditional society and some Pentecostal ministers' attitudes toward the discipline of ethics. In certain cases, I discovered that some of these Christian leaders do not have well-defined or systematized ethical principles to guide their decisions and ministry. Consequently, their response to issues was mainly influenced by their relativist personal opinions.

In terms of institutional support, only a few of the churches surveyed offer any appreciable or comprehensive documented ministerial code of ethics. The portions of some of the church constitutions dealing with ministerial discipline capture useful principles of conduct that reflect positive obligation-based ethics. Nevertheless, the need to maintain institutional integrity has often been pursued at the expense of certain policies' impact on individuals. In some instances, concerns for utility, which considers the human impact of applied ethical principles, seem to have been neglected. The need for tolerance—a major strength of ethical relativity that recognizes individual differences as well as the tension between institutional demands and individual aspirations—is conspicuous in some of the institutional provisions. Furthermore, some of the churches studied overlook the fact that character development is a progressive process of learning that acknowledges human fallibility; consequently, they fail to develop adequate compassionate institutional responses to ministerial moral failure.

Of great concern is the response of the press and public opinion to Pentecostal ministerial ethics in Ghana. In many instances, the press may be commended for their diligent efforts in reporting the constructive contributions of the Pentecostal churches to society. Both print and electronic media often laud the social outreach projects undertaken by these churches to help the underprivileged in society. In addition the press also frequently publishes sermons, articles, and public pronouncements by some Pentecostal leaders with valuable moral import.

This constructive reportage notwithstanding, the press sometimes does irreparable damage to the public image of some ministers, for they often readily publish allegations of scandalous behavior without following the story through to establish the guilt or innocence of the individual involved. Evidently, the media hardly ever publishes retractions to redeem the reputation of such libeled church leaders, who in many cases would never pursue litigation to claim damages.

It has also emerged through this academic investigation that some of the negative opinions the public holds against Pentecostal ministers are either informed by superficial observations or based on exaggerated premises. My interactions with some of these ministers has revealed that the frequent accusations surrounding pastors fleecing their flocks and becoming excessively rich at their expense are not always true. Some such impressions tend to stem from overgeneralization and stereotyping, since the majority of the ministers seem to be honest employees who live on what their churches provide and many pastors struggle to make ends meet. In addition, my fieldwork has revealed that those who patronize the ministries of the Pentecostal leaders give overwhelmingly positive endorsements to their overall positive impact on society.

Nevertheless, the frequency of accusations of immoral behavior, such as misapplication of funds, and abuse of power should serve as a valuable awakening to churches. In some instances, reports of promiscuity, fraud, and violent behavior were discovered to be true. Some of the Pentecostal church administrative structures have also been identified as not being transparent enough, and those in supervisory roles need to be a little more objective and considerate in their dealings with subordinates. In view of the fact that Pentecostal church leaders are supposed to wield moral authority in order to inspire their followers and the wider society to aspire to high ethical standards, a single case of immoral behavior in their fold is one too many.

It is, however, necessary to mention that church leaders are not simply glossing over these concerns. Some have developed institutional structures that respond constructively to ministerial moral failure. And this is coupled with the fact that some ministers appear to be self-critical in consciously striving to approximate high ethical standards. However, the ministers in question may have to consider improving upon their male chauvinist image by offering equal opportunities to women to contribute to the development of the churches. In addition, there is a crying need for policies that hold individuals accountable for the use of church resources in order to curb the frequency of misapplication of funds.

Recommendations

The most plausible solution to some of these problems is likely to be a multidimensional approach deriving from both internal and external sources. Internally, there is a need for more self-evaluation by individual leaders, who may have to more effectively apply biblical moral standards and the principles of responsible decision-making. Secondly, I suggest that the leaders in question could enlist in ministers' associations in order to participate in peer review programs for moral accountability.

Externally, it would help if creative works in the arts and research findings on ministerial ethics could be encouraged in the academy in order to generate useful information for a progressive response to the conduct of Pentecostal leaders. Other strategies—perhaps in the form of social commentary expressed in drama, novels, films, songs, poetry, artwork, and media reports—that praise the positive aspects of Pentecostal leadership and criticize its failures can also make an impact in helping improve ethical behavior in ministry. The recent initiative of His Excellency John Agyekum Kuffour's government in conferring national awards on some outstanding Pentecostal leaders[1] is a laudable effort that will likely motivate other pastors to strive for resourcefulness and moral excellence in ministry. The Ghana Pentecostal Council and other Pentecostal umbrella organizations can take a cue from this action and institute awards to inspire and encourage moral distinction in ministry.

More specifically, umbrella organizations such as the GPC and NACCC have to play more prominent supervisory roles to maintain high moral standards among their ministers. In addition, church leaders can submit themselves to evaluation by their colleagues and other leaders for useful feedback. Furthermore, the need to produce comprehensive documented ministerial ethical codes has to be addressed by many churches in order to provide justification for commending exemplary moral conduct and holding those violating the code accountable (see Appendix 5 for a sample).

Finally, empowering the lay congregation members with information on certain administrative, theological, and ethical issues would help protect them and limit their vulnerability to the schemes of charlatan Pentecostal ministers. This strategy can be enhanced by involving a well-informed laity in church leadership that can contribute meaningfully to the policies that define their institutional structures and respond comprehensively to ministerial ethical concerns.

---

1. Some such ministers who have received the Order of the Volta are Bishop Charles Agyin-Asare, Pastor Mensah Otabil, and Apostle Dr. Michael K. Ntumy.

Appendix 1

Apostolic Church Ghana End-of-Year Performance Review Form For Year: ....

1. Name of Pastor: ....
   A. Staff No.: ....
   B. District: ....
   C. Area: ....
   D. Local: ....

2. Assessment of Employee

Objective	Standards/Factors	Score	Comment
1.	Quality of work Work output Teamwork Human Relations Time Consciousness Initiative Subtotal		
2.	Quality of work Work output Teamwork Human Relations Time Consciousness Initiative Subtotal		
3.	Quality of work Work output Teamwork Human Relations Time Consciousness Initiative Subtotal		

4.	Quality of work Work output Teamwork Human Relations Time Consciousness Initiative Subtotal		
Average Total			

3. Comments and Recommendations on Performance by District Pastor:

....
....
....
....
....

4. Discuss and agree on the specific objectives for the coming year. These objectives must adhere to the SMARTER rules: Specific, Measurable, Agreed, Realistic, Time-bound, Enjoyable, Recorded.

Main Objectives	Targets	Main Standards
Objective 1:		
Objective 2:	1. 3. 4.	
Objective, 3:	1. 2. 3. 4.	
Objective 4:	1. 2. 3. 4.	

A. The training and development support to be given to help the appraisee meet the agreed objectives above:
....
....
....
....
....

Name and Signature: ....

Date: ....

5. Comments and Recommendations by Area Apostle:
....
....
....
....
....

Name and Signature: ....

Date: ....

6. Comments from Head Office (if any):
....
....
....
....
....

Name and Signature: ....

Date: ....

7. Comments by Pastor (Appraisee)
....
....
....
....
....

Name and Signature: ....

Date: ....

Appendix 2

Church of Pentecost Ministers Appraisal Form

Part A (To be completed by Regional/Area/National Head)

Name of Minister: ....

Region/Area: ....

Any Official Duties: ....

Present Status:
    Probationary Overseer/Overseer/Pastor/Apostle/Prophet

Previous Station: ....

Present Station: ....

Date Called: .... Age/Date of Birth: ....

Date of Appointment to Present Status: ....

Other Appointments: ....

Period of Assessment: From: .... To: ....

Key to Grading
[1] Excellent
[2] Very Good
[3] Good
[4] Average
[5] Below Average

Appendix 2

1. Knowledge of work (i.e., understanding of ministerial calling) [1] [2] [3] [4] [5]
2. Initiative and creativity (i.e., understanding or developing ideas and getting things done) [1] [2] [3] [4] [5]
3. Application and industry (i.e., carefulness and continuous attention to work, attendance at meetings, call, etc.) [1] [2] [3] [4] [5]
4. Quantity of work (i.e., retreats/conventions/seminars/rallies held, evangelism, discipling, leadership training) [1] [2] [3] [4] [5]
5. Quality (i.e., thoroughness and accuracy of work) . [1] [2] [3] [4] [5]
6. Supervisory skill (i.e., ability to oversee others' work) [1] [2] [3] [4] [5]
7. Integrity (i.e., extent to which he could be trusted with church resources, e.g., money, property, etc.) [1] [2] [3] [4] [5]
8. Oral and written expression [1] [2] [3] [4] [5]
9. Cooperation:
a) Willingness to work together with or support others
b) Relationship with presbytery [1] [2] [3] [4] [5]
10. Conduct (i.e., friendly, too reserved, indifferent) (Underline the one suitable.) [1] [2] [3] [4] [5]
11. Effective visitation to assemblies in the year [1] [2] [3] [4] [5]
12. How well he manages his family [1] [2] [3] [4] [5]
13. Health (i.e., emotional stability, physical condition and appearance, doctor's report, if any, and environmental cleanliness) [1] [2] [3] [4] [5]
14. Care of Church property [1] [2] [3] [4] [5]
15. Alertness to problem solving (i.e., ability to recognize or anticipate problem situations) [1] [2] [3] [4] [5]
16. Leadership ability (i.e., promptness of action, soundness of decisions, application of good shepherding principles) [1] [2] [3] [4] [5]
17. Personal spiritual development [1] [2] [3] [4] [5]
18. Overall Rating [1] [2] [3] [4] [5]

Statistics

State Number of:	On Assumption of Duty:	Year of Assessment:
Membership	Date	20 ....
Assemblies/Districts		
Converts (Baptized)		
Officers (Ordained)		
Children Dedicated		
Church Building(s) (in-progress/completed)		
Mission Houses (in-progress/completed)		
Tithes		
Missionary Offering		

Activities: Number of Retreats, Conventions, Rallies, etc., Held:

....

19. Spiritual/Moral Life (Your candid assessment; use additional paper if necessary):

....
....
....
....
....

20. Natural Gifting:

....
....
....
....
....

21. Spiritual Gifting:

....
....
....
....
....

22. Potential for Further Development (State further observations and areas where development/training is required; use additional paper if necessary):

....
....
....
....
....

23. Comment on frequency of presence at or absence with/without permission from duty station (Use additional paper if necessary):

....
....
....
....
....

24. Retirement due to:
    a. Age
    b. Health

25. Termination due to health, inefficiency, misconduct, etc.

Head's Name: ....

Signature: ....

Date: ....

26. The Minister:

I have read this report and agree with the views expressed above.

Minister's Signature: ....

Date: ....

Head's Recommendation after Interview with Minister:

Strictly Confidential: (Not to be shown or communicated to Minister)
Would you recommend him for:
Change of Status: [Yes]   [No]

To:
1. Full Overseer
2. Pastor
3. Area Head
4. Missionary
5. Etc.

Name of Head of Region/Area: ....

Status: ....

Signature: ....

Date: ....

(Official Stamp)

For Office Use

1. Further Training (Recommended/Not Recommended)
2. Higher Calling   [Yes]   [No]

Present Grade: ....

Recommended Grade: ....

With Effect from: ....

Approved/Not Approved by: ....

Date: ....

Chairman/Executive Council: ....

Appendix 3

Model Ministerial Code of Ethics of Grace Community Churches by Dela Quampah

Preamble

HAVING RESPONDED POSITIVELY TO God's call to a ministry that transforms sinners into saints, I acknowledge that the core issue of Christianity is character development. I also recognize that the greatest asset of Christian leaders is their testimony. Therefore, guided by this declaration of Jesus, "But seek first his kingdom and his righteousness" (Matt 6:33), I will prioritize moral uprightness above all other concerns in life and ministry. I will strive to develop a personal value system that is based on scriptural principles, guided by love, and inspired by the Holy Spirit. I will also search church history and society for lessons from moral exemplars. However, being conscious of the complexity of contemporary moral issues, I will study ethics in order to make informed and responsible choices that adhere to high Christian moral standards in every decision-making process.

Philosophy of Ministry

I declare my foundational principle in ministry as being called by God to serve the best interest of God's people from God's perspective.

Duty to God

1. I acknowledge the Holy Spirit as my resource-base and recognize my absolute dependence on him for the character development, vision, and ability needed for success in ministry.

2. I will endeavor throughout my life and ministry to nurture a vibrant personal relationship with God through devotional activities such as prayer, meditation, fasting, intensive Bible study, reading inspired Christian literature, fellowship with other believers, and listening to other preachers.

3. I will confess all known sins in my life and endeavor to avoid any acts of wilful disobedience that might grieve the Holy Spirit and obstruct my smooth communication with God.

Personal

1. I will maintain a healthy body by avoiding psychotropic substances such as alcohol, cigarettes, and hard drugs. I will also cultivate healthy eating habits and get adequate exercise as well as optimum rest. I will submit to regular comprehensive medical examinations, take medical prescriptions appropriately, and respond positively to medical advice.

2. I will study to keep abreast with the religious thoughts of the day and keep pace with the challenges of contemporary socio-cultural, political, economic, scientific, and technological issues.

3. I will maintain a high standard of integrity by constantly endeavoring to be pure in thought, transparent in motive, and truthful in speech. I will do my best to keep my word and honor every promise I make.

4. I will place service above money, personal gain, or recognition. I will never manipulate or coerce anyone for financial or material benefit.

5. I will avoid gambling and any shady financial transaction that could tarnish my testimony and ministry.

6. I will strive to live within my means, avoid impulsive buying, and resist the tendency to accumulate unmanageable debts.

Ministry

1. I will seek to serve rather than to be served, and place the welfare of the church above my own personal interests.

2. I will avoid insinuations or exaggeration in my sermons and acknowledge the sources of my information in all honesty.

3. I will promote character development and moral transformation in my congregants by giving due attention to the concepts of holiness, righteousness, and sanctification in both my conduct and communication.
4. I will protect the integrity of my local church and denomination and avoid making unguarded statements about its institutional structure.
5. I will use authority responsibly and try to overcome the attitudes that lead to power abuse, obsession with titles, and a penchant for status symbols.
6. I will appreciate my colleagues in ministry and desist from making disparaging remarks about other Christian leaders.
7. I will respect the rights of other people and avoid discrimination against women, children, and the vulnerable.
8. I will respect people of other tribes, religions, and political affiliations and always be careful not to demonstrate tribalism, fanaticism, partisan politics, or any such divisive attitudes.
9. I will resist any form of destructive superstition that is quick to brand people as witches or wizards and also avoid the indiscriminate branding of objects or locations as demonic.
10. I will regard information received during counselling as sacred and never disclose it, unless to prevent harm to another person or as requested by a court of law.

Relationships

1. I will love, honor, and give my spouse the deserved attention, being always careful not to expose him or her to public ridicule.
2. I will care for and protect every member of my household and discipline them with a loving touch.
3. I will treat the opposite sex with courtesy and decorum and avoid any form of promiscuous behavior.
4. I will cultivate the values of humility, patience, tolerance, and appreciation to promote healthy relationships.
5. I will endeavor to resolve conflicts and maintain a healthy group atmosphere both at home and in ministry.
6. I will express special interest in the welfare of the weak and vulnerable and do my best to help alleviate their suffering.

Appendix 4

Questionnaire on the Ethical Dimension of Pentecostal/Charismatic Church Leadership in Ghana

DELA QUAMPAH IS EXAMINING reports on the conduct of Pentecostal/charismatic leaders in Ghana and would be grateful if you could spare some time to respond to the following questions. It is envisioned that your thoughts on these issues would be useful in shaping people's thinking concerning such church leaders. You are kindly requested to express your candid opinion on each question. Since this work is for academic purposes, strict confidentiality is assured.

A. Personal Information on the Respondent

1. Sex:

M
F

2. Age (Tick the appropriate box below):

15–30	31–45	46–60	61–75	76–90

3. Level of Education:
   Junior High School
   Senior High School
   Tertiary
   Other: ....

4. Religion:
   Christian
   Islam
   African
   Traditional
   Others: ....

5. If Christian, please provide denomination:
   Roman Catholic
   Methodist
   Presbyterian
   Pentecostal
   Charismatic
   Baptist
   Other: ....
   Name of Church: ....

B. Knowledge about the Minister

6. Please name the Pentecostal/charismatic minister you want to assess:
   ....

   a. What is the name of his or her church?
   ....

   b. Where is it located?
   ....

7. How did you get to know him or her?

   a. Personal contact ....

   b. In the media ....

   c. Other ....

8. For how long have you known him or her?
   ....

C. Assessment

Ministry

9. Has his or her preaching been beneficial to you in any way?

Yes	No	Not sure

a. If yes:

　　i. Has he or she helped change your behavior for the better?

　　..

　　ii. Has his or her preaching helped improve your relationship with others?

　　..

　　iii. Has his or her preaching inspired you to do something constructive?

　　..

10. Does he or she preach a lot about demons and witchcraft?

Yes	No	Not sure

11. Has he or she ever accused anyone of witchcraft?

Yes	No	Not sure

a. What do you personally feel about witchcraft accusations?

....

Relationships

12. Does he or she respect other people?

Yes	No	Not sure

13. Does he or she receive people and communicate well with them?

Yes	No	Not sure

14. Does he or she handle confidential information with care?

Yes	No	Not sure

15. Does he or she relate to the opposite sex with decency?

Yes	No	Not sure

16. Do you think his or her leadership style is democratic? (Does he or she seek the views of others?)

Yes	No	Not sure

17. Does the minister you know appreciate material gifts from church members?

Yes	No	Not sure

Attitude to Money and Possessions

18. Do you think he or she has expensive habits in terms of dress code, vehicles, and accommodation?

Yes	No	Not sure

   a. You may please explain your answer to question 18:

   ....
   ....
   ....
   ....
   ....

19. Does he or she manipulate church members for money or property for personal use?

Yes	No	Not sure

20. Does he or she use fundraising methods that you think are unacceptable?

Yes	No	Not sure

a. If yes, kindly describe some of the methods:
....
....
....
....
....

D. General Information on Pentecostal/Charismatic Churches

21. Do you know of a Pentecostal/charismatic minister who practices tribalism?

Yes	No	Not sure

22. Do you know of any Pentecostal/charismatic minister who was involved in sexual immorality?

Yes	No	Not sure

23. Do you know any Pentecostal/charismatic minister who has embezzled church funds or cheated someone out of money or property?

Yes	No	Not sure

24. Have you ever received a prophetic word from a Pentecostal/Charismatic minister? ....

   a. If yes, what kind of message?
   ....
   ....
   ....
   ....
   ....

   b. Do you find the message meaningful?
   ....
   ....
   ....
   ....
   ....

25. Do you know about anyone who has been misled by a prophet?

Yes	No	Not sure

26. Do you agree with the suggestion that women should be ordained as Pentecostal/charismatic ministers?

Yes	No	Not sure

   a. Please give reasons for your answer to question 26:
   ....
   ....
   ....
   ....
   ....

27. Do you consider any particular Pentecostal/Charismatic minister a good example to society?

Yes	No	Not sure

   a. If yes, please provide his/her name: ....

28. What are your general comments on Pentecostal/Charismatic ministers?
   ....
   ....
   ....
   ....
   ....

Thanks a lot for your time!

Bibliography

Abotchie, Chris. *Social Control in Traditional Southern Eweland of Ghana: Relevance for Modern Crime Prevention*. 1997. Reprint, Accra, Ghana: Ghana Universities Press, 2002.

Ackah, C. A. *Akan Ethics: A Study of the Moral Ideas and the Moral Behaviour of the Akan Tribes of Ghana*. Accra, Ghana: Ghana Universities Press, 1988.

Adesina, T. L. *Secession within the Charismatic Churches: Causes and Possible Solutions*. Accra, Ghana: Livingwaters, 2007.

Agyeman-Nkansah, Kwabena. "Deeping the Roots of Christianity in the African Culture through Increased Awareness of the African Identity and Self-Perception." *Maranatha Journal of Theology and Ministry* 1 (2005) 32–42.

Agyin-Asare, Charles. *Pastoral Protocol: A Guide to Ministerial Ethics*. Maitland, FL: Xulon, 2004.

———. *Celebrating the Pilgrimage of Life: The First Forty Years*. n.p.: privately printed, 2002. Copies available from Word Miracle Church International at Perez Chapel International headquarters in Accra, Ghana, http://www.perezchapel.org/6/e-shop.

Akoto, Dorothy. "Religion, Morality and West African Society: A General Overview with a Backdrop in Traditional Religion." In *Religion, Morality and West African Society: Proceedings of the West African Association of Theological Institutions (WAATI) Biennial Conference Held at the Nigerian Baptist Theological Seminary, Ogbomoso, Nigeria, from Sunday, 30th July to Saturday, 5th August 2000*, edited by Joshua N. Kudadjie et al., 83–99. Accra, Ghana: West African Association of Theological Institutions, 2002.

Akoto, Peace Aku. *Ghana: Church Guide and Effective Shepherding*. Tema, Ghana: Smile, n.d.

Akrong, Abraham A. "Religion and Traditional Leadership in Ghana." In *Chieftaincy in Ghana: Culture, Governance, and Development*, edited by Irene K. Odotei and A. K. Awedoba, 193–212. Culture and Development Series 1. Accra, Ghana: Sub-Saharan, 2006.

Allen, Reginald E. *Plato's "Euthyphro" and the Earlier Theory of Forms*. London: Routledge, 1970.

Amankwaa, Alex Ofori. *Assemblies of God Sunday School Prospective Teachers Course*. Accra, Ghana: Assemblies of God Literature Centre, n.d.

Anderson, Allan. *An Introduction to Pentecostalism*. Cambridge: Cambridge University Press, 2004.

———. "The Prosperity Message in the Eschatology of Some New Charismatic Churches." *Missionalia* 15 (1987) 72–83.

Anderson, Robert C. *The Effective Pastor*. Chicago: Moody, 1985.

Anim, Emmanuel. "The Prosperity Gospel in Ghana and the Primal Imagination." Presentation at the Langham-Lausanne Conference on Prosperity Teaching in Ghanaian Charismatic Churches at the Akrofi-Christaller Institute of Theology, Mission and Culture, Akropong, Ghana, October 6–10, 2008.

———. "The Prosperity Gospel in Ghana and the Primal Imagination." *Trinity Journal of Church and Theology* 2 (2009) 30–53.

———. "Who Wants to Be a Millionaire? An Analysis of Prosperity Teaching in the Charismatic Ministries (Churches) in Ghana and Its Wider Impact." PhD diss., All Nations Christian College, 2003.

Anscombe, Elizabeth. "Modern Moral Philosophy." *Philosophy* 33 (1958) 1–19.

"Archbishop's Divorce Rocks Action Chapel." *Ghana Web*, June 30, 2005. Accessed March 8, 2012. http://www.ghanaweb.com/GhanaHomePage/NewsArchive/artikel.php?ID=84859.

Aristotle. *Nicomachean Ethics*. Translated by David Ross. Oxford: Oxford University Press, 1987.

Asamoah-Gyadu, Kwabena J. *African Charismatics: Current Developments within Independent Indigenous Pentecostalism in Ghana*. Studies of Religion in Africa 27. Leiden: Brill Academic, 2004.

———. "'Christ Is the Answer': What Is the Question? A Ghana Airways Prayer Vigil and Its Implications for Religion, Evil and Public Space." *Journal of Religion in Africa* 35 (2005) 93–117.

———. "The Church in the African State: The Pentecostal Charismatic Experience in Ghana." *Journal of African Christian Thought* 1 (1998) 63–81.

———. "Pentecostalism and the Missiological Significance of Religious Experience: The Case of Ghana's 'Church of Pentecost.'" *Trinity Journal of Church and Theology* 12 (2002) 30–57.

———. "Salvation in African Independent Churches and Charismatic Ministries in Ghana." *Trinity Journal of Church and Theology* 2 (1992) 84–98.

———. "'The Way to Pentecost Is Calvary': Martin Luther, the Cross and African Neo-Pentecostalism." *Trinity Journal of Church and Theology* 2 (2009) 69–82.

Asem, E. K., ed. *A History of the Church of Pentecost*. Vol. 1. Accra, Ghana: Pentecost, 2005.

Assimeng, Max. *Saints and Social Structures*. Tema, Ghana: Ghana Publishing, 1986.

———. "Some Reflections on Miracles, Divine Provenance, and Political Economy." *Legon Journal of Sociology* 1 (2004) 117–31.

———. *Understanding Society: An Introduction to Sociology for African Students*. Vol. 87. Accra, Ghana: Woeli, 2006.

Atiemo, Abamfo O. "Deliverance in the Charismatic Churches in Ghana." *Trinity Journal of Church and Theology* 4 (1994) 39–40.

Austin, Michael W. "Divine Command Theory." *Internet Encyclopaedia of Philosophy*. Accessed November 13, 2011. http://www.iep.utm.edu/divine-c/.

Awolalu, J. Omosade, and P. Adelumo Dopamu. *West African Traditional Religion*. Ibadan, Nigeria: Onibonoje, 1979.

Baëta, C. G. *Prophetism in Ghana*. Achimota, Ghana: African Christian, 2004.

Bailey, Tom. "Analysing the Good Will: Kant's Argument in the First Section of the Groundwork." *British Journal for the History of Philosophy* 18 (2010) 635–62.

Barclay, William. *The Gospel of Matthew*. The Daily Study Bible 1. Edinburgh: Saint Andrew's, 1997.

Barnette, Henlee H. *Introducing Christian Ethics*. Nashville: Broadman, 1961.

Barrett, David B., and Todd M. Johnson. "Annual Statistical Table on Global Mission: 1999." *International Bulletin of Missionary Research* 23 (1999).

Barth, Karl. *The Doctrine of the Word of God*. Vol. 1 of *Church Dogmatics*. Edited by G. W. Bromiley and T. F. Torrance. Edinburgh: T. & T. Clark, 1956.

Bassett, Paul Merritt. "Pentecostalism." *Believe Religious Information Source*. Accessed October 10, 2005. http://mb-soft.com/believe/txc/pentecos.htm.
Bayles, Michael. *Professional Ethics*. 2nd ed. Belmont, CA: Wadsworth, 1989.
Bediako, Kwame. *Jesus in Africa: The Christian Gospel in African History and Experience*. Theological Reflections from the South. Yaoundé, Cameroon: Editions Clé, 2000.
Benedict, Saint. *The Rule of Saint Benedict in English*. Edited by Timothy Fry and Imogene Baker. Collegeville: Liturgical, 1982.
Bentham, Jeremy. *An Introduction to the Principles of Morals and Legislation*. Edited by J. H. Burns and H. L. A. Hart. Oxford: Clarendon, 1970.
Betz, Hans Dieter. *Galatians: A Commentary on Paul's Letter to the Churches in Galatia*. Hermeneia. Philadelphia: Fortress, 1979.
Bevans, Stephen B. *Models of Contextual Theology*. Maryknoll, NY: Orbis, 2008.
Bonino, José Míguez. "Changing Paradigms: A Response." In *The Globalization of Pentecostalism: A Religion Made to Travel*, edited by Murray W. Dempster et al., 116–23. Oxford: Regnum, 1999.
Bosch, David Jacobus. *Transforming Mission: Paradigm Shift in Theology of Mission*. American Society of Theology of Missiology Series. Maryknoll, NY: Orbis, 2008.
Bridges, James K. "Introduction: The Pastor's Personal Life." In *The Pentecostal Pastor: A Mandate for the 21st Century*, edited by Thomas E. Trask et al., 105–109. Springfield, MO: Gospel, 2000.
Brown, Montague. *Restoration of Reason: The Eclipse and Recovery of Truth, Goodness, and Beauty*. Grand Rapids: Baker Academic, 2006.
Brueggman, Walter. *Theology of the Old Testament: Testimony, Dispute, Advocacy*. Minneapolis: Fortress, 1997.
Busia, K. A. "The Ashanti of the Gold Coast." In *African Worlds: Studies in the Cosmological Ideas and Social Values of African Peoples*, edited by Cyril Daryll Forde, 190–209. Oxford: Oxford University Press, 1976.
Cairns, Earl Edwin. *Christianity through the Centuries: A History of the Christian Church*. Grand Rapids: Zondervan, 1996.
Camenisch, Paul F. "Clergy Ethics and the Professional Ethics Model." In *Clergy Ethics in a Changing Society: Mapping the Terrain*, edited by James Wind et al., 114–34. Louisville: Westminster John Knox, 1991.
Chadwick, Henry. *The Early Church*. Harmondsworth, UK: Penguin, 1969.
Charlesworth, Max J. *Philosophy and Religion: From Plato to Postmodernism*. Oxford: Oneworld, 2002.
Children's Rights International Executive Director. "Ghana and the Dawn of 50: The Language of Judiciary in Children's Rights." *Ghana Broadcasting News Commentary*, January 23, 2007. Accessed January 31, 2007. http://www.thinkghana.com/tools/printnews/news.php?contentid=2276.
Chittister, Joan. *The Rule of Benedict: Insights for the Ages*. Spiritual Legacy Series. New York: Crossroad, 2005.
Church of God International Offices. "Declaration of Faith." *Church of God*. Accessed February 19, 2013. http://www.churchofgod.org/beliefs/declaration-of-faith.
Coetzee, Pieter H. "Morality in African Thought: Particularity in Morality and Its Relation to Community." In *The African Philosophy Reader*, edited by P. H. Coetzee and A. P. J. Roux, 321–401. London: Routledge, 2003.
Conner, Kevin J. *The Church in the New Testament*. Chichester, UK: Sovereign World, 1989.

Constitution of the Presbyterian Church of Ghana. Rev. ed. Accra, Ghana: Waterville, 2004.

Constitution of the Church of Pentecost. Accra, Ghana: Pentecost Press, 2005.

Cook, David. *The Moral Maze: A Way of Exploring Christian Ethics.* London: Society for Promoting Christian Knowledge, 1997.

Dankwa, Oseadeeyo Addo, III. *The Institution of Chieftaincy in Ghana—The Future.* Accra, Ghana: Gold-Type, 2004.

Danquah, J. B. *The Akan Doctrine of God: A Fragment of Gold Coast Ethics and Religion.* London: Cass, 1968.

Davies, W. D. "Ethics in the New Testament." In vol. 2 of *Interpreter's Dictionary of the Bible*, edited by George Arthur Buttrick, 167–76. Nashville: Abingdon, 1962.

Dayton, Donald W. *Theological Roots of Pentecostalism.* Metuchen, NJ: Hendrickson, 1996.

Deh, K. K., and E. L. Adjei. *Life Story of Rev. Christopher Atta Titriku.* Ho, Ghana: Dickwin, 2007.

De Wille, Marleen. "Altar Media's 'Living Word': Televised Charismatic Christianity in Ghana." *Journal of Religion in Africa* 33 (2003) 172–202.

Dibelius, Martin. *A Fresh Approach to the New Testament and Early Christian Literature.* London: Nicholson & Watson, 1936.

Dovlo, Elom. "A Comparative Overview of Independent Churches and Charismatic Ministries in Ghana." *Trinity Journal of Church and Theology* 2 (1992) 55–73.

———. "The Proliferation of Churches: Its Impact on Established Churches in Ghana." *Maranatha Journal of Theology and Ministry* 1 (2005) n.p.

Driver, Julia. "The History of Utilitarianism." *The Stanford Encyclopedia of Philosophy.* Edited by Edward N. Zalta. Stanford, CA: Stanford University Metaphysics Research Lab, 2011. Accessed November 11, 2011. http://plato.stanford.edu/archives/sum2009/entries/utilitarianism-history/.

Duncan-Williams, Francisca. *Reflections: The Untold Story.* Accra, Ghana: Action Faith, 2002.

Dzobo, N. K. "Values in a Changing Society: Man, Ancestors and God." In *Person and Community: Ghanaian Philosophical Studies I*, edited by Kwasi Wiredu and Kwame Gyekye, 223–42. Cultural Heritage and Contemporary Change Africa 1. Washington, DC: Council for Research in Values and Philosophy, 1992.

Earle, Ralph. *1, 2 Timothy.* Vol. 11 of *The Expositor's Bible Commentary with the New International Version of the Holy Bible.* Edited by Frank E. Gaebelein. Grand Rapids: Zondervan, 1981.

Ekem, John David Kwamena. "Fulfilling Your Ministry: Some Biblical Reflections." *Trinity Journal of Church and Theology* 15 (2005) 26–33.

———. *Priesthood in Context: A Study of Priesthood in Some Christian and Primal Communities of Ghana, and its Relevance for Mother-Tongue Biblical Interpretation.* Accra, Ghana: SonLife, 2009.

Encyclopædia Britannica Online, s. v. "teleological ethics." Accessed January 03, 2014. http://www.britannica.com/EBchecked/topic/585940/teleological-ethics.

Feinberg, Charles L. "Jeremiah." Vol. 6 of *The Expositor's Bible Commentary with the New International Version of the Holy Bible.* Edited by Frank E. Gaebelein. Grand Rapids: Zondervan, 1986.

Feinberg, John S., and Paul D. Feinberg. *Ethics for a Brave New World.* Wheaton, IL: Crossway, 1993.

Fletcher, Joseph F. *Situation Ethics: The New Morality.* Philadelphia: Westminster, 1966.
Folarin, George O. "Prosperity Gospel in Nigeria: A Re-examination of the Concept, Impact, and Evaluation." *African Journal of Biblical Studies* 33 (2006) 79–97.
Frempong, Alexander K. D. "Chieftaincy, Democracy and Human Rights in Pre-Colonial Africa: The Case of the Akan System." In *Chieftaincy in Ghana: Culture, Governance and Development,* edited by Irene K. Odotei and A. K. Awedoba, 379–94. Accra, Ghana: Sub-Saharan, 2006.
Frend, W. H. C. *The Donatist Church: A Movement of Protest in Roman North Africa.* Oxford: Clarendon, 1952.
Freyne, Séan. "The Bible and Christian Morality." In *Introduction to Christian Ethics: A Reader,* edited by Ronald P. Hamel and Kenneth R. Himes, 9–32. New York: Paulist, 1989.
Fuchs, Josef. "The Absoluteness of Behavioral Moral Norms." In *Introduction to Christian Ethics: A Reader,* edited by Ronald P. Hamel and Kenneth R. Himes, 487–512. New York: Paulist, 1989.
Ganusah, Rebecca Yawa. *Christ Meets the Ewe-Dome of Ghana: A Theological Reflection on the Rites of Birth and Initiation into Womanhood.* Ecclesial Studies 5. Legon-Accra, Ghana: Legon Theological Studies, 2008.
———. "Community Versus Individual Rights in Africa: A Viewpoint." *Legon Journal of Humanities* 15 (2004) 1–21.
———. "The Impact of Religion on Morality in West Africa." In *Religion, Morality and West African Society: Proceedings of the West African Association of Theological Institutions (WAATI) Biennial Conference Held at the Nigerian Baptist Theological Seminary, Ogbomoso, Nigeria, from Sunday, 30th July to Saturday, 5th August 2000,* edited by Joshua N. Kudadjie et al., 69–82. Accra, Ghana: Wesley, 2002.
Geisler, Norman L., and Paul D. Feinberg. *Introduction to Philosophy: A Christian Perspective.* Grand Rapids: Baker, 2001.
Ghana Statistical Service. *2000 Population and Housing Census, Summary Report of Final Results.* Accra, Ghana: Ghana Statistical Service, 2002.
Gifford, Paul. "Ghana's Charismatic Churches." *Journal of Religion in Africa* 24 (1994) 241–65.
———. *Ghana's New Christianity: Pentecostalism in a Globalising African Economy.* Bloomington: Indiana University Press, 2004.
Gilkey, Langdon. "Forgotten Traditions in the Clergy's Self-Understanding." In *Clergy Ethics in a Changing Society: Mapping the Terrain,* edited by James P. Wind et al., 37–53. Louisville: Westminster John Knox, 1991.
Green, Ronald Michael. "Religion and Morality in the African Traditional Setting." *Journal of Religion in Africa* 14 (1983) 1–23.
Grenz, Stanley J. *The Moral Quest: Foundations of Christian Ethics.* Downers Grove, IL: InterVarsity, 1997.
Grunlan, Stephan A., and Marvin Keene Mayers. *Cultural Anthropology: A Christian Perspective.* Grand Rapids: Zondervan, 1988.
Gula, Richard M. *Ethics in Pastoral Ministry.* New York: Paulist, 1996.
Gyekye, Kwame. *African Cultural Values: An Introduction.* Accra, Ghana: Sankofa, 1998.
———. "African Ethics." *The Stanford Encyclopedia of Philosophy.* Edited by Edward N. Zalta. Stanford, CA: Stanford University Metaphysics Research Lab, 2011. Accessed July 21, 2011. http://plato.stanford.edu/entries/african-ethics/.

———. *An Essay on African Philosophical Thought: The Akan Conceptual Scheme*. Cambridge: Cambridge University Press, 1987.

———. "Person and Community in Akan Thought." In *Person and Community: Ghanaian Philosophical Studies I*, edited by Kwasi Wiredu and Kwame Gyekye, 101–122. Cultural Heritage and Contemporary Change Africa 1. Washington, DC: Council for Research in Values and Philosophy, 1992.

———. "Spiritual and Moral Leadership: The Role of Theological Institutions." *Trinity Journal of Church and Theology* 15 (2005) 34–40.

———. *The Unexamined Life: Philosophy and the African Experience*. Legon, Ghana: Sankofa, 2004.

Hackett, Rosalind I. J. "Charismatic/Pentecostal Appropriation of Media Technologies in Nigeria and Ghana." *Journal of Religion in Africa* 28 (1998) 258–77.

Hagan, G. P. "Epilogue: The Way Forward—New Wines and Broken Bottles." In *Chieftaincy in Ghana: Culture, Governance and Development*, edited by Irene K. Odotei and A. K. Awedoba, 663–74. Accra, Ghana: Sub-Saharan, 2006.

Harmon, Nolan B. *Ministerial Ethics and Etiquette*. Rev. ed. Nashville: Abingdon, 1978.

Harris, R. Laird. "Leviticus." Vol. 2 of *The Expositor's Bible Commentary with the New International Version of the Holy Bible*. Edited by Frank E. Gaebelein. Grand Rapids: Zondervan, 1990.

Hays, Richard B. *The Moral Vision of the New Testament: Community, Cross, New Creation: A Contemporary Introduction to New Testament Ethics*. Edinburgh: T. & T. Clark, 1996.

Heward-Mills, Dag. *Ministerial Ethics: Practical Wisdom for Christian Ministers*. Iselin, NJ: DgTP, 1998.

Hinman, Lawrence M. *Ethics: A Pluralistic Approach to Moral Theory*. Belmont, CA: Thomson Wadsworth, 2003.

Hollenweger, Walter J. *Pentecostalism: Origins and Developments*. Peabody, MA: Hendrickson, 1997.

———. *The Pentecostals*. London: SCM, 1972.

Horton, Stanley M. "The Pentecostal Perspective." In *Five Views on Sanctification*, edited by Melvin E. Dieter et al., 103–135. Grand Rapids: Zondervan, 1987.

Hughes, Phillips Edgcumbe. *Christian Ethics in Secular Society*. Grand Rapids: Baker, 1983.

Idowu, Emanuel Bolaji. *African Traditional Religion: A Definition*. London: SCM: 1973.

Johns, Jackie David. "Yielding to the Spirit: The Dynamics of a Pentecostal Model of Praxis." In *The Globalisation of Pentecostalism: A Religion Made to Travel*, edited by Murray W. Dempster, Byron D. Klaus, and Douglas Peterson, 70–84. Oxford: Regnum, 1999.

Johnson, Robert. "Kant's Moral Philosophy." *The Stanford Encyclopedia of Philosophy*. Edited by Edward N. Zalta. Stanford, CA: Stanford University Metaphysics Research Lab, 2013. Accessed October 19, 2011. http://plato.stanford.edu/entries/kant-moral/.

Jones, Richard G. *Groundwork of Christian Ethics*. London: Epworth, 1984.

Kaiser, Walter C. *Toward Old Testament Ethics*. Grand Rapids: Zondervan, 1983.

Kalu, Ogbu. *African Pentecostalism: An Introduction*. Oxford: Oxford University Press, 2008.

———. "Shape and Identity in Contemporary African Church Historiography." *Trinity Journal of Church and Theology* 12 (2002) 1–22.

———. "Yabbing the Pentecostals: Paul Gifford's Image of Ghana's New Christianity." *Trinity Journal of Church and Theology* 15 (2005) 3–25.
Kant, Immanuel. *Ethical Philosophy: The Complete Texts of Grounding for the Metaphysics of Morals and Metaphysical Principles of Virtue*. Translated by James W. Ellington, Indianapolis: Hackett, 1983.
———. *The Moral Law*. Translated by H. J. Paton. Senior Series. London: Hutchinson's University Library, 1956.
Kidner, Derek. *The Wisdom of Proverbs, Job, and Ecclesiastes: An Introduction to Wisdom Literature*. Downers Grove, IL: InterVarsity, 1985.
Kpikpi, John. *God's New Tribe*. Accra, Ghana: Hill City, 2003.
Kudadjie, Joshua N., and Robert Kwasi Aboagye-Mensah. *Christian Social Ethics*. Accra, Ghana: Asempa, 2004.
Kuma, Afua. *Jesus of the Deep Forest: Prayers and Praises of Afua Kuma*. Translated by Jon Kirbi. Accra, Ghana: Asempa, 2006.
Kumekpor, K. Tom. *Research Methods and Techniques of Social Research*. Accra, Ghana: SonLife, 2002.
Küng, Hans. "The Criterion for Deciding What Is Christian." In *Introduction to Christian Ethics: A Reader*, edited by Ronald P. Hamel and Kenneth R. Himes, 120–24. New York: Paulist, 1989.
Kunhiyop, Samuel Waje. *African Christian Ethics*. Nairobi, Kenya: Hippo, 2008.
Land, Steven Jack. *Pentecostal Spirituality: A Passion for the Kingdom*. Sheffield, UK: Sheffield Academic, 2001.
Laney, J. Carl. "The Prophets and Social Concern." In *Vital Old Testament Issues: Examining Textual and Topical Questions*, edited by Roy B. Zuck, 108–119. Vital Issues Series 7. Grand Rapids: Kregel, 1996.
Larbi, Emmanuel Kingsley. *Pentecostalism: The Eddies of Ghanaian Christianity*. Accra, Ghana: Centre for Pentecostal and Charismatic Studies, 2001.
Lartey, Emmanuel Y. "Of Formulae, Fear and Faith: Current Issues of Concern for Pastoral Care in Africa." *Trinity Journal of Church and Theology* 11 (2011) 5–13.
Lederle, H. I. *Treasures Old and New: Interpretations of "Spirit-Baptism" in the Charismatic Renewal Movement*. Peabody, MA: Hendrickson, 1988.
Leonard, Christine. *A Giant in Ghana*. Chichester, UK: New Wine, 1989.
Luzbetak, Louis J. *The Church and Cultures: New Perspectives in Missiological Anthropology*. Maryknoll, NY: Orbis, 1988.
Ma, Wonsuk. "Biblical Studies in the Pentecostal Tradition: Yesterday, Tomorrow, and Today." In *The Globalization of Pentecostalism: A Religion Made to Travel*, edited by Murray W. Dempster et al., 52–69. Oxford: Regnum, 1999.
MacArthur, John F. "The Character of a Pastor." In *Pastoral Ministry: How to Shepherd Biblically*, edited by John F. MacArthur, 67–80. MacArthur Pastor's Library Series. Nashville: Nelson, 2005.
Mbiti, John S. *African Religions and Philosophy*. Oxford: Heinemann, 1990.
———. *Introduction to African Religion*. Oxford: Heinemann, 1991.
Meyer, Birgit. "Commodities and Power of Prayer: Pentecostals Attitudes Toward Consumption in Contemporary Ghana." *Development and Change* 29 (1998) 751–76.
———. "Delivered from the Powers of Darkness: Confessions about Satanic Riches in Christian Ghana." *Africa* 65 (1995) 236–55.
Miles, Rebekah L. *The Pastor as Moral Guide*. Minneapolis: Fortress, 1999.

Mill, John Stuart. *Utilitarianism*. Edited by Samuel Gorovitz. New York: Bobbs-Merrill, 1971.

Miller, Donald E., and Tetsunao Yamamori. *Global Pentecostalism: The New Face of Christian Social Engagement*. Berkeley: University of California Press, 2007.

Montoya, Alex D. "Approaching a Pastoral Ministry Scripturally." In *Pastoral Ministry: How to Shepherd Biblically*, edited by John F. MacArthur, 43–63. MacArthur Pastor's Library Series. Nashville: Nelson, 2005.

Mwaura, Philomena N. "New Religious Movements: A Challenge to Doing Theology in Africa." *Trinity Journal of Church and Theology* 13 (2003) 1–19.

Nel, P. J. "Morality and Religion in African Thought." *Acta Theologica* 28 (2008) 33–47.

Njoroge, Nyambura J. *Kiama Kia Ngo: An African Christian Feminist Ethic of Resistance and Transformation*. Ecclesial Studies 2. Legon-Accra, Ghana: Legon Theological Studies, 2000.

Nkansa-Kyeremateng, K. *Akan Heritage*. Accra, Ghana: Sebewie, 1999.

Ntumy, Michael Kwabena. *Financial Breakthrough: Discovering God's Secrets to Prosperity*. Accra, Ghana: Pentecost, 1993.

———. *Struck Down But Not Killed: A Personal Account of God's Deliverance from Unknown Assailants*. Accra, Ghana: Advocate, 2006.

Nukunya, G. K. *Tradition and Change in Ghana: An Introduction to Sociology*. Accra, Ghana: Ghana Universities Press, 2003.

Oden, Thomas C. *Pastoral Theology: Essentials of Ministry*. San Francisco: Harper & Row, 1982.

Odum, Howard Washington, and Katherine C. Jocher. *An Introduction to Social Research*. New York: Holt, 1929.

Ogunewu, Leke "Charismatic Movements and Theological Education: Past, Present and Future." *Ogbomoso Journal of Theology* 12 (2008) 58–82.

Ojo, Matthews A. *The End-Time Army: Charismatic Movements in Modern Nigeria*. Trenton, NJ: Africa World, 2006.

Okyerefo, Michael P. K. "Pentecostalism and the Promotion of Human Capital in Ghana." *Trinity Journal of Church and Theology* 17 (2009) 54–68.

O'Meara, Thomas F. *Theology of Ministry*. New York: Paulist, 1999.

Omenyo, Cephas Narth. "The Charismatic Renewal Movement in Ghana." *PNEUMA* 16 (1994) 169–85.

———. *Pentecost outside Pentecostalism: A Study of the Development of Charismatic Renewal in the Mainline Churches in Ghana*. Zoetermeer, Netherlands: Boekencentrum, 2006.

———. "'The Spirit-Filled Goes to School': Theological Education in African Pentecostalism." *Ogbomoso Journal of Theology* 12 (2008) 41–57.

Onyinah, Opoku. "Akan Witchcraft and the Concept of Exorcism in the Church of Pentecost." PhD diss., University of Birmingham, 2003.

———. *Spiritual Warfare: A Centre for Pentecostal Theology Short Introduction*. Cleveland, TN: Centre for Pentecostal Theology, 2012.

Opoku, Kofi Asare. "Traditional Religious Beliefs and Spiritual Churches in Ghana: A Preliminary Statement." *Research Review* 4 (1968) 47–60.

———. *West African Traditional Religion*. Accra, Ghana: FEP International, 1978.

Osuala, Esogwa C. *Introduction to Research Methodology*. Onitsha, Nigeria: Africana FEP, 1982.

Palmer, Michael. "Social Ethics in the Classical Pentecostal Tradition." In *The New International Dictionary of Pentecostal and Charismatic Movements*, edited by Stanley M. Burgess and Eduard M. van der Maas, 605-610. Grand Rapids: Zondervan, 2003.

Pearlman, Myer. *Knowing the Doctrines of the Bible*. Springfield, MO: Gospel, 1937.

Perbi, Akosua. "Servitude and Chieftaincy in Ghana: The Historical Evidence." In *Chieftaincy in Ghana: Culture, Governance and Development*, edited by Irene K. Odotei and A. K. Awedoba, 353-78. Accra, Ghana: Sub-Saharan, 2006.

Pierce, T. Burton. *Ministerial Ethics: A Guide for Spirit-Filled Leaders*. Edited by Stanley M Horton. Springfield, MO: Logion, 2004.

Plato. *The Republic*. Translated by Benjamin Jowett. *The Internet Classics Archive*. Edited by Daniel C. Stevenson and Web Atomics, 1994-2000. Accessed on March 3, 2007. http://classics.mit.edu/Plato/republic.2.i.html.

Popkin, Richard H., and Avrum Stroll. *Philosophy*. Oxford: Made Simple, 1993.

Quist, Ernestina, "Roles of the Women in the Church of Pentecost in Ghana." MPhil diss, University of Ghana, 2002.

Rae, Scott B. *Moral Choices: An Introduction to Ethics*. Grand Rapids: Zondervan, 1995.

Reeck, Darrell. *Ethics for the Professions: A Christian Perspective*. Minneapolis: Augsburg, 1982.

Riggs, Ralph M. *The Spirit-Filled Pastor's Guide*. Springfield, MO: Gospel, 1948.

Robinson, H. Wheeler. *Inspiration and Revelation in the Old Testament*. Oxford: Clarendon, 1946.

Sarpong, Peter K. "Aspects of Akan Ethics." *The Ghana Bulletin of Theology* 4 (1972) 40-44.

———. *Ghana in Retrospect: Some Aspects of Ghanaian Culture*. Accra, Ghana: Ghana Publishing, 1974.

———. *People's Differ: An Approach to Inculturation in Evangelisation*. Accra, Ghana: Sub-Saharan, 2002.

Schneewind, J. B. "Autonomy, Obligation and Virtue: An Overview of Kant's Moral Philosophy." In *The Cambridge Companion to Kant*, edited by Paul Guyer, 309-341. Cambridge: Cambridge University Press, 1997.

Scutt, Marie Zermatt. "Kant's Moral Theology." *British Journal of Philosophy* 18 (2010) 611-33.

Sinnot-Armstrong, Walter. "Consequentialism." *The Stanford Encyclopedia of Philosophy*. Edited by Edward N. Zalta. Stanford, CA: Stanford University Metaphysics Research Lab, 2012. Accessed November 11, 2011. http://plato.stanford.edu/archives/win2012/entries/consequentialism/.

Soyinka, Wole. *The Jero Plays: The Trials of Brother Jero and Jero's Metamorphosis*. Ibadan, Nigeria: Spectrum, 1995.

Stitzinger, James F. "Pastoral Ministry in History." In *Pastoral Ministry: How to Shepherd Biblically*, edited by John F. MacArthur, 27-46. MacArthur Pastor's Library Series. Nashville: Nelson, 2005.

Stott, John. *The Message of 1 Timothy and Titus: God's Good News for the World*. Leicester, UK: InterVarsity, 1996.

———. *New Issues Facing Christians Today*. London: Pickering, 1999.

Synan, Vinson. *The Century of the Holy Spirit: 100 Years of Pentecostal and Charismatic Renewal, 1901-2001*. Nashville: Nelson, 2001.

Tenney, Merrill C. "John." Vol. 9 of *The Expositor's Bible Commentary with the New International Version of the Holy Bible*. Edited by Frank E. Gaebelein. Grand Rapids: Zondervan, 1981.

Ter Haar, Gerrie. "Standing up for Jesus." *Exchange* 23 (1994) 221–40.

Thomas, J. C. "The Supernatrualistic Fallacy Revisited." *Sophia* 25 (1986) 20–26.

———. "What Is Situation Ethics?" *Ghana Bulletin of Theology* 4 (1972) 26–39.

Ton-Laar, Thompson Yaw. *History: Assemblies of God Ghana, 1931-2011*. Tamale, Ghana: Ghana Institute of Linguistics, Literacy, and Bible Translation, 2009.

Trull, Joe E., and James E. Carter. *Ministerial Ethics: Being a Good Minister in a Not-so-Good World*. Nashville: Broadman & Holman, 1993.

Turner, Harold W. "The Way Forward in the Religious Study of African Primal Religions." *Journal of Religion in Africa* 12 (1981) 1–15.

Van Dijk, R. A. "From Camp to Encompassment: Discourse of Transsubjectivity in the Ghanaian Pentecostal Diaspora." *Journal of Religion in Africa* 37 (1997) 135–60.

Von Rad, Gerhard. *The Theology of Israel's Historical Tradition*. Vol. 1 of *Old Testament Theology*. Translated by D. M G. Stalker. Old Testament Library. New York: Harper & Row, 1967.

Walker, Williston. *A History of the Christian Church*. 4th ed. New York: Scribner, 1985.

Waltke, Bruce K., and David Diewert. "Wisdom Literature." In *The Face of Old Testament Studies: A Survey of Contemporary Approaches*, edited by David W. Baker and Bill T. Arnold, 295–328. Grand Rapids: Baker, 1999.

Waruta, Douglas, W. "Who Is Jesus Christ for Africans Today? Prophet, Priest, Potentate." In *Faces of Jesus in Africa*, edited by Robert J. Schreiter, 52–64. Faith and Cultures Series. Maryknoll, NY: Orbis, 1991.

Weirich, Paul. "Utility Maximization Generalized." *Journal of Moral Philosophy* 5 (2008) 282–99.

Wenham, Gordon J. *The Book of Leviticus*. New International Commentary on the Old Testament 3. Grand Rapids: Eerdmans, 1985.

———. *Genesis 1–15*. Word Biblical Commentary 1. Edited by David A. Hubbard et al. Waco, TX: Word Books, 1987.

Wesley, John. *Wesley's Standard Sermons*. Edited by Edward H. Sugden. London: Epworth, 1951.

Wiest, Walter E., and Elwyn A. Smith. *Ethics in Ministry: A Guide for the Professional*. Minneapolis: Augsburg, 1982.

Wilder, Amos N. *Early Christian Rhetoric: The Language of the Gospel*. Cambridge: Harvard University Press, 1971.

Willimon, William H. *Character and Calling: Virtues of the Ordained Life*. Nashville: Abingdon, 2000.

———. *The Service of God: Christian Work and Worship*. Nashville: Abingdon, 1983.

Wiredu, Kwasi. "The Moral Foundations of an African Culture." In *Person and Community: Ghanaian Philosophical Studies I*, edited by Kwasi Wiredu and Kwame Gyekye, 193–206. Cultural Heritage and Contemporary Change Africa 1. Washington, DC: Council for Research in Values and Philosophy, 1992.

Wood, Allen W. *Kant's Ethical Thought*. Modern European Philosophy. Cambridge: Cambridge University Press, 1999.

Wyatt, C. S. "Soren Kierkegaard: The Original Leap of Faith." *Tameri Guide for Writers: The Existential Primer*. Accessed September 22, 2011. http://www.tameri.com/csw/exist/kierkegaard.shtml.

www.ingramcontent.com/pod-product-compliance
Lightning Source LLC
Chambersburg PA
CBHW062017220426
43662CB00010B/1361